Technospaces

Critical Research in Material Culture

Series editor: Sally R. Munt

Technospaces

Inside the New Media

Edited by
SALLY R. MUNT

CONTINUUM
London and New York

Continuum
The Tower Building, 11 York Road, London SE1 7NX
370 Lexington Avenue, New York, NY 10017-6503

First published 2001

British Library Cataloguing-in-Publication Data
A catalogue record for this book is available from the British Library.

ISBN 0-8264-5004-0 (hardback)
   0-8264-5003-2 (paperback)

Library of Congress Cataloging-in-Publication Data
   Technospaces: inside the new media / edited by Sally R. Munt.
      p. cm. — (Critical research in material culture)
   Includes bibliographical references and index.
   ISBN 0-8264-5004-0 — ISBN 0-8264-5003-2 (pbk.)
      1. Technology—Philosophy. 2. Computers and civilization. 3. Space and time.
I. Munt, Sally. II. Series.

T14.T3955 2001
303.48′3—dc21   00-052355

Typeset by BookEns Ltd, Royston, Herts
Printed and bound in Great Britain by Biddles Ltd, Guildford & King's Lynn

Contents

List of contributors

Rosa Ainley is a writer, editor and photographic artist. Her work includes *New Frontiers of Space, Bodies and Gender* (Routledge, 1998) and *dyke london* (ellipsis, 1999, 2001). She was a contributor to *zed7:Public and Private*, ed. Teal Triggs and Sian Cook (University of Texas, 2001) and *Girls! Girls! Girls! Essays on Women and Music*, ed. Sarah Cooper (Cassell, 1995).

Caroline Bassett is Lecturer in Media Studies at the University of Sussex and course leader for the MA in Multimedia. Her research interests include new media technologies and gender, narrative and culture. Caroline is a member of the Sussex Technology Group.

Michael Bull teaches media studies at the University of Sussex. He has written widely on sound, technology and culture. He has recently published *Sounding out the City: Personal Stereos and the Management of Everyday Life* (Berg, 2000).

Liz Cameron is Community Programme Manager for an environmental regeneration charity in London. Prior to that she set up and managed a youth Internet project in West Sussex which provided young people with access to new technology and the Internet. She has an MA degree from the University of Sussex, and is a member of the Sussex Technology Group.

Peter Dallow lectures in visual media and is Co-ordinator of Research Degrees in the Department of Visual and Media Arts, University of Western Sydney, Bankstown Campus. He has worked in film and television, holds a doctorate in creative arts, and writes fiction.

Andrée Fortin has been Associate Professor in Sociology at Laval University,

Quebec City, since 1982. Her research has been in the areas of sociability, identity and culture in Quebec, with particular emphasis on the spatial basis of these phenomena. She has published several books, the most recent of which are *La Nouvelle Culture régionale* (with Fernand Harvey, 1995), *Nouveaux Territoires de l'art: régions, réseaux, place publique*, and *Produire la culture, produire l'identité*. She is currently co-investigator with Duncan Sanderson in a three-year research project to investigate the links between geographic communities and their uses of the Internet at Université du Québec à Trois-Rivières, Canada.

Radhika Gajjala is Assistant Professor in the Department of Interpersonal Communication/Communication Studies, Bowling Green State University, Ohio. She has published articles in journals such as *Gender and Development* and *Works and Days* and is currently working on a book-length project on Critical Transnational Cyberfeminisms.

Paula E. Geyh is Assistant Professor of English at Southern Illinois University, Carbondale, where she teaches postmodern American literature, critical theory, and film. With Fred Leebron and Andrew Levy, she is the co-editor of *Postmodern American Fiction: A Norton Anthology* (W. W. Norton & Co., 1998), and she is the review editor of the journal *Postmodern Culture* (Johns Hopkins University Press).

Maren Hartmann is a researcher in the Studies on Media, Information and Telecommunication Institute (SMIT), at the Free University, Brussels. She is currently researching language formation on-line (as expressed in individual user metaphors). In the past, she has worked as a research officer for a European research project (EMTEL) and studied in Berlin and at the University of Sussex. Maren is a member of the Sussex Technology Group.

Matthew Hills is a Lecturer in the School of Journalism, Media and Cultural Studies at Cardiff University. He is the author of *Cult Media and Fan Cultures* (forthcoming, Routledge) and is also Co-editor of *Intensities: The Journal of Cult Media*, which is available on-line at www.cult-media.com. Matthew is a member of the Sussex Technology Group.

David Sanford Horner is Senior Lecturer at the School of Information Management, University of Brighton. His teaching and research interests embrace the areas of information policy, communication ethics, innovation, culture and technology, and knowledge structures. He is currently working on a book on theories of information ethics.

Irmi Karl is Lecturer in Media and Communication Studies in the School of Information Management, University of Brighton. She is currently undertaking her PhD at the London School of Economics (LSE) on gender, sexuality, and ICTs, and is a member of the Sussex Technology Group.

Kathleen LeBesco is Assistant Professor of Communication Arts at Marymount Manhattan College in New York. She is co-editor (with Jana Evans Braziel) of *Bodies out of Bounds: Fatness and Transgression* and author of several scholarly essays on resignifying the meaning of fatness. Her research interests include studies of gender, sexuality, and popular culture.

Ben Morgan is Researcher/Project Manager at Keymedia Design, a new media consultancy. Previously, he spent eight years at the University of Sussex, for three of which he was researching the Internet and its social implications in the Graduate Research Centre in Culture and Communication. Ben is a member of the Sussex Technology Group.

Sally R. Munt is Reader in Media and Communication Studies in the School of Information Management, University of Brighton. She has published widely in the fields of spatial theory, identity, and sexuality, including *Heroic Desire: Lesbian Identity and Cultural Space* (Cassell and New York University Press, 1998). Her books and collections include material on crime fiction and culture, narrative theory, lesbian and gay studies, and working-class cultural formations. She is presently writing a monograph on spatial paradigms and shame.

Kate O'Riordan is undertaking doctoral research within the Informatics Research Division, Faculty of IT, University of Brighton. Her research interests are gender, sexuality and cyberspaces. She is a Lecturer in Media Studies for Continuing Education at the University of Sussex.

Per Persson earned his PhD from the Department of Cinema Studies, Stockholm University, with a dissertation on constructivism and spectator psychology. He is presently employed at the Swedish Institute of Computer Science, working with projects on interactive characters, social informatics, and mobile computing.

Judith Roof is Professor of English at Michigan State University and co-director of the programme in film studies. She has written *Reproductions of Reproduction: Imaging Symbolic Change*, and *Come As You Are: Sexuality and Narrative*.

Duncan Sanderson is Assistant Professor at the Université du Québec à Trois-Rivières, where he teaches in the Department of Leisure Sciences and Communication. His research and publications have been in the areas of the social fascination for technology, the organizational dynamics of the introduction of communication technology, mediated scientific collaboration, participatory design of technology, and the social and communication dimensions of engineering work. He is currently co-investigator with Andrée Fortin in a three-year research project to investigate the links between geographic communities and their uses of the Internet.

Zoë Sofoulis (who also writes as Zoë Sofia), from the University of Western Sydney, has published on cultural and gendered aspects of technology, and is currently researching container technologies.

Bridgette Wessels is Senior Research Associate at the School of Management, University of Newcastle, and is a member of the Sussex Technology Group.

Aylish Wood is Lecturer in Film Studies at the University of Aberdeen. Her current research is on images of technoscience in contemporary cinema.

Series foreword

One of the founding figures of Cultural Studies, the historian E. P. Thompson, once claimed that:

> No piece of timber has ever been known to make itself into a table: no joiner has ever been known to make a table out of air, or sawdust. The joiner appropriates that timber, and, in working it up into a table, he is governed both by his skill (theoretical practice, itself arising from a *history*, or 'experience', of making tables, as well as a history of the evolution of the appropriate tools) and by the qualities (size, grain, seasoning, etc.) of the timber itself.
>
> (*The Poverty of Theory* (1978), pp. 17–18)

This series is concerned with the realness of matter, of the substance of culture as a material force that carves, cleaves and sculpts social identities, that forms human experience. Materialist philosophy, since the fifth century BC, has discussed civilization, society and morality in terms of the physical body in motion, offering various sets of explanations for the meaning produced by human activity, in space and time. There are limits to these efforts, and there are effects, for our analysis of the realm of ideas is always embedded in real, material human lives. In this series we offer original research which is intended to critically augment what, in the humanities, has been called 'the cultural turn'. We intend to re-emphasize how culture makes us real, how it confers citizenship, selfhood and belonging, and how it simultaneously inflicts alienation, fragmentation and exile.

Culture is a dynamic process – ambivalent, contradictory, unpredictable; it flows to forge human needs, and is in turn innovated by the vicissitudes of those needs. Culture is intersubjectively produced in the junctures between such oppositional fields as the private/public, the economic/social, the institutional/individual, the material/symbolic, the mind/body. In recent years we have learned how to deconstruct such totemic binaries without losing sight of their specific significance, to trace the relationships between them with critical intelligence. Crucially, because the terrain of culture is constantly changing, emergent and newly distinct structures of feeling demand that we revise our techniques of scholarly engagement. What will be the new strategies, tactics or dispositions to be lived out in the proclaimed Information Age? Does technological convergence really herald the compression of space/time? What will happen to identity *after* the Postmodern? Will cyberlife ensure further fractured forms of consciousness and social atomism? We live in a political moment when the map of the public sphere is being redrawn in terms of rights, yet when we are said to be scurrying towards the post-national, towards the golden goal of globalization. Will hegemony endure, will capitalism reinvent itself using the hoary divisions of race, gender, sexuality and class? What new cultures of dissidence will arise from the bricolage of the twenty-first century? In what senses, and to what effect, is culture 'material' at all?

The series *Critical Research in Material Culture* intends to avoid ephemeral solipsism. Instead, it hopes to illuminate how discourses of representation create embodied experiences, to argue how the matter of life is substantiated in the performance of culture, to disseminate a critique of that culture which engages with its ethical implications, and to ask for an intellectual accountability that recalls that knowledge and power are not dissociated. Our cultural inscriptions can vandalize the tree of knowledge, our pen/knives are out.

Sally R. Munt
Series Editor

Dedicated to my colleagues at the
University of Brighton
for their forbearance and generosity of friendship

Technospaces

Inside the new media

SALLY R. MUNT

Human knowledge passes through two forms of cognition before it can be conceived: space and time. These two forms can be described as intuitive, in the sense that they precede conscious awareness — in other words, we know that, before we experience things, we will perceive them as phenomena in space and time, which are the first filters of knowledge. The eighteenth-century philosopher Immanuel Kant made an important distinction between 'the thing in itself' and 'the thing for me': of the former, we cannot obtain prior and certain knowledge; of the latter, we accept that any knowledge we have is dependent upon knowledge-formations and knowledge-structures, which are fundamentally organized by space and time. To put it another way, humans cannot conceive of their existence *outside* of space and time; therefore, to continue with Kant, space is a *practical postulate* — something that has to be assumed for the sake of 'praxis', or practice. To illustrate, astronomers argue that the universe is infinite and endless, an idea which to humans is inconceivable, something we cannot imagine, and hence cannot know. In deploying space and time in human knowledge we use notions of relativity, i.e., objects are here or there, moments are now or then. These practices are referential in the sense that we know that something is, because of the thing that it is not.

In the last decade there has been a convergence across many academic disciplines — that is to say, in the intellectual formations of knowledge — a concentrated effort, to comprehend spatial paradigms. Most of this work has been concerned with understanding how space organizes human perception, and the practices which emerge from this cognitive framing. This endeavour has studied spatial practices from the macro- to the micro-level: it has studied global configurations, national and geographic structures, societal classifications, art and architectural forms, urban and rural communities, the human body, and the internal psychic mapping of subjectivity (even the opposition external/internal is, of course, a spatial assumption). The contemporary concern with space coincides with the emergence and critical predominance of postmodernism in Western intellectual culture. Postmodernism has refocused the analytical gaze in a sort of horizontal trajectory, to look around at the present, in tandem with a re-evaluation and dissatisfaction with linear models of time and progression. The emphasis has shifted from predominantly historical formulations to theorizing the present, and in particular space has become central to theorizing about identity and culture. Within critical theory as a whole, space has been 'mapped', 'explored', 'contested', and 'colonized', as a metaphorical way of understanding the varied and multiple material effects of oppression and domination. Emerging from these critical and cultural studies is the embodiment of Foucault's project:

> A whole history remains to be written of spaces — which would at the same time be the history of powers (both terms in the plural) — from the greatest strategies of geophysics to the little tactics of the habitat.[1]

Thus a number of academic disciplines, from geography, sociology, philosophy and psychology, to art and architecture, politics and cultural studies, have been preoccupied with theorizing the primacy of spatial structures in new ways.

Space is historically associated with Being, implying a kind of fixity and stasis, as opposed to time, which is conceived of as becoming, as active progress. Traditionally the former is gendered as feminine and hierarchically subsumed under the masculine march of history. Space/Time is aligned with a series of antithetical binary opposites such as passive/active, feminine/ masculine. As Elizabeth Grosz has illustrated though, this binary is to be deconstructed. Space is not passive, fixed, or absolute; it is a relational concept which depends on the position of objects contained within it: 'Space makes possible different kinds of relations but in turn is transformed according to the subject's affective and instrumental relations with it.'[2] There is a certain contingent coherence afforded by the subject's temporal movement through space, which becomes constituent of it, and thus also a constituent of history (time), and politics. Grosz uses the example of the body, which through a perception of itself as a spatial entity is able to manifest and manipulate its corporeality. To paraphrase Grosz, 'a body is what a body can do',[3] and this 'doing' depends on its activity in space.

What Doreen Massey has called 'power-geometry'[4] also gestures to the instability of spaces, which are imbued with partiality. Not only is space contested, any space is always contingent on the space next to it, and so positionality is dependent upon relations of proximity. Spaces are not only gendered, and sexed, they are also moralized. Crucially, territorial activity is established in the way we live our lives, not just in the political grand gesture but in the minutiae of existence, and affective relations. Spatial occupation depends on having a consciousness and an intent: we need to know – in Foucault's sense of the power/knowledge axis – where we are coming from. The strategies and modalities of agency thus become spatial interventions in the field of material culture.

Henri Lefebvre and the production of space

The intellectual paradigm shift into space was pioneered by French Marxist Henri Lefebvre, following Bachelard's *Poetics of Space* (1958), and E. T. Hall's *The Hidden Dimension* (1966). Lefebvre's life work consisted of refocusing critical attention onto the condition of being human, specifically the complex structures and expressions concretized in everyday life. He insisted that the ordinary, mundane level of existence contains within it political meaning, and the utopian potential for a fully lived life. In *The Production of Space* (*La Production de l'espace*, 1974) he argued for the importance of understanding how the spatial character of social life cuts across traditional knowledge-formations. His peerless interdisciplinary synthesis of sociology, philosophy, linguistics, geography and politics was formally predicated on dialectical materialism, even the dialectical style of his writing infers the spatial aspect of communication. Prefiguring later surges in academic research, he discussed the urban and global spaces of capital, and the politics of human geography. Crucially he criticized the myth that space is transparent, neutral, passive, empty, abstract, and objectively 'real', as perpetuated by Euclidean geometry and Kantian ideals of an *a priori* realm of consciousness. He is bluntly critical of 'mental space [that] becomes the locus of a "theoretical practice" which is separated from social practice and which sets itself up as the axis, pivot or central reference point of Knowledge'.[5] So, Lefebvre distinguishes between the representation of space (the 'conceived') and the spaces of representation (the 'lived'). Instead, he demonstrates his formulation of active, operational, instrumental space: 'the role of space, as knowledge and action, in the existing mode of production'.[6] He describes how social space is productive and performative, how it has material effects, how it is first of all lived as a *spatial economy*. Although he would like to see a science of space, he is resolute on how that analysis must be grounded in the specific, how it must take particular productions of space and examine their definitive properties/dispositions. Key for our project here, he argues that 'new social relationships call for a new space, and vice versa',[7] that social/space is dialectical, and historical, that it sets limits as well as defines outcomes:

> (Social) space is not a thing among other things, nor a product among other products: rather, it subsumes things produced, and encompasses their interrelationships in their coexistence and simultaneity — their (relative) order and/or (relative) disorder. It is the outcome of a sequence and set of operations, and thus cannot be reduced to the rank of simple object. At the same time there is nothing imagined, unreal or 'ideal' about it as compared, for example, with science, representations, ideas or dreams. Itself the outcome of past actions, social space is what permits fresh actions to occur, while suggesting others and prohibiting yet others.[8]

However, he also warned against conceptual fragmentation, stressing the urgency of needing a clear distinction between an imagined 'science of space' on the one hand, and real knowledge of the production of space on the other, of negotiating the tension between structural/symbolic and local/illustrative explanations. From Lefebvre, we have gained an understanding of the turbulence of space, that it is a productive and contradictory force.

Spatial practice

French sociologist Pierre Bourdieu's concept of *habitus* provides us with a model for understanding daily spatial praxis. Habitus is the practice of everyday life, which is written on the body. For Bourdieu the body is a kind of mnemonic device upon which culture is habitually inscribed. So, in Bourdieu's habitus, the bodyspace re-enacts its placement — according to social taxonomies such as class, gender and sexuality — in social frameworks; habitus is something which is embodied in the specificities and corporealities of individual lives. It is important to stress the tangibility, perhaps even the nearness, of these theorizations, how they rub up against us, become us, in our particular daily lives, in our mannerisms, in our deportment, in the diaphanous moments/movements of our days. These dynamics become naturalized, made invisible by their ubiquity. Space, as understood through the experience of habitus, is something very ordinary, almost preconscious; it frames the way we live and have our being, and it crucially informs the ways we interact with others. As Elizabeth Grosz has said, we need to look at 'all social relations in terms of bodies, energies, movements, inscriptions',[9] as relations conditioned by spatial forms.

Both Bourdieu and Lefebvre insist upon the intellectual necessity of analysing space in relation to the micro-politics of everyday life; both emerged from leftist French sociology with its commitment to exposing the deleterious effects of capitalism upon the body: human and politic. Lenin and Walter Benjamin were the first to comment upon the spatial characteristics of capitalism, but it was Karl Marx, of course, who instigated the idea of the alienated body as a space inscribed by oppression. The body is thus a product of space and a performance of space, a thing and a process, a configurement of spatial dialectics, crucially a 'lived experience' where conceptualizations materialize, and are materialized, in historically specific ways. The sphere of everyday life is the dynamic arena of spatial practice, but it is not predetermined as radical or progressive, or, conversely, reactionary or regressive; the spatial practices of everyday life, especially those of the body, are to be exposed and fought over in tactical ways.

Space and time

Foucault's assertion that we are living in an epoch (time) of space contains an interesting paradox: namely, that we cannot theorize space without time. While contemporary cultural theory has enthused about space, it has often failed to address its temporal context with the same vigour, often interpreting space as a kind of static void, deprived of political content. The present is troubled: Fredric Jameson, for example, sees the postmodern as characterized by a spatiality of 'chaotic depthlessness'.[10] Within the endless proliferation of the commodified present, past and future have been subsumed to the apparently voracious desire to have things *now*: it is a fairly terrifying simultaneity. Space without time is a disabled concept: a moving body occupies space, but these spaces are not fixed moments with individually recoverable co-ordinates; they are acts of duration, of space-in-time. The moving body has succeeded in being (spatial) and becoming (temporal) by expressing duration, a concept proposed by Bergson and elaborated by Ann Game:

> A moving body occupies successive positions in space, but the process by which it moves from one position to another is one of duration which eludes space (Bergson, 1950: 111). Motion itself, the act, is not divisible, only an object is; space which is motionless can be measured but the motion of bodies cannot. Movements cannot occupy space, they are duration ... To think of a body occupying points in space is to do so from a perspective outside the body, not from the perspective of the moving body. To be *in* the body is to be in time.[11]

There is a particular meaning of time being deployed here, one that is experienced as a body in motion, which in Bergson's formulation is a kind of creative evolution. As Game discusses it, this evolution is a process without an end, a proliferation of experience without finality or conclusion, a kind of infinite differentiation without negativity or denial. As she says, Bergson's theory of time is compatible with positive desire, reproducing itself for its own sake, moving for pleasure. It is infused with an attitude of openness. It is an entering of time, rather than a measurement of it. This is to deconstruct the binary of time/space, where they collapse to form a moving present; it is 'space that is lived and is transformed by imagination'.[12]

The present, though, is also in an important sense utopian: since utopian desires attempt to change the present by integrating possible futures, it is the quality of hope that transforms this present. The recognition that possible futures are latent within the present simultaneously enables belonging and becoming. This is not about predicting a future, neither does it resort to a myth of inevitable progress; it is about animating a kind of optimism, philosopher Ernst Bloch's anticipatory consciousness − a consciousness of possibilities that have not yet been, but could eventually be realized. Utopias are not fixed entities, or static spaces; they generate utopian thinking, or speculations, the reader's own projection of and response to desires for a better present. These desires are never 'utopian' in the derogatory sense of too distanced to be real; rather, they are very real, and express a yearning, a movement towards possibilities. Utopian desires lean into potential futures, and in doing so those futures elaborate the present, they create moments of transition. If we reconsider Althusser's definition of ideology − 'Ideology represents the *imaginary* relationship of individuals to their real conditions of existence'[13] − we can conceive how necessarily compelling this re-visioning of the present, in opening up potential futures *and spaces*, becomes.

New technologies and space

What has all this got to do with technology? Science and technology have had a profound effect on the way humans perceive space and time − think, for example, of the way information technologies such as the telephone have reduced our former perception of the world as inaccessible, unknowable and exotic to a sensibility of nearness, friendliness, fellowship and instantaneity (the so-called 'global village'). Think how the invention of the microscope opened up the 'inner worlds' of the body. Since the nineteenth century, science and technology have been driven by a utopic imagination, with hope for a future. Science has also rhetorically anticipated that technological change will be synonymous with social progress. Perhaps the first way of approaching the link between science, technology and space is to consider the evolution of the genre of science fiction. Robert Scholes and Eric Rabkin have claimed that 'The history of science fiction is also the history of humanity's changing attitudes toward space and time'[14] — consider, for example, how Victorian colonialism formed the context for Jules Verne's conquests of 'foreign' space in that 'hardware romance'[15] *20,000 Leagues Under the Sea* (1870). Between science and science fiction there exists a blurry realm: science fiction is the imaginative space where scientific futures are extrapolated. Remember that science fiction defines itself against fantasy: as the literature of the 'possible' it is an idealist, speculative fiction that explores the plausible relationship between the present and the future. Science fiction has often proved itself to be the literature of the probable and the achievable (think of Verne's *Nautilus* as an early submarine, of H. G. Wells' scientific training in Darwinism); it can be interpreted as a kind of poetics of reason. The tradition of utopian fiction — ideal worlds invented to illustrate political ideologies — is as old as the classics, in which the invention of 'another place' ('Once upon a time, far far away ...') allows for a kind of rationalist hypothesis of causality to be held up to the present. Think, too, of the scientific method of 'probability'. Crucially, technological changes exist first as experimental fictions, they are hallucinative leaps which can only exist if imaginative spaces are opened up — hence, the 'scientific method' is as much visionary illusion as reason. The spaces of the universe ('outer space', discovered in 1643), and of the atom, are still imaginary, alien zones.

The scientific knowledge which produces technology remains a system of beliefs, the perspectives of science are thought-structures, that is ideologies, which organize the world into sets of believable fictions. Scientific knowledge does make a conscious effort to test beliefs for their validity, but that testing is also constrained by the practices of knowledge-formations which have their own characteristics. Returning to Kant, then, although science has tried to define 'the thing in itself', it ends up exploring 'the thing for me', through the practical postulate — the praxis — of space/time paradigms. This has had a practical effect upon our invention, and our use, of new technologies.

Michel Foucault died before the Internet was born as a global communication network. One wonders what he would have made of it. In his later work he discusses technologies of the self, and perhaps the present euphoria of identity-play in electronic cultures would have been the logical development — the (dis)embodiment — of this self-fashioning. His words are just too temptingly prophetic. Here he introduces his concept of heterotopias, which he saw as 'something like counter-sites, a kind of effectively enacted utopia in which the real sites, all the other real sites that can be found within the culture, are simultaneously represented, contested, and inverted'.[16]

Heterotopias are kinds of mirrors to utopias, a counterpoint of the real to the unreal, in which the utopic glance returns to reconstruct the real, in a new way of seeing. Heterotopias are the conceptual space in which we live, six principles of which are identified by Edward Soja[17]: 1) they are found in all cultures, although no type is universal; 2) they change over time, and have a genealogy as well as a geography; 3) they are dynamic places where many different, incompatible spaces/sites may intersect; 4) they can occur at particular temporal and spatial axes; 5) they presuppose systems of territorial opening and closing which make them subject to the disciplinary technologies of power; 6) they function in relation to the spaces around them, either through the creation of an illusion or out of the sensibilities of compensation. Heterotopias allow a slippage of meaning, they

> make it impossible to name this and that ... because they shatter or tangle common names, because they destroy syntax in advance, and not only the syntax with which we construct sentences but also that less apparent syntax which causes words and things ... to 'hold together' ... [heterotopias] desiccate speech, stop words in their tracks, contest the very possibility of language at its sources; they dissolve our myths, sterilize the lyricism of sentences.[18]

It is this juxtaposition that produces a kind of space-play, out of which can emanate a new kind of semiotic, new practices, and, by extension, new kinds of identities and subjectivities. They are simultaneously, and paradoxically, both here and nowhere; perhaps they can be best described as an enabling idea which permits the imagination to reconfigure space, rather than affording a real place we can actually go to:

> The present epoch will perhaps be above all the epoch of space. We are in the epoch of simultaneity: we are in the epoch of juxtaposition, the epoch of the near and far, of the side-by-side, of the dispersed. We are at a moment, I believe, when our experience of the world is less that of a long life developing through time than that of a network that connects points and intersects with its own skein.[19]

What a prescient prophecy of the spatial properties of the new information and communication technologies.

New media technologies function by appropriating space as a framing metaphor to enable consumption and use. Visual technologies such as cable, satellite and closed-circuit television (CCTV), and digital cinema provide spaces of meaning for the consumer to occupy, in which s/he interacts through processes of identification and subjection. Depth, surface, liminality, transcendence, emplacement, positionality – these spatial concepts are intrinsic to organizing visual consumption, and thus central to the way modern identities are formed. By making more visible the parameters of spatial practices in new technologies, we can stimulate their more critical deployment. Spatial metaphors suffuse our technological, social, and cultural environments; by analysing these conceptual underpinnings we can further develop conscious modes for technological interaction.

Within technologically grounded disciplines such as computer science, human computer interaction (HCI) and information science, spatial models are increasingly used to gain insight into the complex configurations of people, information and representation made possible by new generations of communication apparatus. Spatial metaphors are now established intellectual tools for designing and analysing new systems, with the desktop metaphor and the World Wide Web as primary examples. Technology users refer easily to interfaces and knowledge bases as spaces in which they operate; sophisticated games and virtual reality environments allow users to experience alternative three-dimensional worlds; and technological and organizational developments such as portable computers, electronic village halls, teleworking and hot-desking are blurring the traditional picture of such separate spheres as real/virtual, and private/public.

Although aspects of spatial theory have been implicit in conceptualizations of technology use, they have not been coherently identified and interpreted by current research. Lefebvre asked in 1974:

> where, how, by whom, and to what purpose is information stored and processed? how is computer technology deployed and whom does it serve? We know enough in this area to suspect the existence of a space peculiar to information science, but not enough to describe that space, much less to claim close acquaintanceship with it. [20]

Each discipline has brought its own applied insights. In particular, HCI foregrounds the notion of technologies as designed artefacts: not simply ready-made objects which people adopt and adapt but products which bear the mark of spatial thinking in their very design. We need to investigate how we use notions of space to appropriate novel technologies and to translate them into extensions of ourselves and our cultural life, through sequences of mental mapping which allocate often unconscious concepts such as here/there, public/private, home/work and translate them into technological practices.

The understanding of new technologies, especially computer-based technologies, draws on notions of spatial configuration and location in multiple ways. On the purely physical and literal level, there is the siting and use of the more visible/tangible instruments of new technologies in the landscape. Some examples of new practices brought about by such technological innovation include the ubiquity of the laptop and the personal organizer, which move the computer out of the office and into the train, the meeting room and the home; the creation of cyberbars, which integrate computers into recreational spaces; the trend towards home computers as toys and educational tools; and the move to teleworking from home. These new cultural practices raise questions about the changing conventions surrounding attitudes to the spatial setting or place of particular technologies. In an office context, we have seen the beginnings of a reconceptualization of the workplace which accompanies the increasing acceptance of new communication and information technologies. A related aspect is the move to wearable and ubiquitous or ambient displays and devices, which are designed to blend into conventional land/cityscapes.

The graphical user interface originally made popular by the Apple Macintosh has given currency to the notion of the screen as a place: interface developers, for instance, routinely speak of the screen as 'real estate'. Spatial notions play an important role in the design and use of software interfaces, allowing people to grasp the relationships between functions and objects which otherwise would remain insubstantial and largely incomprehensible. The so-called 'desktop metaphor' is arguably the greatest advance ever in HCI, allowing a user to envisage programs and files, essentially collections of bits and bytes, as objects laid out in a two-dimensional space which has features in common with an office desk. Spatial aspects of two-dimensional screen layout such as proximity, sequencing, orientation and position are very often pressed into service by individual computer users to bring order to their work artefacts. Three-dimensional interfaces can go further, offering conceptualizations of information of all kinds — databases of stocks and shares, World Wide Web pages, design ideas — in terms of constantly evolving stylized representations of real-world landscapes. The idea of the site or the Home page, the notion of 'going to' or 'visiting' an HTML document (when in fact any movement is in the inverse direction), the provision of site maps and exit signs and the idea of being 'lost in hyperspace' all point to the prevalence of the notion of web pages as places in space; while on the producer side of the Web, the notion of spatial constructs for presenting information and services has been taken up enthusiastically by constructors of the Web equivalents of shopping malls, museums, university auditoriums, laboratories, social clubs and other relatively familiar settings, creating the possibility of peopling these virtual spaces and forming virtual communities. The feasibility of connecting work colleagues via the Internet has created interest in interfaces which would make it possible to work more easily at a distance. This effort has been informed by spatial concepts, with the development of interfaces allowing images of people working apart to appear on a single screen, even in a virtual reality setting. Here, rather than the computer merging into the workplace, as in the desktop metaphor mentioned above, the entire workplace is reproduced inside the computer itself.

Technospaces

Technospaces are those temporal realms where technology meets human practice. Significantly, technospaces are lived, embodied fluctuations in human/machine interaction. At the momentary intersection of the human being and the machine there is spatial praxis: there is technospace. This book intends to introduce the reader to a number of cognate themes within this conjunction technology/human/space. The collection aspires to initiate debate around a number of conceptual questions:

- How are spatial metaphors implicated within the design of innovation technologies and user/consumer paradigms?
- Do the 'real' spaces of the body, or the city, intersect with conceptual spaces of 'virtual' reality? Is there a clear distinction between real/virtual to defend?
- How are virtual communities dependent upon grounded spatial metaphors of near and far, us and them?
- How are the real and metaphorical spaces of electronic cultures quantified, qualified, and regulated?
- How is information packaged according to spatial practices of consumption?
- How do navigational metaphors transfer between spatial domains?
- How do subject/object relations become practised in the new media technologies, and do they affect constructions of self?
- How does the concept of duration inform emergent practice in technospace?
- How do we understand user movement as an unfixed phenomenon within time and space?
- How is habitus experienced in technospace? What forms of embodiment are practised in technospace?
- Must an 'ethics of technospaces' be realized?

The book consists of two sections: Part I, 'Spatial Modelling: Critical Paradigms in New Media Technologies', in which the chapters are generally concerned with the perception of spatial models and spatial formations in new media technologies; and Part II, 'Smart Spaces: Strategies and Tactics in New

Media Technologies', which seeks to analyse spatial practices within those formations. Roughly speaking, the essays in the first half of the book are primarily concerned with conceptualizing and critiquing models, while those in the second half prioritize the patterns of experience within those domains, although of course material common to both approaches appears in each section.

The first two essays in *Technospaces* offer a historical context for understanding how we conceptualize spatial models within technologies. Judith Roof explores how the metaphor of depth has accrued meaning in Western perceptions of technology, becoming synonymous with truth and mastery. She discusses the association of depth with visual technologies, discussing depth as cued through illusion, creating a 'depth effect', where depth is rendered discursively as the site of knowledge made accessible through visual technologies. Per Persson also reflects upon the historical correlation between the emergence of early cinema and the nascent development of digital interfaces, discussing how both technologies similarly engaged with spatial visualization processes. He explores how cinematic space changed and stabilized into the now dominant frames of representation, in order to extrapolate how digital space may or may not stabilize in analogous ways: for example, in graphical user interfaces, desktop metaphors, WYSIWYG, hyperspace, and virtual environments. Several of the essays refer to film, and we might wonder how far our competence in navigating cinematic space — through depth of field, for example — has and will influence similar imaginative journeys in digital media.

Peter Dallow, like Persson, reminds us of the importance of human performance within digital media. New digital communications technologies initiate new spatial practices, but often carry with them nostalgia for old human orientations. He raises the negative effects of speeded-up time and the diminution of geographic space that seem to lead to confusion and uncertainty in finding agency in a rapidly globalizing virtual life. The massification of digital media forms is leading to a logic of visualization and consumption embedded within capitalism, within paradigms of power which offer the human being limited spaces of negotiation in which to find a self. Dallow concludes with an exploration of the dilemmas that 'post-human digitality' present; alluding to Dante, he prefigures the morality of mind/body dualism which David Sanford Horner focuses upon in his chapter on the ethics of eulogizing cyberspace. Horner critiques the anti-somatic urges of the often utopian hyperbole deployed by cyber-idealism, and reminds us of the trenchant presence of bodies and the real boundaries they impose. The discourse of new technologies proffers an ontology which desires to escape from physical space; this idea of identity as something fluid, free and incorporeal is invested in ideologies of immaterial transcendence that go right back to the Platonic/ Cartesian hatred of the flesh. Horner, too, contextualizes his analysis of contemporary digital formations in historical thought traditions; many of the essays in this book temper the present infatuation with space with admonitions on the importance of time, and Horner reintroduces the notion of accountability to the space/time conjunction (a life has a life history). Material continuity constitutes a necessary condition of moral accountability, it is a vital counterpoint to the illusion of abstract mental mastery which has suffused the fictions of cyberfutures.

In her chapter, Rosa Ainley writes of the architectural techtronics of CCTV. Linking the scopophilic tendencies of CCTV to panopticism, she has produced a critique of how urban space is visualized and policed by a technology that is more symbolic than actual. The surveillance industries have grown exponentially in recent years, and the resultant popular response has vacillated between Orwellian disquiet and the vaunted rhetoric of the desirability for 'safe zones'. Ainley exposes how the mechanics of displacement, and the concomitant creation of 'other spaces', relocates criminal behaviour rather than controls it. She outlines how social coercion succeeds through categorization and specularization, these visual techniques reinforcing the spaces of belonging/non-belonging in urban life. Like Horner, she recognizes the need for further moral debate on the spatial implications of new media technologies. Whereas Ainley takes as her object of study the scopic structures of the built environment, the next chapter, by Paula Geyh, extends this interest into electronic representation by discussing what she calls the 'city/cyberspace interface'. Commencing her discussion with the technologies of memory introduced by classical rhetoricians, she shows how old the link between urban architecture and information is, asking why it is that data should be represented as physical space at all. The three-dimensional spatiality of the Internet is a given; we 'dimensionalize' information constantly, projecting human cognitive frames onto an essentially imaginative domain. Geyh addresses the interaction of these spatial logics that exist between the 'virtual' and 'real' specifically in order to raise political questions about the power implicated by their reproduction. She presents two competing visions of the city: the city as fortress and 'scanscape', in which the spatial logics are those of control and surveillance; and the city as polis, in which the spatial logics are those of democratic access and free movement. It is the Cartesian, carceral, grid of the former which is ascendant in cyberspace. Geyh warns us of the potential power of the abstracted space of the disciplinary electronic matrix to affect the 'real' landscape in alarmingly material/political ways.

The following two chapters introduce feminist perspectives to our critical understanding of media technologies. Radhika Gajjala takes an overview of

Internet studies, highlighting how they often reinvest hegemonic readings of binarized gender, race and class formations on-line. Reminding us, like Horner, how material power relations are reproduced uncritically in celebratory cyberdiscourse, Gajjala asks us to look carefully for the silent or unrepresentable speech acts on-line for signs of resistance or radical potential. Thus, forms of dis-identification, exclusion or abjection can symbolize an other-discourse of democratic contestation, can provide other-spaces, margins, through which the subaltern can speak. Zoë Sofoulis looks at some of the implications of the 'smart spaces' represented in the television series *Star Trek: The Next Generation*; specifically she foregrounds the fictional fantasies of the Starship *Enterprise*, its bridge, and its holodeck, observing how highly gendered cultural anxieties are played out in their design and representation. A smart space is intelligent, agentic, and productive, rather like good old Mum, to whom Captain Picard relates as good old Dad ('Make it so!'). Through a close reading of the episode 'Emergence' (1994) Sofoulis illustrates how heterosexual gender relations frame the narrative, and yet how, as with all dominant discourses, these predeterminations can occasionally be undermined. Sofoulis thus leads us into Part II of this collection, by drawing to our attention the practices of agency latent within the spatial paradigms of new media technologies.

The three essays by Sofoulis, Hills, and Wood make connections between mass media forms, specifically television and video, and information technologies. Each discusses the different ways in which ICTs (Information and Communication Technologies) are deployed within visual narratives as technologies of resistance, or are used to create alternative sites/routes of reflection to the cardinal narrative. Matthew Hills is concerned with how fan activities are being transformed by new media technologies, taking the Internet newsgroup as its focus in his case study of the US-oriented newsgroup alt.tv.X-Files. He argues that virtual fan communities constitute a novel 'affective space' which sustains a *community of imagination*, extending Benedict Anderson's concept of the nation as an 'imagined community'.[21] He engages directly with Michel de Certeau's writing on 'strategies' and 'tactics', exploring the temporal, spatial, and affective implications for these concepts when applied to virtual communities.[22] Aylish Wood takes the video-feature *Fresh Kill* (1994), and describes how the non-classical narrative is arranged in distinct spatial groupings which interconnect through the use of ICTs. The theme of the film is environmental activism, and Wood is able to show how strategies and tactics of resistance are practised through the mediation of technologies. Space is represented as contingent and productive, as the physically disconnected become attached, and social spheres combine, in processes of assemblage and territorialization. She describes this interpretation as 'textual spatiality'.

In Kathleen LeBesco's chapter, the theme of resignification is continued. She investigates the experience of fatness on a newsgroup and a listserver, arguing how these zones simultaneously and ambiguously construct fat subjectivity, and fat subjection. These Internet sites have thus become contestatory spaces where the virtual subaltern speaks – or not, following Gajjala's thesis – where her struggle for identity is also her right to dis-identify. LeBesco resumes the debate centred around the place of embodiment in cyberspace, so here we are continuing to ask where the body 'fits' in digital domains. In this, the body as mediated by technology remains one that is unstable and othered – represented as text – something which is at once enabling and constraining. Size is also a concern of Duncan Sanderson and Andrée Fortin, namely in their interest in the relationship between traditional place-based communities and their 'localization' in cyberspace. They note the difference between the geographic significance of a place and the projection of its image on the World Wide Web, drawing attention to how its virtual presence may exceed or misrepresent its physicality in the real. This is another form of virtual resignification; Sanderson and Fortin explore the tensions, absences, and distortions in virtual rendition, raising again the spectre of identity-formation and its perlocutions.

The following three chapters by the Sussex Technology Group, Kate O'Riordan and Michael Bull take three technologies as case studies – mobile phones, computer games and personal stereos respectively – exploring the spatial practices embodied in each. The Sussex Technology Group's study of mobile phone users during their first phase of adoption in the UK reveals how self-consciously that use was practised, in the seaside town of Brighton. They describe four distinct zones of mobile telephony that variously display that awareness, explaining that the tactics deployed by users in these zones reveal highly spatialized performances. Kate O'Riordan explores the use of computer games in domestic space, specifically in order to articulate the relationship between the player and the game, and concentrates on how spatiality affects the construction of self. O'Riordan stresses that the temporal identity of the player enters into a symbiotic space of identification with the game, and that this formation needs further elaboration, as it has both physical and psychic elements. Michael Bull's essay takes up the idea of aural space, through his ethnography of personal stereos. He notes that this technology's intrinsic mobility raises a challenge to the dichotomous conception of space as either public or private, and has implications for the transitorial construction of users' subjectivities. In sympathy with the Sussex Technology Group's analysis of mobile phones, he illustrates the high degree of strategic mediation involved in his interviewees' adoption of these machines. Writing on the spatial experience of sound technologies, Bull describes the embodied practices of autobiographical travelling that the associations of music provoke, practices which make the urban *flâneur* feel more privatized, more secure.

When Fredric Jameson called for 'a new kind of spatial imagination'[23] he was arguing for a perception of the spatial as invested politically and historically in power. What we explore in this project are some of the implications, and contingencies, raised by the currently emergent new spatial practices. Historically, the reception of new technologies has often been constituted by fantastic predictions, and as a result they become invested with romantic idealism, or panic and threat. The social implications residual in these practices are key — utopian dreams need to be tempered by ethical, humanistic needs — thus these new technospaces need to be above all revealed and reflected upon, and evaluated for our potential futures. We hope to have contributed to that work.

Acknowledgement

The editor would like to thank Lyn Pemberton, University of Brighton, for her involvement in the earlier stages of this project, and in particular for her input into the writing of this introduction.

Notes

1. Michel Foucault, 'Of other spaces', *Diacritics*, Spring (1986): 22–7, quoted in Edward W. Soja, 'Heterotopologies', in S. Watson and K. Gibson, *Postmodern Cities and Spaces* (Oxford: Blackwell, 1995), pp. 13–34.
2. Elizabeth Grosz, *Space, Time, and Perversion* (New York: Routledge, 1995), p. 92.
3. *Ibid.*, p. 214.
4. Doreen Massey, 'Power-geometry and a progressive sense of place', in *Space, Place, and Gender* (Cambridge: Polity Press, 1994).
5. Henri Lefebvre, *The Production of Space*, trans. Donald Nicholson-Smith (Oxford: Blackwell, 1991), p. 6 (first published 1974).
6. *Ibid.*, p. 11.
7. *Ibid.*, p. 59.
8. *Ibid.*, p. 73.
9. Elizabeth Grosz, 'Refiguring lesbian desire', in *Space, Time, and Perversion*, p. 182.
10. Fredric Jameson, *Postmodernism; or, the Cultural Logic of Late Capitalism* (London: Verso, 1991), quoted in Doreen Massey, *Space, Place, and Gender* (Cambridge: Polity Press, 1994), p. 251.
11. Ann Game, 'Time, space, memory, with reference to Bachelard', in Mike Featherstone, Scott Lash and Roland Robertson (eds), *Global Modernities* (London:

Sage, 1995), pp. 192–208, p. 200. She is referring to H. Bergson, *Time and Free Will*, trans. F. L. Pogson (London: Allen & Unwin, 1950).

12. *Ibid.*, p. 202.

13. Louis Althusser, 'Ideology and ideological state apparatuses', in *Lenin and Philosophy and Other Essays*, trans. B. Brewster (New York: Monthly Review Press, 1971), pp. 127–87, p. 162.

14. Robert Scholes and Eric Rabkin, *Science Fiction: History. Science. Vision.* (London: Oxford University Press, 1977), p. 3.

15. *Ibid.*, p. 14.

16. Foucault, 'Of other spaces', p. 24.

17. Edward W. Soja, 'Heterotopologies', in S. Watson and K. Gibson (eds), *Postmodern Cities and Spaces* (Oxford: Blackwell, 1995), pp. 13–34.

18. Michel Foucault, *The Order of Things* (New York: Vintage, 1980), p. xvii.

19. Foucault, 'Of other spaces'.

20. Lefebvre, *The Production of Space*, p. 86.

21. Benedict Anderson, *Imagined Communities: Reflections on the Origin and Spread of Nationalism* (London: Verso, 1991).

22. Michel de Certeau, *The Practice of Everyday Life* (London: University of California Press, 1988).

23. Fredric Jameson, 'Postmodernism, or the cultural logic of late capitalism', *New Left Review*, 146 (1984): 53–92.

Part I

Spatial Modelling

Critical paradigms in new media technologies

1

Depth technologies

JUDITH ROOF

Depth has become profound even as it has become increasingly superficial. The idea that the deep harbours the truth is an old one; surfaces have prevaricated since the Greeks, appearances deceive, and it is foolhardy to trust the eyes. Even if seeing is believing, belief is far from knowledge, which is an altogether more recondite state of affairs. In fact, in order to know, one must penetrate the surface, delve into recesses, body cavities, cell walls, the earth's crust, DNA, atoms, and ancient monuments, dive beneath the ocean, scan luggage, all because the truth either hides (as in disease, suitcases, or murder mysteries) or is really hard to find (as in oil or the *Titanic*). Technologies for scanning the depths of everything from the atom to the ocean and deep space have developed in proportion to techniques for producing the surface illusion of depth. Just as the anatomical studies of modern medicine began in late Renaissance Italy, so did Leonardo da Vinci's exposition of the techniques of portraying depth. Just as Freud's *fin-de-siècle* insights about the relations between surface behaviour and psychic constructs played upon depth as a topographical metaphor, cinema, which emerged at the same time, began almost immediately to toy with methods for producing three-dimensional illusions.[1] While DNA may hold the key to life, its exploration has been coterminous with the development of such three-dimensional imaging techniques as holograms.

But does depth still hold sway as a repository of meaning? Given that there is very little that we cannot see by means of one technology or another, is there any depth left or has depth itself become a surface phenomenon? In what ways do the technologies by which depth is explored (optics, X-ray, sonar, psychoanalysis) relate to the methods which produce the visual illusion of depth (depth cues, linear perspective, stereoscopy, holography)? Do both instrument and illusion perpetuate a belief in the topographical figuration of truth as existing within, beneath, beyond, or somehow in depth, whether that truth is knowledge or merely an increasingly sophisticated ('realistic') representation of the depth cues of the physical world?

Depth perception

The idea of depth is obviously not simple. Not only is it a relational term dependent upon spatial analogies but it also slips easily from the literal to the figurative, from location to metaphor, from the minute to the grandiose, from perception to rendition. Depth refers to what is hidden and inside (either literally or metaphorically), what is deep (in the earth, in space, or in profundity), and what is distant or far from the immediately perceivable. It refers to the presence of multiple dimensions in relation to one another (depth of field, volume) as well as to the illusion of presence marked by the cues of three-dimensionality. But in all of these various manifestations, the traditions of Western physiology and optics suggest that depth is somehow difficult to perceive. Depth requires labour: the brain's work to produce an image neither eye sees, the necessity for a prosthesis, or the travail of making the illusion. And because depth is understood as relational, its fabrication is never a singular endeavour; it always takes at least two — two eyes, two objects, two fields, two images.

The idea of depth as a supplemental third dimension is mainly a Western concept. In the East, 'space is seen as an extension, created by unfolding through the dimensions, involving various degrees of freedom to move'.[2] Western notions of dimension are premised on the right-angled squares appurtenant to Western graphic drawing rather than to the sphere used as a basis for rendition in Islamic culture; thus, anything beyond the flat plane requires the imaginary addition of another flat-plane square attached at a right angle.[3] The idea of dimension itself in its etymological connection to measuring suggests the co-existence of multiple, superimposed flat planes, whose area and volume are calculable simply by shifting orientation. Mathematical computations of volume depend upon the serial combination of measurements from multiple planes quite literally added on to one another.

The right-angled square and flat plane also dominate notions of how vision works; from the Renaissance on, ocular processes have been explained as analogous to the operations of the camera obscura as a passive receptacle for light focused by a lens. The flat plane of the camera obscura surface served as a model for the eye's retina, likening the eye to the canvas (or wall or paper) of two-dimensional graphic rendition.[4] Departing from earlier ideas of vision as an active process where the eyes send out rays, the camera obscura analogy reinforced the primacy of the two-dimensional perceiver as the basic condition of perception. But because two-dimensional perception means that depth is difficult both to perceive and render, the perception of depth itself became a sign of civilized sophistication thought to belong only to the West. One of the early issues in perception research was the extent to which depth perception might be culturally conditioned – whether subjects, such as Subcontinental Asians, unaccustomed to seeing depth cues portrayed in fine art are able to see depth cues in three-dimensional space, or whether their art takes the forms it does because the groups do not perceive depth in the same way.[5]

Given the standard Western assumption of two-dimensionality, depth is an add-on, a complication, a difficulty whose presence must either be accounted for or laboriously produced. Depth perception – the mechanisms by which sentient beings discern (whether in real space or on a flat plane) the presence of a third dimension defined from the point of view of the perceiver – is an arduous production. Depth perception as difficult depends again on the ways visual processes are understood as analogous to the techniques of graphic rendition; part of the challenge of explaining depth perception comes from trying to explain three dimensions in terms of the two readily available for graphic representation.[6] Even the idea that there is such a process as 'depth perception' and that such perception consists of a complex set of additional processes is linked to the Western idea of depth as a supplement enhancing meaning and power. This is not to say that we do not see or need to perceive volume and space; it is to suggest that depth perception's labours are linked to cultural ideas about depth as something beyond the capacities of flat-plane technologies.

As it is currently understood, depth perception utilizes both monocular cues and binocular dynamics. Monocular depth cues are those elements that can be rendered on a flat plane and include the interpretation or deployment of cast and attached shadows; texture, detail, colour, and size gradients; scale; and overlap (see Figs 1.1 – 1.4). These are *cues* about the likely relation of objects

Figure 1.1

Figure 1.2

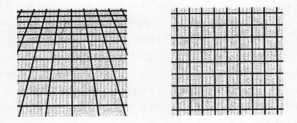

Figure 1.3

Figure 1.4

in a third-dimensional space that contribute to the illusion of depth; seeing cues does not mean that depth itself is perceived, but rather that depth can be deduced. Since these monocular cues are the same as those deployed to render an illusion of depth in drawing and painting, it is difficult to tell whether we understand these as depth cues because we are already familiar with the conventions of artistic rendition or whether artistic convention deployed what the culture thought the eye saw.

Since monocular depth cues are defined as two-dimensional strategies, it is difficult to accept that such cues are sufficient to explain the apprehension of three-dimensional depth. Researchers make recourse to a more dynamic process through which the two eyes and brain interact to produce the perception of a third dimension. Depth goes from a comparative process requiring only two elements (shadow and object, a large object and a small object, one object behind another) to a dynamic process requiring three elements – an object, divergent angles of sight, and a brain processor. The binocular perception of three dimensions is enabled by binocular parallax, which depends upon the anatomy of the head: the fact that two eyes of presumably comparable acuity see two different images by virtue of their slightly different angles (binocular parallax) enables the brain's perception of a three-dimensionality that is not perceived by either eye alone. In this optic geometry, three-dimensional objects produce two disparate images (one for each eye), which are merged into one stereo image by the brain. If we agree that we exist in a three-dimensional world, and if we agree that our eyes work two-dimensionally, then the illusion produced through binocular parallax matches the conditions of the real world, making binocular parallax a kind of compensatory illusion machine that brings us up to speed with the 'real' state of affairs. Given the limitations of our anatomy, truth is already an illusion, or so our conceptual reliance on two-dimensional models would suggest.

But given that the eyes can perceive a dimension that is, within a flat-plane system, theoretically not available to them, that process then provides the model for more sophisticated representations of space. Renditions of the illusion of three-dimensionality (as opposed to depth) essentially attempt to reproduce on flat planes the binocular parallax disparities of distance and volume, then utilize some prosthetic mode of combining them. The stereoscope, invented by Sir Charles Wheatstone in 1838, used two disparate images placed side by side on a binocular viewer that when seen together produce a depth effect. [7] The same effect is produced by presenting two slightly disparate images, one in red, the other in green, side by side, offset slightly on the horizontal and viewed through glasses with one red and one green lens. This anaglyphic system is the same principle used in early cinematic attempts to produce 3-D; pioneer filmmakers such as the Lumière brothers projected strips of red- and green-tinted film simultaneously for a glasses-wearing audience.

Another method by which the illusion of three-dimensionality is produced through binocular parallax is polarization, where two slightly disparate images are photographed, projected through, and viewed with differently polarized lenses. Cinema deployed this method, called 'Natural Vision' in the 1950s, but because it was gimmicky and inspired mostly action films that took advantage of the shock effect of elements seeming to come at the audience out of the screen, most filmmakers abandoned it for the benefits of anamorphic wide-screen processes such as CinemaScope, which 'exploited depth through peripheral vision'.[8] This same polarizing technique was used to make stereoscopic toys in the 1950s and 1960s: tiny strips of two different images were intercut and separated by tiny plastic ridges. When the object was turned, the shifts in polarity produced the illusion of depth and movement.

Both monocular depth cues and the dynamics of binocular parallax depend on an idea of the third dimension as an extension of the first two dimensions (both of which are themselves idealized — neither one nor two dimensions can actually exist materially without the third). If we depart momentarily from the dominance of two-dimensionality, we might also see that just as there are depth cues, there are flatness cues (flatness being one aspect of depth).[9] Flatness cues are those hints which suggest that objects do not have much volume or do not exist at disparate distances. They would be the cues that tell us that an illusionist painting is in fact a painting, or that disparate elements exist on the same plane. This suggests that what we are always dealing with is never two dimensions but simply gradations of three. The question of depth perception then becomes not how we can possibly see depth given our visual apparatus, but how we can possibly ever see anything but depth in differing degrees. If this is the case, then the labours involved in trying to render depth as a two-dimensional process, labours intrinsic to the rendition rather than the perception of depth, signal depth's more metaphorical and metaphysical functions as a locus of a difficult-to-gain truth as those functions inflect our conceptions of perception. Perception and perceptual machines (such as ocular and optical models), then, become suspiciously loaded analogies when transferred into the realms of science, knowledge, and mental functioning. Instead of representing some objective understanding of the relations between perceptions and the geometry of space, they represent a particular way of understanding those relations that is already grounded in the difficulties of rendition. Thus, the very ways we understand metaphorical depth are conceptually tied to attempts to render three-dimensionality graphically. What this suggests, then, is that deep understandings exist only in so far as the human subject can wield, represent, or reproduce them. That indeed is the lesson of the scientific method. The insight of theory is far less impressive than the manifestations of practice; the over-valuation of practice not only underwrites capitalism in its emphasis on tangible results but also perpetuates capitalism's attendant anti-intellectualism by undervaluing the intangible.

Perspectives on depth

What is at stake in issues of depth is rendition disguised as a function of perception, when in fact it is probably the other way around. Depth becomes a matter of extending perception beyond the bounds of what is literally or metaphorically visible or fashioning the perceived so that aspects which are in fact not present (such as extended volume in a limited space) are nonetheless perceivable. This pairing of perception/rendition is the necessary condition of our understandings of what depth might be; depth as a desirable quality to perceive or render is a part of cultural ideology that already locates depth as a difficult and sought-after quality. Within the extended realism/scientifism of Western culture that has existed at least since the Renaissance, depth perception and rendition have become signs of sophistication and technical mastery that lead to progress, greater truth, deeper understanding, and more profound meaning. It is no surprise, then, that the evolution of graphic depictions of depth also traces the evolution of machines by which various kinds of depth could be perceived.

Techniques for portraying depth in graphic arts began to re-emerge in the work of Italian Renaissance painters in the thirteenth century, but their reappearance was already coincident with the rebirth of science as an exploration of both literal and figurative depths. Classical Greek art had already employed depth cues on ceramics and wall paintings. Some art historians cite thirteenth-century Cimabue (1240–1302) as the artist whose works begin to manifest some new attempts to render depth. At the beginning of the fourteenth century the work of Giotto reproduces perspective and a century later Leonardo da Vinci (1452–1519) wrote about ways to produce a sense of depth. Around 1500 da Vinci instructed painters about how to produce a sense of distance through colour gradation: 'paint the first building beyond the aforesaid wall in its own proper color and make the more distant building less sharply outlined and bluer, and a building that is twice as far away, make it twice as blue'. [10]

The genius Leonardo, however, was also simultaneously engaged in dissection experiments that built upon the anatomical work that had begun with Renaissance artists' interest in physiology as necessary to the rendition of the human form. An interest in anatomy as a scientific practice probing depth was tied to the more accurate and in-depth rendition of the body. From the fifteenth century on, painters pursued anatomy as 'a matter of course'; science and art met in the body and sought therein their various truths. Leonardo in particular brought together scientific anatomical research and painting, knowledge and rendition. [11] Though not as devoted an artist as his contemporaries Michelangelo and Albrecht Dürer, who used anatomy exclusively for art, Leonardo combined perspectives, as Roy Porter describes, 'comparing anatomy with architecture, and using it to probe the mysteries of the microcosm'.[12] At roughly the same time, Copernicus (1473–1543), a Polish medical student turned astronomer, deduced the workings of the solar system, beginning attempts to understand the depths of space. While looking into the body and out into space would seem to be looking in opposite directions, both activities are attempts to find a truth that is quite literally out of normal sight and thus figuratively 'deep'. The desire to find truth in the depths continued through the Renaissance with Galileo's (1564–1642) development of the telescope and the work of Hooke (1635–1703), Malpighi (1628–94), and van Leeuwenhoek (1632–1723) with the microscope. Slightly later, Canaletto (1697–1768) perfected the use of linear perspective to produce the illusion of depth.

As perspective drawing and depth renditions became a commonplace in Western art after the Renaissance (*trompe-l'oeil* is perhaps its most extreme expression, popular from the Renaissance through the seventeenth century), the metaphor by which truth is linked to unseen depths persisted in science and medicine. By the nineteenth century, the search for scientific truth about human behaviour and feelings (the psyche) already preoccupied with forces deep in the body, became, with Freud, a 'depth psychology', a method by which the 'unseen' metaphorical depths of the psyche could be deductively discerned.[13] Working first with hysterics, dreams, and the slips of everyday life, Freud tracked 'surface' symptoms to 'deeper' unconscious etiologies. Freud's method depended upon the idea of the subject as multi-layered and 'deep'. Linked both to theories about the location of the soul (as in the heart, the brain, the stomach) and to early nineteenth-century ideas of consciousness as a faculty that develops through time, the unconscious was understood as that which is buried both in history and the body.[14] Freud's dilemma was how to excavate what was figuratively buried, material that he believed affected (and even effected) individual choice and action. Conceptually, Freud's methods involved using the dynamic between subject and analyst as a way to make what resides in the depths appear. It may be only a coincidence that this very much resembles binocular parallax's two angles producing a third, but Freud's own reliance on ocular models suggests that psychoanalysis, too, assumes the idea of depth as the difficult supplement to be produced from multiple vantage points.

Freud had difficulty finding analogies for psychic processes that were metaphorically more than two-dimensional. Trying to account, for example, for a memory/repression system that required a surface that retained impressions but was also receptive to new stimuli, he first deployed the model of the microscope or telescope. In *The Interpretation of Dreams* (1905),

Freud compares 'the mental apparatus' to a 'compound instrument', in which the 'systems' of the apparatus 'may perhaps stand in a regular spatial relation to one another, in the same kind of way in which the various systems of lenses in a telescope are arranged behind one another'.[15] To explain 'the relation between memory and perception in the memory trace', Freud later suggests the following:

> I propose simply to follow the suggestion that we should picture the instrument which carries our mental functions as resembling a compound microscope, or a photographic apparatus, or something of the kind. On that basis, psychical locality will correspond to a place (*Ort*) inside the apparatus at which one of the preliminary stages of an image comes into being. In the microscope and telescope, as we know, these occur in part at ideal points, regions in which no tangible component of the apparatus is situated.[16]

Freud's problem, like the dilemma of many who investigate depth perception, is that he must account for processes whose workings defy two-dimensional representation. Just as those explaining binocular parallax utilize the non-existent third image as a way to account for the perception of depth, so Freud uses the idealized site within the optical apparatus to represent imperceivable locations in the psyche — in fact, locations that should not, according to Freud, even be located:

> thoughts and psychical structures in general must never be regarded as localized in organic elements of the nervous system but rather, as one might say, *between* them ... Everything that can be an object of our internal perception is *virtual*, like the image produced in a telescope by the passage of light rays.[17]

The mystic writing pad is the closest analogy he can employ which renders multiple dimensions within essentially two planes whose layers provide the combination of depth and proximity through which Freud formulates the workings of the perception/memory system.

So while Freud developed a depth psychology through recourse to spatial analogies, his models, like those of depth perception, depended upon renditions of prosthetic apparatuses that make the literally deep visible. But while surfaces can render depth, they can also reveal it — a hypothesis Freud deploys to analyse Leonardo da Vinci.[18] Freud is interested in why it is that da Vinci quit painting to pursue scientific knowledge — in other words, why he quit his genius manipulation of surface illusion in favour of probing the depths.

Using an analysis of da Vinci's paintings combined with his biography, Freud deduces that da Vinci sublimated his erotic feelings into a quest for knowledge. While the paintings reveal a highly charged relation between mother and child, they were mainly incomplete and often abandoned. Freud's analysis of one of da Vinci's anatomical drawings of coitus concludes that da Vinci had repressed sexuality and instead become a platonic homosexual. 'He had', Freud notes, 'merely converted his passion into a thirst for knowledge.'[19] Surface gives way to depth. The truth about Leonardo is that his fascination with the deep (knowledge) comes from the deep (repressed sexuality) and only incidentally translates into da Vinci's brilliant manipulation of the surface appearance of depth.

Freud's recourse to a surface/depth model, while reiterating traditional conceptions of the psyche also inflected surface/depth relations with a new complexity. The analogy between the surface and consciousness and depth and the unconscious and the need for a third party (the analyst) to sort it all out both set surface and depth somewhat at odds and related them through a difficult dynamic process by which the surface could also be made to reveal depth. The surface bore 'depth cues' in the form of symptoms which bear a rational and traceable relation to deep material and personal history.[20] Freud's connection between surface and depth, and the coincident augmentation of the importance of depth as the site of knowledge, established an idea of the subject as an entity with depth and reinforced the idea of depth as a locus of knowledge that was accessible through technologies of vision, deduction, and insight.

In depth

The rendition and exploration of 'depth' not only signifies advanced artistry but also the 'right' and proper concern of an empirical science that seeks knowledge by locating causes and mechanisms within normally imperceptible depths – the minute, the distant, the hidden. From the perspective of Western cultures generally, the absence of proper depth cues bespeaks primitivism or radical difference, especially since progress has been measured in terms of depth – how deeply we can perceive, what insight we have. Even though the connection between depth and truth is a Western cliché, we continue to believe that scientific truth resides in molecules of DNA or in atomic particles discerned through the traces they leave when rousted from their atomic security by a supercollider. And we continue our archaeologies, thinking to uncover the truth of humanity through what we can deduce from its material history.

Why has the metaphor of depth and its various literalizations and figurations become so central to a Western *Weltanschauung*? Why depth? Part of depth's appeal comes, I think, from the way the apparatus of depth perception constructs a centred viewer in a rather singular and privileged vantage point. Even if many persons might share this vantage, it is still the best seat in the house, the place for which the depth is produced in the first place. Perspective drawings and lenses, which either render or make visible a depth, position the viewer in the optimal vantage point at the centre of the image. This inevitably suggests that viewing depth is a powerful process enacting humanity's aegis over that which is either proportionately too vast or too minute. Depth implies both power and individual control, reinforcing capitalist notions of individualism as the site where power is exercised and the locus from which technology is controlled.

Another aspect of depth's appeal is its prosthetic extension of human capabilities — or the prosthetic effect of the apparatus by which depth can be produced. This is another version of depth as empowerment, but as an effect of devices which appear simply to extend powers humans already wield, such as vision. In the twentieth century, this prosthesis becomes the more literal application of the older idea of vision as the extension of rays. X-rays or Roentgen rays, named after their discoverer, reveal what is unseeable by recording the patterns of X-rays shot through an object (like a body). Since heavier materials absorb more of the rays, fewer rays reach the sensitive plate and the areas will register as lighter than those bombarded with many rays. This produces a shadow-like image that reveals relative density rather than three-dimensionality, but which also reveals the unseen both within the body and in outer space. Radar, developed in the early twentieth century, sends out a beam of electromagnetic waves and tracks the patterns produced when they bounce back to the transmitter. It enables perception at great distances. Sonar utilizes the reflection of underwater sound waves and is also employed medically as ultrasound. With such apparatus, human perception outstrips the capabilities of unaided vision (at least for the expert who can interpret the data), knowledge exceeds insight, the truth seems both objective and available.

But depth is also attractive as a supplement, as the locus whose access unravels the dilemmas posed by surface appearance's sometimes contradictory cues. This, of course, depends on a pre-existing notion of surface/depth as opposing and different sites, which is itself not only a product of Platonism but is also a necessary corollary of post-Renaissance mechanistic thinking. If we believe that all phenomena have a rational and discernible mechanism, that we have not yet discerned the mechanism means that it must be hidden. Science means making the hidden visible, even if the concept hidden may also refer to simple ignorance rather than literal depth. If a Western sense of what can be perceived is premised on a model of two-dimensionality, depth becomes the impossible, but completely significant, supplement, the dimension whose perceptions give life to the flat façade of superficial existence.

In all of this, depth's centrality depends upon privileging vision as the key metaphor of understanding, a metaphor made literal through the operations of depth technologies whose display is entirely visual and whose probing revelations seem to answer questions. Depth technologies conflate vision and perception, making the former equivalent to the latter and transforming the metaphorical into the all too literal. The unacknowledged transmutability between vision and perception makes depth (insight) a privileged site, because it is not easily seen (literally viewed). Finding means of seeing the unseeable transforms depth and mystery into an available and revealing surface, while it transforms the perceiver into an omnipotent seer who can penetrate the mysteries of the universe. Via depth technologies the human shifts from the position of wondering suppliant to wise observer, whose optical apparatus substitutes for the complexities of understanding.

Depth reflections

The saga of depth is not finished, however. Wielding the digital codes of computers provides a whole new arena for rendering depth, even if the depths of the computer reveal finally no depth at all, but only an architecture of alternations between 1 and 0, on and off. The computer's calculating abilities enable the operation of diagnostic prostheses such as the CAT scan and MRI, both of which are premised upon three-dimensionality. CAT scanners combine multiple X-rays taken from different angles to image (again two-dimensionally) in greater detail and more thoroughly the body's internal structures. MRI (Magnetic Resonance Imaging) deploys nuclear magnetic resonance to map the body's interior in detail. Using radio waves to change the magnetic state of the body's protons, the MRI then 'reads' and renders the changes in electro-magnetic transmissions that come back from different protons. Because the protons are scattered throughout the body, the MRI is multi-dimensional, literally reading the depths, though its rendition of spatial distribution is rendered in a colour-coded flat image.

Just as techniques for perceiving depth become so sophisticated that they function on the atomic level, so techniques for rendering depth refine to the pixel the monocular depth cues and illusionist practices of two-dimensional graphic art. Computer 3-D graphics cards enable personal computers to process the geometrical calculations, rasterization, z-sorting and z-buffering, texture mapping, pixellation, MIP mapping, perspective correction, fogging, alpha blending, and bilinear filtering calculations that must occur for the smooth depiction of animated 3-D graphics. The virtue of these graphics is that they can produce the illusion that one is moving in and through a space by rapidly altering perspective and depth cues to correlate with the changing perspective of a moving eye. But the computer, like all forms of depth rendition, still depends on a two-dimensional model, deploying triangles (an economy move, producing the same effect as square planes, but requiring fewer calculations) as a way of locating points in two-dimensional space. Computer programs combine triangles to produce complex shapes and the electronic equivalents of traditional depth cues to render the illusion of depth.[21] While its mode of rendering is finally virtual rather than material and its problems with rendition are related to the speed with which the computer can process the calculations, the computer represents merely a translation of traditional two-dimensionally based strategies for presenting an illusion of three-dimensionality. The amount of calculation and difficulty necessary to achieve a three-dimensional effect on a computer, however, suggests not only the infinitely more complex and refined mathematical science by which both electrical impulses and flat planes are organized into an illusion but also the market value of such illusions. At this point in time, 3-D graphics cards are sold with computers and sophisticated programs (especially games) are popular commodities.

The hologram, however, seems finally to represent a method for producing three-dimensional images that relies on the reflections of three-dimensional surface differences rather than the two-dimensional rendition of depth. A hologram is made by recording the interference pattern made when the waves of light produced by an object scattering a laser beam meet the laser light that has been deflected through a mirror. When the photographic plate is illuminated, it reveals the actual degrees of light refraction produced by the surfaces of the object. This produces a three-dimensional effect based on the wave fronts that were originally created by the beam hitting the object. The result is an image that when viewed from different angles presents different planes of the object or a three-dimensional rendering.

The hologram's curious resonance with binocular parallax (two beams coming from different angles) suggests that even the hologram is premised upon the same two-dimensional ideation as graphic art, but that it combines parallax with the idea of photography as a record of the action of actual light waves to produce what might be seen as an objective artefact, the actual wave tracings of an object's existence in time and space.[22] Science fiction's versions of the hologram, such as the holodecks in *Star Trek*'s USS *Enterprise*, project the hologram into three-dimensional space as a kind of free-standing image that reproduces an even greater range in depth than in actual space.[23] Holodecks enable humans to inhabit a three-dimensional illusion produced by combining holographic imagery with three-dimensional force fields. Imagining this ultimate three-dimensionality suggests the continued stake in rendition as digital technology labours to reproduce the depth effects we imagine.

That the phenomenon of the hologram, the technologies of 3-D photography, and the continued scientific explorations of depths – rendition, reproduction, and knowledge – are completely interdependent phenomena is manifested most clearly in a recent issue of *National Geographic* (August 1998) where images from both the Mars rover *Sojourner* and the wreck of the *Titanic* were reproduced in anaglyphic 3-D, complete with 3-D glasses (brought to you by Nissan). Both terrains are deep sites, viewed only with great labour, technological advances, and much expense. Perhaps to bring literally home the reality of these two deep sites, 3-D photographic renditions emphasize not only the existence and appearance of the surface of Mars and the pathos of the shipwreck, but demonstrate (or at least attempt to) the technical virtuosity of high-tech rendition which is a synecdoche for the technical advances signified by the exploration of such extremes. The acquisition of knowledge from the deep is again integrally tied to its rendition. The purpose of the *Pathfinder* Mars mission was to determine more about Mars' surface, including what it looked like. The rover was equipped with a stereoscopic camera, an instrument to record weather and an instrument to analyse the make-up of soil and rocks. It was simply another, albeit very expensive, prosthesis. Its stereoscopic camera was an advanced version of the double-lens camera invented in the nineteenth century.

National Geographic's images of the *Titanic* wreck were acquired, again prosthetically, but with another version of stereoscopic photography. Deploying two submersibles, each with four high-intensity lights, the photographic expedition wanted to get 'the clearest, highest resolution pictures of the Titanic possible'. [24] It used paired video cameras to achieve the same kind of 3-D effect produced by a stereoscopic camera. Pictures of *Titanic's* wreckage, however, might be read two ways. On the one hand, the *Titanic* represents the blindness of modern hubris; on the other hand, photographing the ship's carcass represents the triumph of a technology that can now discern enough to assess the deep meaning behind the *Titanic's* tragedy by simply seeing deeply and in lifelike 3-D. The technologies of rendition, which have always underwritten imaginings of the profound, finally substitute for knowledge even as they seem to provide it, making everything surface. Rendition is, finally, everything.

The increasingly technological nature of renditions of depth demonstrates that what has been at stake with rendition all along has not simply been portrayal, but rather a specific kind of realistic portrayal. Realism is one mode or fashion of rendition among many, but it is a mode that attempts to erase the differences between portrayal and a version of a real-world model. Realism is not necessarily more realistic or true than other modes of rendition; it selects certain ideologically 'objective' aspects of a visual scene to reproduce in a way that emphasizes the illusion of volume, space, and detail. Realism more thoroughly and assuredly centres the viewer and appeals to the reassuring similarities of photographs, graphic art, computer simulation that come to stand in place of what other things we might also see (and in fact substitute for some things we probably don't see). In preferring representational spatial relations and volume over other qualities such as colour variation, texture, pattern, asymmetry, or non-representational possibilities, realism implants a mode of viewing that emphasizes not only the centralized viewer but also the ascendancy of objects over qualities, space over colour, singular objects over pattern, even if these various elements work together in paintings and photographs. The question this raises is the same question posed by early depth perception researchers: do we see the world the way we do because that is the way our eyes work or do we see it that way because that is how Western representations since the Renaissance have organized visual space? Representational realism appears to give us an immediate world, one that needs no interpretation or adjustment – in fact, the truth.

Technology's and realism's equation of visual power and immediate meaning, however, is itself a lure that distracts us from the real object of our fascination: the operation of the technologies by which depth is seemingly penetrated, produced as an illusion, or reproduced as a presence. Believing we can see the unseeable and render illusion immediately real is a lure that erects technologies of depth in place of the meaning that depth seems to guarantee. Thus, instead of depth as a substantial, complex, sometimes obscure, mysterious possibility, technologies of depth render it as not only totally superficial but also as entirely about surface appearances. In the twenty-first century, depth is no longer a supplement, an out-of-sight locus containing the keys to mysteries, but has become a part of the surface – of the panoply of loci instantly available for view, detached from relations, and exhibiting the traces of the technology by which it has become superficial. With depth just another perspective, meaning is always available, the product of technologies which bring everything into view; depth and meaning are technology and we need go no further than that. [25]

When depth rises to the surface, the model of the multi-layered complex subject shifts to a model where all that is important is not only immediately perceivable but is also marked as a surface attribute. Three-dimensional comes to mean heavily accessorized, tattooed, pierced, tanned, muscled, or displaying the many commodity signifiers of wealth and power (clothes, jewellery, cars, beepers, cell phones) – or, in American culture, revealing personal and family secrets on commercial television. While the idea of commodity culture as superficial is rather hackneyed, the relation between surface, commodity and the disappearance (and/or over-availability) of depth would signal the ultimate disappearance of any tension or dichotomy between surface and depth, which suggests that if depth is now written completely on the surface, there is no mystery left.

Notes

1. In *A History of Narrative Film* (New York: Norton, 1990), pp. 484–94, David Cook summarizes cinema's various efforts to achieve three-dimensional effects from Cinerama to 3-D to wide-screen.
2. Cynthia Dantzic, *Design Dimensions: An Introduction to the Visual Surface* (Englewood Cliffs, NJ: Prentice-Hall, 1990), p. 77.
3. *Ibid.*, p. 85.
4. For further argument about the model of the camera obscura and the operation of the homunculus in concepts of perception, see Myron Braunstein, *Depth Perception through Motion* (New York: Academic Press, 1976).
5. See Marshall Segall, Donald Campbell and Melville Herskovitz, *The Influence of Culture on Visual Perception* (Indianapolis: Bobbs-Merrill, 1966).
6. Braunstein, *Depth Perception*, p. 1.
7. Sir Charles Wheatstone, a physicist primarily interested in electronics, invented the stereoscope in 1838 and in 1852 invented a kine viewing device which produced the illusion of 3-D movement by mounting stereoscopic images on a drum. In 1848 Sir David Brewster invented a binocular camera that would make stereoscopic pictures. See C. W. Ceram, *Archaeology of the Cinema* (New York: Harcourt, Brace and World, n.d.), Fig. 134; and Braunstein, *Depth Perception*, p. 15.
8. Cook, *Narrative Film*, p. 487.
9. Braunstein argues that because of a focus on depth and a belief in flat-plane ideologies of vision, we have ignored flatness cues.
10. See generally Daniel Weintraub and Edward Walker, *Perception* (Belmont, CA: Brooks/Cole Publishing, 1966), pp. 20–38.
11. Roy Porter, *The Greatest Benefit to Mankind: A Medical History of Humanity* (New York: Norton, 1998), p. 176.
12. *Ibid.*, p. 177.
13. Henri Ellenberger notes that Eugen Bleuler is credited with coining the term 'depth psychology', a term Ellenberger says 'was popular at the time when psychoanalysis was equated with the psychology of the unconscious'. Henri Ellenberger, *The Discovery of the Unconscious: The History and Evolution of Dynamic Psychiatry* (New York: Basic Books, 1970), p. 562. Bleuler's book, *Depth Psychology and a New Ethic* (New York: G. P. Putnam's Sons, 1969), originally appeared in 1949.

14. Both Ignaz Troxler and Carl Carus, nineteenth-century precursors to dynamic psychiatry, see the unconscious as a part of an early developmental stage. Carus believed that a 'formative unconscious' developed in the womb. See Ellenberger, *Discovery of the Unconscious*, pp. 206–7.
15. Sigmund Freud, *The Interpretation of Dreams*, trans. James Strachey (New York: Avon, 1965), p. 575.
16. *The Interpretation of Dreams*. See also Jacques Derrida, 'Freud and the scene of writing', in *Writing and Difference*, trans. Alan Bass (Chicago: University of Chicago Press, 1978), pp. 196–231, where he discusses Freud's recourse to both optical metaphors and the magic writing pad.
17. Freud, *The Interpretation of Dreams*, p. 649.
18. Sigmund Freud, *Leonardo da Vinci and a Memory of His Childhood*, trans. Alan Tyson (New York: Norton, 1964).
19. *Ibid.*, p. 24.
20. Many 'New Age' therapies are also premised on this intimate interrelation between surface and depth.
21. For a complete explanation of how 3-D graphics and virtual reality devices work, see Ron White, *How Computers Work* (Indianapolis: Que, 1998), pp. 230–7.
22. See André Bazin, 'The ontology of the photographic image', in *What Is Cinema? Vol. 1*, trans. Hugh Gray (Berkeley: University of California Press, 1967), pp. 9–16.
23. Though this technology does not exist, it is described in some detail in Rick Sternbach and Michael Okuda, *Star Trek Next Generation Technical Manual* (New York: Pocket Books, 1991), pp. 156–7.
24. *National Geographic*, August 1998, p. 123.
25. I write this as someone who actually cannot perceive literal depth, since I lack binocular parallax. While that might account for other lapses of insight, it also suggests that, finally, vision isn't really necessary to any of this.

2

Cinema and computers

Spatial practices within emergent visual technologies

PER PERSSON

Introduction

In spite of its radical transformation over the last fifty years, digital technology is still embryonic. Something is emerging from computer business and professionals, but there are few clues as to what it is, to what purposes it best fits, or to the appropriate framework in which to understand it. Considering this, it is surprising that the computer community has not turned to other technologies — of which the last two centuries are so rich — in pursuit of some answers. While historical comparisons with other emerging technologies may not perhaps provide exact answers as to where digital technology is heading, they may sketch some recurrent patterns, and at least provoke the right sorts of questions. This is what the present chapter aims to accomplish.

I will be occupied with the technology of recording and displaying moving images, which first appeared around 1895. The comparison between cinema and digital technology is apt in so far as both are primarily visual practices. The emergence of both displays striking similarities:

- Both emerge from a scientific context: cinema was — among other things — spurred on by Eadweard Muybridge's extremely thorough empirical and physiological investigations of body movement; computers arose from a mathematical and engineering setting, often accompanied by a close involvement with the military.
- Both are technologies imbued in commercialization and consumption: cinema and digital technology are commodities in themselves as well as channels to stimulate other forms of consumption. Both transferred quickly from cottage industries to large multinational production and distribution practices, due to the exploding demand for their commodities.

- The emergence of both was intimately associated with juridical and commercial fights over patents, standards and copyrights, effectively eliminating alternative technologies early on.
- Both instigated the emergence of institutionalized metadiscourse in the form of academic departments, publications and conferences.
- Debates around censorship and governmental control were prevalent within emergent cinema as well as digital technologies. The arguments almost invariably centre on protecting children from violence, pornography or other forms of 'moral decadence'. The advocates, on the other hand, often emphasized (and still emphasize) the educational and social identity-creating functions of the technology in question.
- Contemporary debates about the best function and purpose of the cinematic medium (as scientific, informational, aesthetic, educational, etc.) parallel today's discussion about the social uses of digital technologies.

My ambition here, though, is not to trace all of these economical, industrial, legal or cultural correspondences, but to focus on one particular parameter: the spatial practices and visualization processes in which cinema and digital technology are engaged. First, I will argue that today's digital interfaces, like early cinema, handle space in similar ways. Then I will explore the ways in which cinematic space changed and finally stabilized into what we today call *mainstream cinema*. On the basis of this analysis I will finally make some speculative predictions about the future of digital space.

Early cinema

Cinema was the first technology to render moving images based on photographic technology. The transfer from peep-show to white screen projection made the act of viewing a social rather than individual experience, providing one of the prerequisites for mass consumption. During the first few years, it was the technology itself that was the major attraction rather than the content of the films, and this technological wonder was displayed at world fairs alongside other inventions. Although films were shown in museums, amusement parks, circuses and fairs, perhaps the major exhibition outlet was the vaudeville. This efficaciously affected themes and motives, which were predominantly composed of sketches, conjurers, singers, tableaux, dancing numbers, wrestlers and gags. There were also non-fiction genres – travelogues, panorama films and newsworthy events – which appealed to the educational functions of the new medium. Films were short, often no more than one or two minutes, and were put together in a programme of ten to fifteen minutes. They were presented with black leader or image slides in between, containing short descriptions of the contents of each film. During the first ten to fifteen years, the projectionist often also functioned as lecturer, providing a verbal accompaniment. This mimicked the slide lecture, which was an important genre at the time, not only in vaudeville but also in museums, fairs and churches. The block of films would then be inserted into an evening programme together with other features of singing, dancing and conjurers. Not until the nickelodeon boom of 1905–6 were films shown in a separate context of their own. Thus, staged vaudeville was the framework within which cinematic space came to be understood and received, particularly the fictive genres, which will be my major concern here.

In terms of the visual space within the frame, a modern spectator is struck by the lack of realism displayed in these films. In typically vaudeville manner, the scenery often consisted of flat backdrops on which the landscape or features of the room were painted, creating a stark contrast between actors and background (Fig. 2.1). Sometimes that backdrop was all black – like Muybridge's – abstracting the object or actor from background (Fig. 2.3). The acting style was that of the pantomime with exaggerated and often coded gestures and expressions (Bordwell, Staiger and Thompson, 1985: 189).

Figure 2.1 *The Great Train Robbery* (1903). Interior of a cargo train wagon. The postmaster has just discovered the thugs behind the door to the left and shows his fear by looking at the camera/spectator and making a pantomime gesture.

Another important dimension of early cinematic space was its constant communication with the space and spectators of the auditorium (Gunning, 1994: 261). Just as in vaudeville, characters acknowledged the presence of the spectators by looking into the camera, gesturing towards them, seeking empathy or sympathy in difficult situations and sharing a joke or a prank with them, in a manner sharply different from the characters of today's mainstream cinema (Fig. 2.1). This practice effectively erased the division between stage/ screen and auditorium space in a manner similar to the circus, stand-up comedy or televised news, in which the address is direct and characterized as face-to-face. Cinema simply adopted a practice already established within vaudeville. It is curious to note that theatres and nickelodeons probably were not darkened to the same extent as today. Whereas today's total darkness effectively 'erases' the auditorium space, early cinema treated screen space and theatre space as one and the same.

The close relationship with vaudeville space also becomes apparent in the camera work, or rather its absence. The camera was considered to be a replacement for the spectator in the theatre seat, which meant that camera movement and editing were extremely rare. As in the theatre, all action was presented without any fragmentation or disruption of the time/space continuum of the single shot. This 'respect' for the wholeness of the event depicted also manifested itself in terminology. Contemporary filmmakers and scholars use 'scene' to denote a segment of a narrative film that takes place within the same spatial location (e.g. a bar) without changing or omitting time (ellipses, for instance, usually separate two scenes although they may occur in the same space). 'Shot' or 'take', on the other hand, refers to one uninterrupted run of the camera. The combination of shots from different angles and distances make up a scene. Before the 1920s, however, every shot was called a 'scene' (Bordwell, Staiger and Thompson, 1985: 196). The fact that there was no need to make distinctions between shots and scenes marked early cinema's high esteem for the autonomy of the pro-filmic event.

Another feature that is a direct consequence of the vaudeville context is the resistance to anything but long shots, containing whole bodies and objects within the frame (Fig. 2.1). Moving characters or camera closer to one another so that feet or other body parts disappeared outside the frame (so-called 'medium shots' or 'close-ups') elicited complaints from critics:

> Pictorial art is composition. A picture is a combination of several factors into a complete and harmonious whole. An arrangement with the feet cut off is not a complete and harmonious whole. There is something lacking. Most people cannot tell exactly what is wrong, but they feel it

nevertheless. Neither can they analyze and tell why a composition is correct, but they realize it unconsciously because it satisfies.

(Hoffman, 1912: 53)

Thus, in early cinema all 'scene' space was contained within the 'screen' space. Nothing of the action or the objects in the scene overlapped the 'off-screen space'. The fictive space did not continue beyond the edge of the screen, but was like a self-contained box, very much like a theatre stage. The space immediately outside the frame belonged not to the fictive world, but to the space of the theatre (which, again, was not entirely dark). In this conceptualization of space, closer framings of characters 'cut off' at the feet, waist or neck were more or less universally described in terms of 'grotesqueness' and 'vulgarity' (Bordwell, Staiger and Thompson, 1985: 191; Tsivian, 1994: 196).

In combination with the painted backdrops, these constraints made the space of action extremely flat, void of depth. As actors were unable to move forwards or backwards very much, action was stretched out horizontally rather than in depth, generating the striking frontality with which these films are associated.

The approach to editing also suggests that early spectators did not think of off-screen space in the same way as we do. Whereas viewers of today make spatial inferences between different shots, early cinema and its audience did not conceive of relations between shots in spatial terms. At the end of *Dr Jekyll and Mr Hyde* (1912), Hyde trashes his lab and picks up a bottle of poison (Fig. 2.2),

Figure 2.2 *Dr Jekyll and Mr Hyde* (1912).

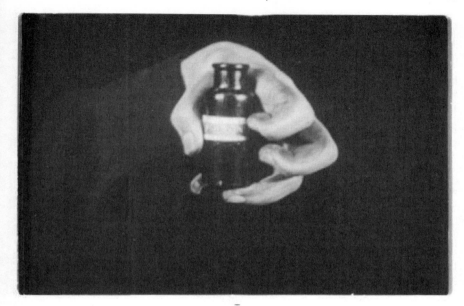

Figure 2.3 *Dr Jekyll and Mr Hyde* (1912).

shown in a close-up insert (Fig. 2.3). Next, we cut back to the long shot in which Hyde drinks the content and is later found dead by his fiancée and the police. The filmmakers make no obvious effort to create spatial continuity between these shots. The hand is shown against a neutral black background and there is a stark contrast between Hyde's violent movements in the long shot and the completely still hand in the insert. The two shot segments seem to inhabit two different spaces. This conceptualization of space also surfaces in descriptions of editing, where inserts are treated as something 'separate' from the long-shot space, here explained by an anonymous Russian critic from 1917, discussing the film *Tsari birzhi* [*Kings of the Stock Exchange*] (1916):

> The actors playing Velinsky and Nadya, badly made up around the eyes, often pull terrible faces. The director ought not to have fastened the audience's attention on these grimaces, which are shown separately from the rest of the picture and much enlarged.[1]

Whereas a modern spectator would see the hand or facial insert as a segment of a larger space extending outside the frame, early cinema audiences and filmmakers interpreted the insert as being outside of *any* spatial realm. Whereas a modern audience would interpret the insert of the hand as the camera/spectator moving closer to the object or face (reflected in the term 'close-up'), the early spectator would have rather conceptualized it in terms of the object magically popping out *towards* the spectator (reflected in their terms 'enlargement' or 'magnification') (Olsson, 1998). The camera was still perceived as a stand-in for the immobile spectator in the theatre seat. The relations between shots were thus associational and conceptual in character rather than spatial. If we are to find modern analogies to this kind of non-spatial reception, perhaps music videos or commercials, with their often fleeting, unstable and sometimes more 'message-oriented' space, may provide us with examples.

In an early historical practice, in which the screen contained all the action and space did not extend beyond the frame, shot changes were experienced in terms of suddenness and abrupt shifts. Images were conceived of as conjured up by the magical machine; many commentators seemed unwilling to make spatial connections between these appearances and disappearances. The space of early cinema was a very unreliable one, from which the unexpected could pop out at arbitrary points in time. It is perhaps no coincidence that conjurers and magicians, with their obsession with presence and absence, constituted a rather important genre at the time. Cinematic space was indeed a magical one.

GUIs: digital space emerges

One of the most revolutionary and commercially successful transitions in computing history was the changeover from command-based interfaces (e.g. DOS) to Graphical User Interfaces (Preece *et al.*, 1994: 18). GUI, which has for years remained the dominant paradigm of human–computer interaction, enabled the *direct manipulation* of objects (Shneiderman, 1992) and forced designers to consider space and spatial practices. The user was here confronted with a radically new form of space, in a way analogous to an early cinema audience. The desktop metaphor was one framework within which this space could be understood, but although it was used by designers as a guide (Erickson, 1990), it is difficult to estimate whether users actually and actively used the analogy in their interaction with computers.

At first sight, the connection between early cinema and GUIs seems somewhat strained. Whereas cinema is photography-based and objects and humans are represented in a realistic style, digital space contains abstracted and highly symbolic objects, such as icons, menus and buttons (Fig. 2.4), which are often marked with text that indicates the nature and function of that object.

However, just as early cinema displayed actors and objects against neutral

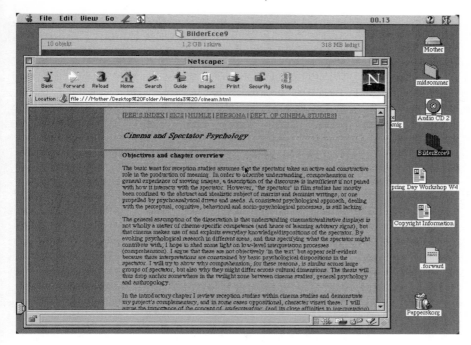

Figure 2.4 A Mac GUI. Reprinted by permission of Apple Computer, Inc. Portions © Netscape Communications Corporation, 1998. All rights reserved. Netscape, Netscape Navigator and the Netscape N logo are registered trademarks of Netscape in the United States and other countries.

or flat backgrounds, thus abstracting the object from it, so do GUIs. Objects seem to be 'floating' without spatial anchors (is it a room? an exterior?), rather like the hand insert in *Dr Jekyll and Mr Hyde*. Also, GUIs display little depth; there is no variation in size between icons to indicate background/foreground relations, and the only depth cue used is spatial overlap (windows stacked upon one another). The flatness of this space is most clearly felt when we replace the neutral single-colour background with a photograph of, for instance, a landscape. Like early cinema, the predominant movement of objects is not in depth, but rather parallel to the screen surface.

The GUI 'camera' is also extremely static. In accordance with early cinema's respect for the wholeness of events, GUIs have no ambition to change visual perspectives or disrupt the time/space continuum. Occasionally there might be some zoom in/out functions, but one still has the impression that it is the document that is coming out towards us, not the other way around.

Overall, 'the camera' maintains immobility and refuses to show us any space beside, beneath or above the screen space. Like early cinema, there is no off-screen space, and all of the action and objects are contained within the frame (no or very few close-ups/enlargements). There is no sound to indicate the presence of things off screen, and since the space is not reducible to any particular environment (except perhaps in the vague desktop analogy) it is impossible to have any expectations of what off-screen space should look like: 'what-you-see-is-what-you-get' (WYSIWYG). Links and buttons clearly hide other information spaces, but these do not exist to the right/left or beneath/above the present space, but somewhat magically 'pop up' and replace 'the old' information space. It would be interesting to investigate the ways in which users conceptualize this form of space: does the text of a document continue beneath the screen or window, or does it just 'disappear' (in accordance with the scroll metaphor)? Is browsing really experienced in terms of travelling *through* hyperspace or is the information coming *to* the user (cf. Maglio and Matlock, 1998)? Does the user make geographical connections between different web pages ('this info is placed in Sao Paolo'; 'this in Stockholm') or are the relations exclusively associational or conceptual in nature ('they relate to a common theme')? Do users interpret windows or web pages as shown 'separately' from some master space or do they belong to the same space? My guess is that such investigations would reveal that the experience of spatiality is subdued in ways similar to early cinema audiences' understanding of relations between shots.

The absence of off-screen space makes the computer screen a self-contained entity, a box in the office, that makes no effort to engulf and surround the user with its spatial practices. Where the screen ends, 'real' office space takes over, in a fashion similar to early cinema space and its relation to the auditorium space. Perhaps it is no coincidence that computer use and early cinema both take place in lit environments, where real space interplays with space on the screen. Another example of this is the way most digital characters (to the extent that there are any) address the user in face-to-face situations: the Microsoft Assistant, for instance, gazes and gestures out towards the user. There is little or no voyeurism in GUIs (see below).

GUIs and digital space are also magical spaces, characterized by sudden changes, appearances and disappearances. The viewpoint is static, and windows and web pages pop out at the user, not unlike the way a rabbit emerges out of a conjurer's hat. There is no spatially realistic interpretation for what is happening when users click on icons and links. However, although there is a common magical denominator between GUIs and early cinema, the magic is somewhat reduced in GUIs, since the (dis)appearances in most cases are felt to be triggered by the user's activities, and not by some other force of narration.

Narrative cinema and spatial immersion

Cinema changed radically during the years from 1905 to 1915. Vaudeville attracted mainly a working-class audience, but in order to secure a more stable and reliable source of income, the industry turned to high-class narrative art forms like theatre, classical literature, myths and religious anecdotes. It was by no means 'natural' for cinema to become 'narrativized', but the economical determinants paved the way for a generic and formal integration (Gunning, 1994; Bordwell, Staiger and Thompson, 1985; Elsaesser, 1990; Musser, 1990; Burch, 1990). In contrast to the 'punctual' nature of magic and short sketches, narratives extend over time and affect the cognition and emotions of the spectator in a more temporal fashion. Indeed, the mainstream cinema that emerged during the period from 1910 to 1920 aimed at being a 'cognitive-emotional roller coaster'. With longer films (around ten minutes by 1910, and feature-length by 1914) and a strongly character-centred form of narrative enabling processes of identification, cinema created the 'narrative immersion' of the spectator. These modes of storytelling were mirrored in the spatial practices they employed, which in a more literal sense sought to engulf the viewer. It is those spatial practices that will be my concern here.

First of all, the bonds between fictive space and auditorium were erased. Characters started to ignore the spectator in the theatre seat by turning their backs to the camera and refusing to look into it. Through the camera, the spectator was allowed to move freely within the fictive space, undetected by the people inhabiting this space, thereby creating a voyeuristic impression: spectators were suddenly able to look into the most secret events of other people's lives without 'being caught'. This created a sharp division between the auditorium space and the 'aquarium world' of the characters, which was to persist into the mainstream cinema of today.

Second, the decor evolved from painted backdrops or black neutral backgrounds to elaborate settings, often shot outdoors. As a consequence, space started to recede perpendicular to the screen, as is seen in Figure 2.5 in the distances between the professor, the fake mummy and the door at the very back. Particularly in Europe, where editing did not achieve the same stronghold as in the USA, staging in depth and moving characters between background and foreground became important narrative and dramatic devices, in strong contrast with the horizontal composition of early cinema (e.g. Fig. 2.1).

Most importantly, however, space was allowed to continue outside the frame. Close-ups and medium shots contained objects and bodies which were only partially visible within the frame (see Fig. 2.6). This did not mean that they were 'cut off', but the spectator cognitively 'filled in' their off-screen presence on the basis of his or her knowledge about objects. In this way, closer

Figure 2.5 *The Egyptian Mummy* (1914). The ignorant professor intends to inject a poisonous embalming liquid into the vagabond ...

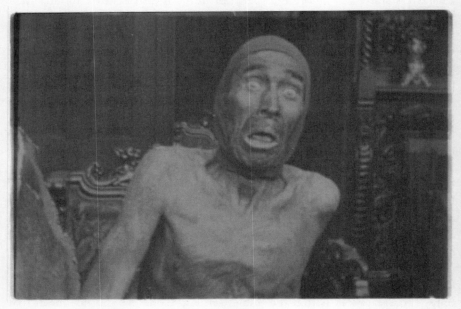

Figure 2.6 ... who fearfully realizes what is about to happen.

shots 'burst the frame' of the vaudeville stage and allowed cinematic space to expand into and overtake theatre space, which then of course had to be pacified and erased by compact darkness and a quiet audience. Tighter shot scales and the notion of off-screen object parts represented the first crucial steps in creating a 'surround' space of cinema.

These immersive strategies of modern cinema become most obvious when considering the different editing techniques established during the transition from early to narrative film. '*Spatial overlap*' refers to inserts like that of Figures 2.5 and 2.6, where the insert covers a part of the larger space in the wider shot. In contrast to the hand insert in *Dr Jekyll and Mr Hyde*, the filmmakers here have a clear ambition to maintain continuity of space, utilizing a background that is similar to that of the long shot, with the door and the mantelpiece acting as landmarks. When the spectator reaches the medium shot (Fig. 2.6), the memory of the space of the long shot (Fig. 2.5) creates an awareness and expectation of the surrounding off-screen space. This sort of shot scale transfer, in combination with the spatial inferences of the spectator, creates an immersive space.

Another commonplace device in mainstream cinema and television is the 'shot/reverse-shot' convention (SRS), cutting back and forth between one gazing/talking person to another. On the basis of the father's gaze and discourse in Figure 2.7, the viewer expects something/someone off screen, and the cut to the son in Figure 2.8 makes that space visible. Now it is the father who is occupying off-screen space. In this way, editing and spectator, in combination, create a common space of 'the father and son looking at each other', although the actors may actually have been filmed on different occasions and locations. Moreover, the spectator also has expectations on the specific *location* of the off-screen presence. On the basis of the direction of gazes the viewer infers that the son must occupy off-screen *right* in Figure 2.7 (somewhere 'behind my back'), and the father off-screen *left* in Figure 2.8. Father and son are looking *at* each other, and not *away* from each other. Keeping directions of gazes and movements consistent across shots (the 180° rule) is one of the most pivotal techniques in creating a space that is coherent and without spatial contradictions and ambiguities, which is essential in order to produce an experience of immersion.

Other techniques can be employed to spatially engulf the spectator (Persson, 1999), most of which were introduced and stabilized by 1915 and are still very much in force. Suffice it here to mention sound, introduced in 1928, which has an inherently 'surround' character unbound by frames and thereby supporting the immersive strategies of the visual track. It is also interesting to note recent technologies like Surround Sound and IMAX, which in essence continue the ambitions to create an increased feeling of spatial immersion.

Figure 2.7 *Ladri di bicilette* (1948). Ricci talks to . . .

Figure 2.8 . . . his son Bruno.

I do not think that filmmakers and producers consciously planned to create immersive space. Rather, they were interested in getting across the story as clearly as possible. To this end inserts and close-ups were important devices to direct the attention and comprehension processes of the spectator to the most important aspects of a given scene. The long shots of early cinema often contained many people and much bustling action, to the point where it was difficult to discern the major protagonists and their activities. Closer framings became necessary to control the flow of story information to the spectator, and thereby manipulating his or her emotions. Thus, immersive space was rather a spin-off effect of the striving for narrativization and comprehensible plot structures.

The future of digital space?

There are some indications that practices in digital space are following the trail of cinematic space. In virtual environments (VR) and 'caves', the abstract, flat and non-immersive space of GUIs is replaced by a deep and simulated surround space, enabling the spectator to − if not tactilely, at least visually − 'move' through space. In flight simulators, mystery games and 'shoot-'em-up' games, screen space can be traversed by the player, who can project space 'behind oneself'. Text-based chat and MUDs (multi-user dungeons) are being replaced by 'rooms' and environments like *Palace*, *Active Worlds* or, in more sophisticated cases, VR teleconferencing systems.

Also, some VR systems seem to employ automatic 'camera control' which chooses angle and view for the user according to an algorithm, trying to predict what the user is doing and what segment of space is most important for the moment. This may be helpful to a user who, for instance, has both hands occupied with other tasks during the interaction and cannot navigate on her or his own (Bares and Lester, 1997). This might include surgeons performing operations, chemists manipulating virtual molecules, submarine personnel mending ship hulls or users moving a creature in the virtual world by manoeuvring a real plush doll (see Johnson *et al.*, 1999, and their *Swamped!* system developed at the MIT Media Lab). Here the system employs many of the editing techniques developed within mainstream cinema, such as the 180° convention. All of these systems burst the screen frame of the GUI and create similar relations between screen and off-screen space as do cinema and real-world perception.

Perhaps GUIs will follow and introduce a mobile 'camera' with which the user can scan the desktop, look left or right in search for objects. Instead of an abstract ICQ indicator blinking when a friend is on-line and wants to chat, perhaps cigarette smoke will pour into the visual field from off-screen right (or an off-screen grunting), indicating the arrival of your friend's avatar on your desktop. Perhaps the abstract icons will become more realistic in appearance and shape as well as in their spatial relations. Maybe GUIs will find a way to properly exploit perpendicular space.

Based on the different functions of cinema and computers, I think some of these trends are more probable than others. Take editing, for instance, which is extremely useful for a narrator in order to present a clear and coherent story. S/he knows best what information and segment of space is most important for the moment. Digital space, on the other hand, is a *performative* space; it includes many objects with endless and complex possible connections and relations between them, the importance of which depends on the momentary purpose of the user. Whether the user is concerned with writing documents, graphical design, information seeking or talking to other people via the keyboard, it is extremely difficult for the system to 'know' exactly what the user is doing, what s/he plans to do next and what segment of space is most important for the moment. The *narrative* function of cinema and the *tool* function of digital space place radically different requirements on the design of these spaces. As cinema *spectators* we have to understand space, but as computer *users* we both have to understand and *act* within digital space, and this makes things much more complicated. Thus it is not surprising that users of *Swamped!*'s automatically controlled camera editing sometimes felt frustrated when the camera 'cut when I was about to do something' (Johnson et al., 1999: 157).

Another case in point would be the spatial immersion of cinema, which contributes to the strong emotional and cognitive engagement of the spectator with the story and its characters (cinema's 'narrative immersion'). Although games may have similar emotional ambitions, most digital spaces do not. Take, for instance, so-called '3-D' browsers or desktops, often rendered in the form of intergalactic space or cities/landscapes. Here, the crucial question is not if immersive space enhances the emotional experience of the interface, but rather if it supports navigating large information spaces (such as the World Wide Web). Navigation involves the semantic structure of the information space, goal formulation, knowing where one is and where one is going and whether one has really reached the goal or has located the correct information for the task at hand (see Dahlbäck, 1998). Neither of these processes seems to be significantly enhanced by the transfer from window-based to '3-D' browsers/desktops. Thus, for this particular function, immersive space makes little sense.

It is easy to be seduced by the 'reality effect' produced by many VR and '3-D' systems, and forget the benefits of abstract and non-immersive space.

Abstraction simplifies and makes some aspects of space more visible than others. The efficiency of visualization techniques is dependent on the purpose to which it is put, and realism might not always be the best option. Consider the discussion group environment *Babble*, developed by IBM Research Centre (Erickson *et al.*, 1999), in which each participant is represented as a coloured blob in a circle. As the participant makes contributions to the discussion, which may be synchronous or asynchronous, the blob will move towards the centre; if a user stays inactive, his blob will drift to the margins of the circle. In this way, a new user entering the discussion may at a quick glance determine the history of the discussion, observing which participants are most active for the moment. This system does not visualize avatars in realistic space with actual distances between them, and as an immersive representation of a multi-participant discussion, *Babble* is extremely poor. As a visualization of the number of contributions made by each participant, however, it works perfectly well.

This points to a general observation: digital spaces with virtual objects are not constructed in order to imitate reality, but to enable the user to accomplish tasks which are impossible or more difficult in reality. Writing software is designed to make text editing, index making and automatic spelling correction more convenient than dealing with typewriters and paper. The abstracted, symbolic and non-realistic visualization techniques of GUIs, will, I think, thus not necessarily follow the realistic and immersive space of cinema, since they are valuable and highly functional within their context. Neither do I believe that digital spaces will become voyeuristic or that avatars, agents and other forms of character will stop acknowledging the user. Many systems that are now exploring the possibilities of anthropomorphic creatures in the interface focus on the dialogic nature between user and interface. *Rea* (Cassell *et al.*, 1999), for instance, is a computer-generated real-estate agent who senses the user through cameras and audio input, understands and generates simple discourse about houses and house buying. In this restricted domain, users/buyers can have dialogues with Rea in real time and she can provide the user with appropriate information. Since dialogue is such a powerful way of interface interaction, it is hardly likely that digital characters will turn away from the user and only attend to their own affairs (like cinematic characters once did).

Although I have only discussed information technology in the form of screen interfaces, one could expect this to change in the future. Computers will become smaller and will be implanted in everyday objects like clothes, kitchen utensils, flower pots and white goods. We will probably be unable to see them, and they will be able to communicate with each other and make decisions for us without our awareness. Specifically how this 'ubiquitous computer space'

will be experienced and what spatial practices it will involve remains to be
seen.

Conclusion

History is an open hypertext with a number of possible paths at any moment
in time. In retrospect it is easy to forget those discarded routes and see history
as a 'natural', linear and therefore Hegelian progress. But in order to get a
better understanding of the technological choices we encounter today,
previously discarded paths may provide important cues. I have maintained that
early cinema and GUIs employ similar spatial practices and that we may learn
something from the way in which cinema later adopted other forms of
visualization techniques. Such historic comparisons do not necessarily provide
answers to what should or should not be done with computers, but they will
hopefully develop and nuance the vocabulary of and sensitivity to different
forms of space and spatial practices, within business as well as research
communities. It is to this endeavour that I hope to have contributed.

Acknowledgements

The author is grateful to archivist Maxime Fletcher and the Wisconsin Center
for Film and Theater Research for supplying all the photographic material. All
still enlargements are from 16-mm prints. The author has been unable to
identify the present copyright holders of the photographic material. Screen
shot reprinted by permission from Apple Computer, Inc. Portions Copyright
Netscape Communications Corporation, 1998. All rights reserved. Netscape,
Netscape Navigator and the Netscape N logo are registered trademarks of
Netscape in the United States and other countries.

Note

1. From '*Tsari birzhi*', in *Kulisy* [*The Wings*] (1917), 9/10: 15–16. Cited in Tsivian
   (1994: 197).

Bibliography

Bares, William H. and Lester, James C. (1997) 'Cinematographic user models for automated realtime camera control in dynamic 3D environments', in *User Modelling '97*, (Sardinia, Italy), pp. 215–26.

Bordwell, D., Staiger, J. and Thompson, K. (1985) *The Classical Hollywood Cinema: Film Style and Mode of Production to 1960* (New York: Columbia University Press).

Burch, Noel (1990) *Life to Those Shadows* (London: BFI Publishing).

Cassell, J., Bickmore, T., Billinghurst, M., Campbell, L., Chang, K., Vilhjálmsson, H. and Yan, H. (1999) 'Embodiment in conversational interfaces: Rea', in *Proceedings for CHI'99 Conference on Human Factors in Computing Systems* (Pittsburgh), pp. 520–7.

Dahlbäck, Nils (ed.) (1998) *Exploring Navigation: Towards a Framework for Design and Evaluation of Navigation in Electronic Spaces*. Deliverable for the Persona project; available at [http://www.sics.se/humle/projects/persona/web/publications.html].

Elsaesser, Thomas (ed.) (1990) *Early Cinema: Space – Frame – Narrative* (London: BFI Publishing).

Erickson, Thomas D. (1990) 'Working with interface metaphors', in Brenda Laurel (ed.), *The Art of Human Computer Interface Design* (Reading, MA: Addison-Wesley), pp. 65–73.

Erickson, T., Smith, D., Kellogg, W., Laff, M., Richards, J. and Bradner, E. (1999) 'Socially translucent systems: social proxies, persistent conversation, and the design of "Babble"', in *Proceedings for CHI'99 Conference on Human Factors in Computing Systems* (Pittsburgh, PA), pp. 72–9.

Gunning, Tom (1994) *D. W. Griffith and the Origins of American Narrative Film* (Chicago: University of Illinois Press).

Hoffman, H. F. (1912) 'Cutting off the feet', *The Moving Picture World*, 12(1) (6 April): 53. Reprinted in George C. Pratt (1973), *Spellbound in Darkness. A History of the Silent Film* (Greenwich: New York Graphic Society), pp. 97–8.

Johnson, M. P., Wilson, A., Blumberg, B., Kline, C. and Bobick, A. (1999) 'Sympathetic interfaces: using a plush toy to direct synthetic characters', in *Proceedings for CHI'99 Conference on Human Factors in Computing Systems* (Pittsburgh, PA), pp. 152–8.

Maglio, Paul and Matlock, Teenie (1998) 'Constructing social spaces in virtual environments: metaphors we surf the Web by', in *Proceedings of Workshop on Personalized and Social Navigation in Information Space* (Stockholm, Sweden), pp. 138–47.

Musser, Charles (1990) *The Emergence of Cinema: The American Screen to 1907* (New York: Charles Scribner's Sons).

Olsson, Jan (1998) 'Magnified discourse: screenplays and censorship in Swedish cinema of the 1910s', in John Fullerton (ed.), *Celebrating 1895. The Centenary of Cinema* (Sydney: John Libbey & Co.), pp. 239–52.

Persson, P. (1999) 'Understanding representations of space: a comparison of visualization techniques in mainstream cinema and computer interfaces', in

A. Munro, K. Höök and D. Benyon (eds), *Social Navigation in Information Space* (London: Springer), pp. 195–216.

Preece, J., Rogers, Y., Sharp, H., Benyon, D., Holland, S. and Carey, T. (1994) *Human-Computer Interaction* (Reading, MA: Addison-Wesley).

Shneiderman, Ben (1992) *Designing the User Interface: Strategies for Effective Human-Computer Interaction* 2nd edn (Reading, MA: Addison-Wesley).

Tsivian, Yuri (1994) *Early Cinema in Russia and Its Cultural Reception*, trans. Alan Bodger (London: Routledge).

3

The space of information

Digital media as simulation of the analogical mind

PETER DALLOW

What is 'familiarly known' is not properly known, just for the reason that it is 'familiar'.

(Hegel, 1967: 92)

Jean Baudrillard warned that there is no worse mistake than taking the real for the real. How much more cautious then need we be in attending to the properties of the *virtually* real. In significant parts of (post)industrialized societies, the mediated world has so invaded the world of everyday life that the two have become indistinguishable, so that *mediated* experience has become imbricated with *immediate* experience. Progressively the media in certain ways have replaced a lived sense of our world. As reality gradually has mutated into hyperreality, notions of simulation, cyberspace and virtual reality, once taken as abstract theoretical premises or science fantasies, have been successively overtaken by technological fact, so that they now appear as the logical expression of contemporary consciousness, and of how we inhabit our lived world.

In introducing new spaces into the existing mediascape, into the existing social spaces, the new digital communications technologies bring with them a new set of spatial practices. But as with all media, what is offered cannot be satisfied. What is virtually real and interactive may seem to pass as real (familiar) experience and as genuine (lived) activity, but of course they are not. Oddly enough, it is the very impossibility of what is offered through digital media – of seemingly direct access to (unmediated) reality and of open-ended activity – which creates a new, 'impossible' space, like that of an M. C. Escher drawing, and which gives rise to new possibilities, requiring a reassessment of older attitudes, to 'get real' about our present circumstances. The emergent interactive media spaces are expressive of the disjuncture between mediated and not-mediated experience, and serve as an analogue of our efforts to reconfigure the 'I'/'not I', existential, spatial conundrum. The on-line media offer us not only a range of site options but also seem to reinstate a nostalgic sense of social interconnectedness. The new visual forms of digital media in particular do afford us a technologically generated notional space, a 'matrix', within which we can (virtually) exercise our identity, analogically, and paradoxically.

When we engage with the new media, we are in a sense present inside a synthetic mediated environment. We experience a sense of actualizing the gridded space of digital information and the associated network of 'pathways' into and through this technologically facilitated structure. Even without the aid of sophisticated forms of (so-called) immersive technologies, we now routinely participate in modifying the form and content of the digitally mediated environment, in real time. This is truly a spatial as well as a temporal experience where *hyperreality* becomes normalized as *virtuality*. Our relation to information, and by extension, to knowledge, has been very rapidly redefined.

Face to (inter)face

Web-based information is dispersed around the planet, in geographic space, along certain vectors. This information is experienced, or at least accessed, via a 'browser', a type of graphical user interface, a flâneuresque shopping metaphor predicated upon two-dimensional pages, which alludes to the architectural spaces of shopping malls, arcades, libraries, galleries, and the like. The browser interface software offers access to these virtual spaces by way of an *informational event*, based upon user-initiated (inter)actions which are predicated upon the uploading and downloading of data. According to Townsend (1998: 7), this generates a participatory event between the user and the computer which emphasizes the present.

The space around this ephemeral event, this computer-generated time-frame, is (momentarily) constructed around the viewer/interactor's point of view. Rather than recuperating the experience of a coherent, single-point perspectival space, or remaining stuck in the flat, anti-perspectival visual space of modernism, with its lack of fixed reference points, the space entered is conditioned by the individual user's experience of an interactive space, *within* the rhyzomic network of networks. The immediacy of this new virtual participatory space, although fractured, weaves its 'web' into a variable, relational spatial realm. We can gain an idea of the (simultaneously) dispersed and atomized qualities which this *differential* space offers from the ways it confounds our experience of near and far, connected and disconnected. The space appears to be *unified through change* (interactivity).

Townsend describes the immediacy of interactive media as working metonymically by instantly shifting positions within 'the containing analogy': 'What is relevant to speed and interconnection is the index and structure as part of the information event, as being specifically subjective, or to show multiple positions or viewpoints to information' (Townsend, 1998: 9–10). We are positioned inside the deep space of the *informational structure* provided, ephemerally, by way of a unique 'event' or viewpoint in time. The factoring of the informational event (time) by the informational space of interactive media offers a sense of a (virtual) identity. Though not 'real', this spatial experience of the immediacy and interaction offered in this virtual space assumes the force of reality, in a Baudrillardian sense. Arguably, this in turn serves as a metaphor for more general interactions, which define so much of who we are, or who we think we are. This hybrid space, delineated by mediated immediacy, is akin to Baudrillard's third order of simulacra, where 'referential reason disappears' and 'production is no longer sure of itself' (Baudrillard, 1983: 102). But in this hyperreal condition which interactive digital media sets up, has referential reason truly disappeared, or has it been virtualized?

Like our 'reconfigured' relation to photographic imagery in the 'post-photographic' era, which Mitchell described (1992), Baudrillard suggests there has been a change in the situation we find ourselves in, which is typified by the 'reversibility of reality and information' (Baudrillard, 1994: 110). Even at the visual representational level of the 2-D flat screen we are confounded with epistemological and ontological problems around digitality. When we look at the image generated from a digital visual media device, for instance, what we see is actually an analogue version of digital information. That is, we see the non-segmented visual appearance of a highly segmented information structure which is based upon numeric values, digits, billions of 'bits' or 'bytes' of data. Thus we see the 'digital' images via the system we most readily comprehend – the illusory visual space of (analogue) representation. But if we attempt to go beyond the 'dot matrix' of this contradictory 'apparent' representational space, into digital space, to try to reach the other world of digitality behind 'the image', as exemplified in the ending of the film *The Matrix*, we would see only the machine code, the patterns of numeric data, 'bits' of digital information, which 'lies' behind the interface. Is it not then the metaphoric 'image' of referential reason itself which appears at the metatextual, metatechnological and metacognitive levels with the advent of digital media? Do 'interactivity', 'virtuality' and 'immersive' not reveal themselves as the mirrored regression of referentiality?

The (inter)play of (inter)activity

In a sense we experience time spatially within the informational structures of interactive media via the simulated information event. Cameron (1998) suggests that the interactive media 'product' can be considered more as a 'model', a spatially defined entity or condition, rather than in terms of the more conventional rhetorical 'proposition', or message, generated by older forms of media. The form of in-*form*-ation – the 'representational space' which emerges or 'appears' in the (inter)activity of new media – is, he suggests, an open-ended engagement, rather than an already enunciated message: 'The design "product" is a representation within which the audience explores and discovers information for themselves, rather than being given it directly in the form of a message' (Cameron, 1998: 7). This is the literalization of McLuhan's aphorism of the medium being the message. With interactive media, we are (relatively) free to explore the medium of the Web, say, without any explicit overarching message having been constructed for us: '(A) quality of playfulness is essential to all engaging interactive representations: play and interactivity are connected at a deep level' (*ibid.*: 8). Thus (inter)*play* is a characteristic of the (inter)*action* with/in new media. Our experience of the information event may be the message, conveyed by the structure of the Internet, but it should also be borne in mind that for the structure of the medium to become apparent, some content must come into play, in the play of randomly accessible 'memory' across the computational space, once uploaded. The 'parts' dis*played* may seem to be formally organized into a 'whole' (experience), in and through play. The global synthetic 'stretch' of the matrix of the new interactive media, however, sits in an uneasy dialogical relation to the immense volumes of data 'in waiting' within it. The ephemeral information event, which emphasizes the organic quality of playfulness, of 'changeability', offers us a way into the chaotic excess of information in the structure of the new media.

Navigating by design in the architectures of light

As we begin to make our way into the information structure of interactive media, what becomes revealed is the '*enframing*' of the web of frameworks, of linkages. This is quantitatively and qualitatively different from the sense of engagement or involvement offered by older media. In the digital realm, we experience being immersed in information, rather than merely retrieving information, as Tofts has argued (Tofts and McKeich, 1997: 73). This reinforces the notion of the new digital visual media consisting of a spatial condition, of entering an 'enframing', a synthetic space. This constitutes a new relation to information, as constituting a virtual structure, constructed in an almost geometric or algorithmic sense by forms of data: 'The historical understanding of "information" as being static, materialistic in the sense of the creation of the physical artefacts of print, and linear has been superseded' (Townsend, 1998: 5). By participating in modifying the form and the content of the mediated environment in real time, we experience the sense of actualizing the networks of pathways, the potential routes through the informational space presented on the screen and facilitated by the technological and textual structure of the hardware and software. We inhabit these digitally created 'vibrant architectures of light', for a 'time'.

If information characterizes much of this new digital domain, then navigation, or some other as yet unnamed equivalent, allows us to interact among the potentially unlimited set of options and pathways through the vibrant space 'described'. The modality of interactivity is nodal: 'In the electronic apparatus, place is a plateau, a temporary stasis achieved while one is in transit between one node and another' (Tofts and McKeich, 1997: 73). Interactivity, in notionally moving us through the (virtual space) of the informational field which appears to surround us, allows us to make choices from the options deployed in real time. Rather than merely looking on, interactivity draws us into a place of enactment, a *mise-en-scène*. We have the sense of 'visiting' sites, of restlessly moving about in the 3-D gridded (cyber)space, while remaining rooted to the one physical place, or 'station', staring at the 2-D flat screen for hours at a time. Ironically we quickly feel frustrated waiting for 'links' to open these remote 'sites', which only a short time ago would have taken hours, days or even weeks to access by previous forms of communications media, if they were accessible at all without physically travelling *there*.

It is the in-between-ness, though, the postponement, which most typifies the viewer's 'Lost in Space' response to the excessiveness of the Web, of being positioned between texts, in the designer geometries of cyberspace, rather than being caught up by individual texts. This is consistent with Steve Pile's 'metaphorical logic of spatialisation' in the way in which 'bodies are caught in webs of analogons such as images, signs and symbols' (Pile, 1996: 165). In *hyper*textuality, *inter*textuality is literalized.

Interactive media, despite seeming to enclose us in their architectonics of light, in the glowing web of connections which wrap around us, also, paradoxically, afford us emotional detachment. It is not just hip to go on-line, but in McLuhan's terms 'cool'. We have a far greater sense of being in control of the shape of what is being negotiated in the representational space of the new media than we might in a film or television programme, where we would be engaged more by the feel of what is being presented. There is an even

greater sense of form predominating over content, although content may be
what we initially go in search of. The structure of the Web, the links, seem to
dominate any sense of the specific detail of the immense volumes of
information stored digitally and available on-line. Little wonder we require a
'search engine' to 'navigate' by.

Functional design considerations may be paramount in issuing iterative
'applications' into the glowing processual space of the new media, but more
than meaning is deferred until reception — the performance of interaction
'structures' the informational experience as an event in the space of
consumption, so that both form and content can be different with each
'launch'. Reproduction becomes production. Cameron proposes that interactive
media can be viewed as affording a space waiting to be played with, so to
speak:

> An interactive representation is information *in waiting*; it refers to a
> principle, a set of rules, an algorithm, a stasis outside time, that can
> simulate events and information in time. The referent, the thing other
> than itself to which the simulation refers, is the condition for
> communication, not the message itself.
>
> (Cameron, 1998: 7, my emphasis)

The distinctions between production and reproduction and consumption
become blurred in the 'information in waiting' condition of interactive media.
There is no formal separation of the interactive experience from the spectator's
desire. Reception becomes enunciation. The author is not so much dead, as the
user has also become writer/designer.

In the way that analogue representations (so-called digital images) of digital
space serve as a metaphor of the ways in which human intelligence
accumulates 'bits' of experiential information about the chaos of the
phenomenal world and attempts to construct this into a subjective 'image'
of that world, so too interactivity serves as a metonym of the ways in which
we constantly test that knowledge through hypothesizing. This interactive
methodology of higher-order cognition, of trying to connect different bits of
information together into certain patterns or pictures, and in turn into abstract
'conceptions', is consistent with a view of new media which emphasizes
signification and performativity, and of the potential which the process
possesses for creating a new (third) processual space. The cultural process of
information dispersal as articulation, on the one hand, and 'acts' of engagement
with these new media on the other, revise and hybridize the conventional
locale and locations of the user's social activity (which gives rise to 'avatars'
and other parallel forms of cyber-identity). But every deterritorialization, every

effort to transcend our present relation to space and time, necessarily involves a reterritorialization. There is no outside, no place we can reach 'there', outside of culture, however much we may desire it. Lefebvre writes of the 'gestural simulation' of travel:

> So what escape can there be from a space thus shattered into images, into signs, into connected-yet-disconnected data directed at a 'subject' itself doomed to abstraction? For space offers itself like a mirror to the thinking 'subject', but, after the manner of Lewis Carroll, the 'subject' passes through the looking-glass and becomes a lived abstraction.
>
> (Lefebvre, 1991: 313–14)

Although discursive space cannot be left behind, the new media spaces may offer new opportunities, new spaces, for dialogically reworking older binaries.

From geography to infography

The characteristics of contemporary life, according to Paul Virilio, are the speeding up of (historical) time and the effective diminution of (geographic) space, so that: 'the *far* horizon of our planet's antipodes has finally become an apparent, or more precisely, "trans-apparent" horizon, through the effects of audiovisual techniques' (Virilio, 1995: 142–3). Thus a new frontier, one that is not geographic, but infographic, makes itself felt. Distance on the globe yields to 'the instrumental imagery of a computer that can generate a virtual otherworld, thanks to the computing speed of its integrated circuits' (*ibid.*: 143). This virtual 'other world' can be accessed by an interface, a 'doorway to other worlds' which is both personal and portable.

This spatio-technological discourse also suggests a way of considering some of the means by which the new 'cultural technologies', which Jody Berland speaks of, produce a 'continuous sensory and spatial reorganization of social life' (Berland, 1992: 43). It is our relation to information which increasingly effectively defines the space we inhabit, and many of the events which occur in that space. Virilio suggests that confusion between real space and virtual space, and between action and 'retroaction', in turn leads to uncertainty about 'the place of effective action'. Thus the possibilities for locating and controlling the virtual environment are in doubt. The possibilities of the informational space of digital media may be as limitless and uncertain as those of reality, yet the potentiality of the virtuality of new media spatiality, like temporality, is conditional. It cannot exist without a perceiver. Aristotle observed that time cannot exist without a soul to count it. In a similar way space, unlike place, has to be lived, as de Certeau pointed out. The informational space of the new media has to be *actualized* through human agency.

Our physical relation to information has been altered through new forms of technological mediation. We can access centralized spaces – mainframes, libraries, stores – and everyday spaces – banks, libraries, databases, books, disks, journals, and so on – from any telephone point or mobile phone, from domestic spaces, cafés, beaches. This new relation to information has atomized and splintered older social and political spaces, and redefined workplace and domestic spaces, for example through such practices as teleworking. The new media have, as McKenzie Wark (1992) observed of the vectors of other global media, spread rapidly and unpredictably. They have become a medium of the everyday for many of us in post-industrial societies, far exceeding the entertainment and informational possibilities of older media. They have also significantly transformed the experience of space through the almost instantaneous feedback loops of the digital global information environment.

Like all media, digital interactive media are a product of 'an institutional matrix', according to Wark, and not merely a cultural artefact. The representational spaces of digital media, like other mental, social and physical spaces, are both medium and message, especially in articulating the workings of power (see Pile, 1996: 153). That is, the spaces produced in and through digital media reinscribe the forces which materially give rise to them. Debord said of 'the spectacle' that it is capital 'to such a degree of accumulation that it becomes an image' (Debord, 1994: 24). The media, a key institution in the constellation of corporate capitalism, thus reveal themselves as the mirrored image of the invisible 'moving totality of relations of power and communication' in society (Wark, 1992: 149). Harvey put it that capitalism perpetually 'strives to create a social and physical landscape in its own image and requisite to its own needs at a particular point in time' (Harvey, 1985: 150).

So the dispersed condition of the digital web, with its invisible, rhyzomic links, serves as an analogue of the decentred market system. It generates a mimetic space for that analogue of the intrinsic operations of the decentred global market system, which conceals itself, even as it is brought into view. Virilio presciently observed:

> How can we fail to notice that the imminent reign of computer-generated virtuality was made possible, indeed necessary, by the long-awaited advent of globalization? If the world is closing in on itself and becoming a finite world, according to Merleau-Ponty, the necessity of overtaking it becomes patently obvious.
>
> (Virilio, 1995: 142)

The massification of digital media forms, and the World Wide Web and Internet in particular, reveals the image of the need for post-Cold War capitalism to remap and reterritorialize both itself and the world. This mapping/territorialization is enacted through various representational practices, which vary from time to time, and from medium to medium. For instance, global capital reproduces itself through the 'image' of the global information economy, most readily typified by its emergent subset, the Internet economy. It can, of course, in turn also be seen to reinvent itself through the various forms of on-line trading, none the least the regressing mirror image of on-line trading in shares in new technology 'start-ups'.

A different kind of space

If each phase of history is marked by a particular logic of visualization, as Lefebvre has argued, then as we move deeper into the digital era, where images are more widely dispersed throughout the everyday world than ever before, we seem to be moving towards a logic of visualization in which images are frequently no more than the entry point to the (informational) matrix. Here visual representations represent representational space itself, so to speak. Instructional texts in 'doing' new media, such as Stansberry, emphasize the way interface design is about creating a visual screen environment which is sufficiently consistent and familiar that we might want to 'enter' the metaphoric interface space, and hence pass through the 'cognitive wall' between computer and user, seemingly gaining direct access to the 'site' (Stansberry, 1998: 36). This illustrates the shift that is under way from the organization around a 'text', which Kress has identified, to a newer form of organization around an informational 'resource'. That is, there is a shifting away from a concern with *knowledge* to one with gathering *information* (Kress, 1997: 66). The graphical forms of new media, for instance, offer a display, rather than an image as such. 'Clickable' icons and image 'hotspots' offer user-selectable entry points to the informational space.

In Lefebvre's terms, the employment of certain (spatial) practices to create the illusion of representing space generates a space of representation, a virtual space which is not fixed, and hence that we experience subjectively. This seemingly individualized space is analogous to the lived space/s of subjectivity, and, by extension, to life: 'People look, and take sight, take seeing, for life itself' (Lefebvre, 1991: 75).

If every mode of production has its own space, and hence, operationally, must have its own spatial practices, as Lefebvre argues, then the nature and dimensions of the spaces of new forms of digital media, far more than for older forms of media, are more overtly articulated and (redetermined) in the act of consuming, and the space of consumption. Rather than being caught up in the binaries of subject–object, it is the in-between-ness of these conditions in new media which seems to typify or convey the sense of the spatial dynamic at work. Pile's account of spatio-visual regimes refers to Lefebvre's 'metonymic logic of spatialization', in which 'a continual to-and-fro ... between the part and the whole' appears to give rise to the dialectical topography of the implied space (Pile, 1996: 165).

The spatial practices, the way these practices codify and hence represent space, and the symbolism by which meaning accrues to those representations in the process of interaction is how subjectivity is primarily perceived to be brought into relief. It is through the particular chains of associations with the metaphors and metonyms at work that we reveal our 'selves': 'The interactions between these associations produce intricate and dense matrices of meaning which are "topographical" in the sense not only that difference is produced "spatially", but also that matrices are played out in specific sites' (Pile, 1996: 177). This seems to be particularly true of the informational spaces opened up by/with the new forms of media. This informational 'web' in waiting exists like a proscenium arch which we enter – a space of enactment and performance, a 'theatrical space'. This virtual proscenium of new digital media, which William J. Mitchell describes as 'a hole cut through the membrane separating the space of our bodies ... from cyberspace' (Mitchell, 1999: 33), is not merely to do with the physical parameters of the computer screen which operationally becomes the centre of attention, rendering all else peripheral, but describes a much broader spatial potentiality, a 'third space', which is actualized as we log on.

So-called immersive digital media (VR) put a monitor in miniaturized form in front of each eye, literally monopolizing vision, as the theatre and cinema attempt to do through dramatic, cathartic devices. But here the proscenium arch becomes a headset, which then slips out of view. We are 'inside'. Here, the addition of seeming real-time physical interactivity is further enhanced by the interactor wearing head-tracking devices which synchronize the 'computed scene' with the motion of the wearer. The perspective of the viewpoint being presented, or actualized, is 'refreshed' to match the viewer's movements, conveying the sense of three-dimensional virtuality. This virtual reality gear affords the sensation of actually being inside cyberspace.

The virtual proscenium of cyberspace seems to literalize the aspirations implicit in the employment of perspectivally rendered space. As the camera lucida gave rise to the Renaissance perspectival scopic regime, which 'imaged' the individual-focused, secularized modern world-view emerging at the time, VR technology serves to 'render' reality in its virtual scopic regime, and also serves as an analogue of the way we now experience space as a convolution of the mediated and the immediate. Mitchell describes something of this: 'In a world of proliferating screen space and speakers, smart surfaces, video-projected displays, virtual reality, and augmented reality, luminous digital information is ubiquitously overlaid on tangible physical reality' (Mitchell, 1999: 41).

Informational space, in the sense in which I am using the notion here, is about the conceptual experience of a mediated potentiality which overlays the whole environment of the digital era. The construction of these new cultural spaces, however, does not so much enable us to transcend the old cognitive distinctions as serve as metaphors for the desire to do so. Pile articulates a notion of third spaces being produced through the dialectical processes of 'public/private, seen/unseen, fictions/real, experienced/perceived' (Pile, 1996: 161). 'Negative' spaces are created in the interstices between these bi-polar distinctions, and in the interrelationships between body/machine, time/space, local/global, form/content. Although the architectonics of the new media space may seem set or fixed by these distinctions, they are instead 'made fluid by difference', through repetition − 'differentiation endlessly produces difference' (*ibid.*: 162). Perhaps the most significant of these differentiations in relation to the spatial practices of new digital media is that between human and information, which, according to Mitchell, will increasingly become 'the enabler of new social constructions' (Mitchell, 1999: 14). The informational environment, the immense collective construction of computational hardware and software, of communications systems and of network protocols, will increasingly and significantly not only reflect our real, imaginary and symbolic spaces but also help to reshape them.

The dream of technology

The essence of modern technology, Heidegger implies in *The Question Concerning Technology*, is not to do with the technological apparatus itself, or the representations from the technology, but shows itself in 'enframing'. Enframing in turn is nothing technological but the way 'the real reveals itself as standing-reserve' (Heidegger, 1977: 23). That is, 'the real' reveals itself as a 'mode of ordering', a 'gathering together', which is revealed in the 'bringing-forth' of *poiesis*: 'Always the unconcealment of that which is goes upon a way of revealing' (*ibid.*: 25). In a sense as we stand within our increasingly sophisticated technological enframing, we are not necessarily getting any closer to 'that which is'. The new media provide a new space, as the older arts and media did before, a space for bringing forth from the depths, not what is there, but 'what is sayable', for encountering 'what is susceptible of figuration', as Lefebvre (1991: 139) termed it.

What is brought forth into presence through virtuality, then, is not so much reality, as the mind's image of it. What is revealed in the space opened up by the new media, in part, is the figure of the mind, an analogue of some of its workings and its aspirations to exceed itself, to attempt to transcend being a *mere species being*, as Benjamin termed it. Thus Mitchell writes of the 'smart objects' being equipped with cameras and microphones as 'eyes' and 'ears', of 'smart artefacts' with 'embedded memory and machine intelligence' to process information and respond (Mitchell, 1999: 45).

If psychoanalysis was, among other things, an attempt by Freud to 'reinstate mind or "psyche" back into the realm of scientific discourse', as Wertheim (1999: 233) has proposed, then, a century later, interactive media also appear to attempt to reinscribe the notion of subjectivity into the supposed objectivity of the machinic apparatus of instrumental logic. Cyberspace can be seen as 'a new realm for the "self" '. Wertheim suggests 'a new space for the playing out of some of those immaterial aspects of humanity that have been denied a home, in the purely physicalist world picture' (*ibid.*: 232).

The relativistic space of individually focused new media is in part a product of the microchip, the algorithm and the quest to literalize the web of meanings unravelled upon the therapist's couch. As the photographic camera arguably was the inevitable consequence of the single-point perspectival visual regime, with its vanishing point, interactive media can be seen as the inevitable consequence of hybridizing the digital void of computing science with that of psychoanalysis. Our sense of being, of illumination, is relocated in relation to the space of information, and, conversely, of disinformation.

In a Lacanian sense, what we see in the mirror of the digital mediascape is the metaphorical image of the workings of our minds, the abstraction of the metaphoric and metonymic aspects of the new spatio-visual regime. It is analogous to the ways in which our subjectivity itself is abstracted, and of the relational dimensions of community, and its construction. New digital-analogue technologies which permit the wearing of visors that allow us to see the world before us and simultaneously view on-line information will challenge and extend the 'I' and 'not I' differential, as will the advent of the cyborg, a hybrid human clone/machine, in which technology and media, human and machine, will merge. In this even more hybridized informational and cultural space, the 'smart' (digital) sensibility will struggle to confront its own (analogical) limits.

The new space of information of the digital era may metaphorically speak of power, and metonymically represent our aspirations to hold sway over the social world through particular spatial practices, to control 'others', but it also serves as a space where we encounter our own image, and enact narratives of self, our own desire to achieve a post-human digitality, the 'virtual, derisory immortality' Baudrillard (1994: 119) wrote of, in which we upload our (digital) consciousnesses to cyberspace so that we may inhabit a technological dreamscape, while our material (analogue) body lies cryogenically frozen in limbo, in Purgatorio, waiting to be 'beamed up' to reunion in Heaven. Or Hell.

Bibliography

Baudrillard, J. (1983) *Simulations* (New York: Semiotext(e)).

Baudrillard, J. (1994) *The Illusion of the End*, trans. C. Turner (Cambridge: Polity Press).

Berland, J. (1992) 'Angels dancing: cultural technologies and the production of space', in L. Grossberg, C. Nelson and P. Treichler, *Cultural Studies* (New York: Routledge), pp. 38–51.

Cameron, A. (1998) 'The medium is messy', *Eye*, 30(2): 6–7.

Debord, G. (1994) *The Society of the Spectacle*, trans. D. Nicholson-Smith (New York: Zone).

Harvey, D. (1985) *The Urbanization of Capital* (Oxford: Blackwell).

Hegel, G. W. F. (1967) *The Phenomenology of the Mind*, trans. J. B. Baillie (New York: Harper Torchbooks).

Heidegger, M. (1977) *The Question Concerning Technology and Other Essays* (New York: Harper Torchbooks).

Kress, G. (1997) 'Visual and verbal modes of representation in electronically mediated communication: the potentials of new forms of text', in I. Snyder (ed.), *Page to Screen: Taking Literacy into the Electronic Era* (St Leonards, NSW: Allen & Unwin), pp. 53–79.

Lefebvre, H. (1991) *The Production of Space*, trans. D. Nicholson-Smith (Oxford: Blackwell).

Mitchell, W. J. (1992) *The Reconfigured Eye: Visual Truth in the Post-Photographic Era* (Cambridge, MA: MIT Press).

Mitchell, W. J. (1999) *The E-topia: 'Urban life, Jim – but not as we know it'* (Cambridge, MA: MIT Press).

Pile, S. (1996) *The Body and the City: Psychoanalysis, Space and Subjectivity* (London: Routledge).

Stansberry, D. (1998) *Labyrinths: The Art of Interactive Writing and Design: Content Development for New Media* (Belmont, CA: Wadsworth).

Tofts, D. and McKeich, M. (1997) *Memory Trade: A Prehistory of Cyberspace* (North Ryde, NSW: Interface).

Townsend, S. (1998) 'Unfolding the surface of information', *Design Issues*, 14(3): 5–18.

Virilio, P. (1995) *The Art of the Motor* (Minneapolis: University of Minnesota Press).

Wark, M. (1992) 'To the vector the spoils: towards a vectoral analysis of the global media event', in E. Jacka, *Continental Shift: Globalisation and Culture* (Double Bay, NSW: Local Consumption), pp. 142–60.

Wertheim, M. (1999) *The Pearly Gates of Cyberspace: A History of Space from Dante to the Internet* (Sydney: Doubleday).

4

Cyborgs and cyberspace

Personal identity and moral agency

DAVID SANFORD HORNER

Cyberspace has been characterized as 'a utopian vision for our post-modern times' (Robins, 1996: 1). The creation of new technologies of the virtual holds out the promise of deliverance from the limitations of existence in physical space. The ontology of this virtual space is an ontology without bodies. In the metaphysics of virtuality 'cyberspace supplants physical space' (Heim, 1993: 99). Cyberspace has come to represent for its proponents a counter space where, as Sadie Plant ironically pointed out, freedom is only limited by imagination:

> Virtual reality (VR), cyberspace, and all aspects of digital machines are still said to promise 'a freedom that is limited only by our imaginations ... mastery of a realm of creation (or destruction ...) a realm of the mind — seemingly abstract, cool, clean, and bloodless, idealistic, pure, perhaps part of the spirit, that can leave behind the messy, troublesome body and the ruined material world'. Cyberspace emerged as a disembodied zone wilder than the wildest West, racier than the space race, sexier than sex, even better than walking on the moon. This was the final of final frontiers, the purest of virgin islands, the newest of new territories, a reality designed to human specifications, an artificial zone ripe for an infinite process of colonization, able to satisfy every last desire, especially to escape from 'the meat'.
>
> (Plant, 1997: 180)

This is very much a case of old wine in new bottles. The ideas of personhood, identity, inner and outer space, which are expressed in these new technological visions, have deep roots in Western culture. For example, they tap into a

Platonic-Cartesian view of persons as somehow incorporeal, disembodied and ultimately otherworldly. At other moments the identity which is invoked echoes David Hume's account of personal identity as defined by 'nothing but a bundle or collection of different perceptions, which succeed each other with an inconceivable rapidity, and are in a perpetual flux and movement' (Hume, 1967: 302). The idea of identity as something fluid and incorporeal appears in various strands of postmodernist thinking, exemplified in cyberfeminist and post-humanist writing, and is underpinned by the apparent potentialities offered by the technologies of virtuality (Robins, 1996).

The world, the flesh and the devil

To establish some cultural perspective let me begin with an earlier utopian vision which engages with the transcendence of inner and outer space. In 1929 the British scientist J. D. Bernal published *The World, the Flesh and the Devil*, a speculative vision of a future which could be shaped, if we so chose, by the planned application of science and scientific method. The book was a manifesto for the replacement of a religious vision of the world by a scientific one – reflecting Bernal's own conversion from Catholicism to Marxism in the early 1920s. This was emphasized by the ironic use in the title of the words of the Litany from the *Book of Common Prayer*: 'From all the deceits of the world, the flesh, and the devil, Good Lord, deliver us'. The subtitle of the book, 'An enquiry into the future of the three enemies of the rational soul', indicates the architecture of his argument. Bernal's dream was of an abstract, disembodied scientific intelligence which would be triumphant over 'the three enemies of the rational soul'. Bernal sought to show, by extrapolating from the then current trends in science and technology, how these would subdue 'the world' in the interests of human needs. Bernal forecast the conquest of (literal) space: he proposed the construction of a human habitat in space consisting of a three-dimensional, gravitationless, spherical shell, ten miles or so in diameter, made up from the substance of one or more smaller asteroids, the rings of Saturn or other planetary detritus. Under competitive pressures or in anticipation of the death of the sun, human beings would pass eventually beyond the solar system. Therefore, by intelligent organization we would ultimately cheat the finitudes of the universe.

As for the conquest of 'the flesh', Bernal proposed an even more radical vision: he argued that modern mechanical and chemical discoveries would make the current skeletal and metabolic functions of the body redundant. The human species was an evolutionary dead end, but our further development could be predicated upon a break with organic evolution in favour of 'mechanical' evolution. To some extent, like McLuhan, Bernal saw technology as 'the extension of man' – technology as prosthetic. The increasing complexity of human existence demanded a much more complex sensory and motor organization, and a better organized cerebral mechanism:

> Instead of the present body structure we should have the whole framework of some very rigid material, probably not metal but one of the new fibrous substances. In shape it might well be rather a short cylinder. Inside the cylinder, and supported very carefully to prevent shock, is the brain with its nerve connections, immersed in a liquid of the nature of cerebro-spinal fluid, kept circulating over it at uniform temperature. The brain and the nerve cells are kept supplied with fresh oxygenated blood and drained off deoxygenated blood through their arteries and veins which connect outside the cylinder to the artificial heart-lung digestive system . . . The eyes will look into a kind of optical box which will enable them alternatively to look into periscopes projecting from the case, telescopes, microscopes and a whole range of televisual apparatus . . .
> (Bernal, 1969: 38)

Here Bernal anticipates the cyborg – the hybrid of the technological and the human. Sense organs would tend to be less and less attached to bodies, and the host of subsidiary, purely mechanical agents and perceptors would be capable of penetrating those regions where organic bodies cannot enter or hope to survive. The interior of the earth and the inmost cells of living things would be open to consciousness through these 'angels' (messengers), as would the motions of stars.

For Bernal the criterion of living is the capacity for conscious thought associated with the brain. However, this new evolution would lead in the direction of 'the permanent compound brain', which would be a networking of several individual brains. This opened up the possibility that death might well be postponed beyond current life horizons. Through this cerebral merging an immortal, multiple individual would emerge with older components being replaced by newer ones. The technical problem was 'simply' that of providing the most favourable environment for the survival of brain cells.

Bernal envisaged that somehow the continuity of individual selves would be maintained in spite of these cerebral mergings. Within the network of the 'compound brain' he believed that the identity and continuity of the human individual would somehow be maintained but with a new transparency of communication. Such directness of communication would transcend the normal limits of human relationships; feelings and memories would be held in common, division of labour would set in, and there would develop a hierarchy of minds, which could extend their perceptions and understanding far beyond those of the individual:

> The new life would be more plastic, more directly controllable, and at the same time more variable and more permanent than that produced by the triumphant opportunism of nature. Bit by bit the heritage in the direct line of mankind – the heritage of the original life emerging on the face of the world – would dwindle, and in the end disappear effectively, being preserved perhaps as some curious relic, while the new life conserves none of the substance and all of the spirit of the old would take its place and continue its development ... consciousness itself may end or vanish in a humanity that has become etherialised, losing the close-knit organism, becoming masses of atoms in space communicating by radiation, and ultimately perhaps resolving itself entirely into light.
>
> (Bernal, 1969: 46)

Bernal's fantasy can be read as an anticipation of, or a metaphor for, 'the networked society' with its celebration of instantaneous communication and the creation of new types of non-spatial communities (Rheingold, 1994). It is even more suggestive of Gibson's *Neuromancer*, where cyberspace was originally defined as:

> A consensual hallucination experienced daily by billions of legitimate operators, in every nation, by children being taught mathematical concepts ... a graphic representation of data abstracted from the banks of every computer in the human system. Unthinkable complexity. Lines of light ranged in the nonspace of the mind, clusters and constellations of data. Like city lights, receding ...
>
> (Gibson, 1995: 67)

Bernal's utopia, however, is not that of an earthly paradise designed for the ultimate satisfaction of the 'pleasure principle'. The conquest of want and scarcity through science and technology provides only the basis for further challenge and exploration. The devil is understood by Bernal, in crudely Freudian terms, as the power of the Id, the inner impulse of the pleasure principle. The devil was symbolic of sexually unrepressed humanity and its quest for sensual bodily pleasures. Only when the devil was expelled could the world be abandoned and the flesh subdued. The chief danger to his progressive vision might be the turning away from science. Sexuality needed to be balanced by rational activity in recognition of the reality principle. The ideals of the super-ego should be brought in line with external reality – using and rendering innocuous the power of the Id — technologizing the psyche and transforming inner space. For Bernal, to live more fully would be to live a more intense intellectual life. This translates into the idea of constant action, perpetual self-transformation and the transformation of the natural world (Easlea, 1981: 19). Curiously what begins as an apotheosis of scientism becomes increasingly mystical and religious, imbued with a kind of Faustian spirit of (masculine) conquest, and so 'Bernal's dream of the abstract disembodied intelligence stands as the antithesis of feminism's dreams of an embodied situated knowledge' (Rose, 1994: 217).

Trends in cyber-idealism: ghosts in the machine

Bernal's vision was linked to a political project of social transformation inspired by a fusion of science and socialism, the belief in the creation of a planned social order. *The World, the Flesh and the Devil* provides an anticipation of the preoccupations of current prophets of cyberspace, virtual reality and cyborgs. In the same way, current futuristic thinking about information and communications technologies (ICTs) resembles a utopian project which I will call 'cyber-idealism'.

For an example of contemporary heirs to this Bernalian dream we need look no further than the posthumanist visions of the Extropians. Their celebration of the possibilities of new technologies similarly gestures towards the transcendence of the body and of space (literal and metaphorical). Dery writes that:

> Cybercultures's most vocal proponents of consigning the body to the scrap heap of the twentieth century are Extropians who espouse a form of transhumanism based on an explicit contempt for the body and the material. This Manichaean project proposes a transformation of the species based on 'downloading' and 'nano-medicine'.
>
> (Dery, 1996: 302)

The Extropy Institute, founded in 1992 in the USA, acts as a catalyst for the promotion of Extropian principles. For example, the first principle of the Institute's 'Transhumanist Declaration' states:

> Perpetual progress — Seeking more intelligence, wisdom, and effectiveness, an indefinite lifespan, and the removal of political, cultural, biological, and psychological limits to self-actualization and self-realization. Perpetually overcoming constraints on our progress and possibilities. Expanding into the universe and advancing without end.
>
> (More, 1999: 1)

Extropianism is a radical vision of the transformation of what it means to be human through the use of advanced computing technology and nanomedicine (atomic-level medical interventions to 're-engineer' the human body); what emerges, however, as a central theme is contempt for the body. Hans Moravec (Director of the Mobile Robot Laboratory at Carnegie-Mellon's Field Robotics Center) is a key figure for such posthumanist visions in promoting the belief that the mind can be technologically separated from the body. Moravec proposes that the mind can be 'downloaded'. The idiosyncratic neural networks of human minds can be mapped on to computer memory – rendering the body superfluous.

The Extropians, like Bernal, believe that the harnessing of technology as 'the extension of man' will lead to a breakthrough in the evolution of the species. This evolutionary step may even involve the division of the species into those who embrace the potential of new technologies and those who remain rooted and constrained by the human:

Rather than simple exploitation of VR technology Extropianism envisages nano-computer implants – integrated into the brain to provide additional memory, processing power and the ability to run sophisticated decision-making programs. Extropians wish to exploit genetic engineering, smart drugs and cryogenics and self-transformative psychology to produce a quantum jump in the evolution of the human species.

(Dery, 1996: 302)

In contrast to the socialism of Bernal, however, the Extropians champion laissez-faire capitalism and express an enthusiasm for all forms of new technology. Their philosophy, imbued with Nietzschean ideas of the will to power, emphasizes individualism and criticizes statism and collectivism as the roots of social and political evil. The great evolutionary change, producing some higher form of being, brings with it the end of morality and the transvaluation of values:

Posthumanist visions of the mind unbound, of the Earth dwindling to a blue pinpoint in the rearview mirror, are a wish fulfillment fantasy, situated (at least for now) in a world of limits. The envisioned liftoff from biology, gravity and the twentieth century by barging, morphing, 'downloading', or launching out minds beyond all bounds is itself held fast by the gravity of the social and economic realities, moral issues, and environmental conditions of the moment. Try as they might to tear loose from their societal moorings and hurtle starward, the millennium science fictions of 'transcendental' posthumanists ... remain earthbound.

(Dery, 1996: 315)

Cyber-idealism has its feminist form, but in contrast to Extropians this alternative set of discourses on identity and cyberspace is formulated on a central premise of postmodernism – the concept of the fractured, plural condition of the subject. As Robins notes:

> Weaving together a blend of post-structuralist theory and cyberpunk fiction, this other discourse charts the emergence of cyborg identities. In the new world order, old and trusted boundaries – between human and machine, self and other, body and mind, hallucination and reality – are dissolved and deconstructed.
>
> (Robins, 1996: 8)

Cyberfeminism seeks to liberate technoculture from its patriarchal origins. The *locus classicus* here is Haraway's 'A manifesto for cyborgs' (1990), which was first published in the mid-1980s in *Socialist Review*; it exploits a utopian tradition of imagining a world without gender by the fusing and transcending of the natural and the artificial, the biological and the technological, much in the same way that Bernal sixty years earlier harnessed the science and technology of the day to his political project. The cyborg for Haraway is an ironic political myth, which seeks to subvert the 'informatics of domination' – the macho militarized, commercialized world of advanced capitalist technologies (Haraway, 1990: 205). Claudia Springer (1991) sees the cyborg as the consummate postmodern concept – cyberspace as an insulated place for unconstrained, omnipotent experience. For Sadie Plant (1993) cyberspace provides the opportunity for exciting new adventures with off-the-shelf identities and, according to Jaron Lanier (1990), the new technologies will deliver us from the limits and defeats of physical reality and the physical body.

As Dery (1996) points out, cyberfeminism is convergent also with Derridean post-structuralism in that it argues that Western systems of meaning are underwritten by binary oppositions: body/soul; other/self; matter/spirit; emotion/reason; natural/artificial and so on. These binary oppositions are constructed so that the first term of each hierarchical dualism is subordinated to the second and privileged one. Haraway criticizes trends in feminist theory which simply seek to reverse such binary oppositions: biology rather than technology, for example. However, much against her own initial materialist intentions, the cyborg manifesto quickly became assimilated into cyber-idealism as the projection of a future untroubled by ambiguity and difference which reconciles mechanism and organism, culture and nature, simulacra and original, science fiction and social reality (Squires, 1996).

Cyber-idealism and the Form of the Good

If these future states of cyber-idealism are more desirable than the present, then we are, of necessity, confronted by a moral vision — a vision of the Good Life. As Nowell-Smith points out:

> What sort of principles a man [sic] adopts will, in the end, depend on his vision of the Good Life, his conception of the sort of world he desires, so far as it rests with him, to create. Indeed his moral principles just *are* this conception.
>
> (Nowell-Smith, 1965: 313)

Heim, for example, attempts to show how the Form of the Good (its essential nature and ideal template) in Platonism might be realized by the technology of the virtual as cyber-entities:

> The ideal Forms in early Platonism has the allure of a perfect dream. But the ancient dream remained airy, a landscape of genera and generalities, until the hardware of information retrieval came to supplant the mind's quest for knowledge. Now with the support of the electronic matrix, the dream can incorporate the smallest details of here and now existence. With an electronic infrastructure, the dream of perfect Forms becomes the dream of Information.
>
> (Heim, 1993: 89)

Heim attempts to shape Platonic idealism to the contours of the networked, virtual society — the physical world being only a pale reflection of the perfect, incorporeal world of the virtual. The good society will take the form of an electronic community or communities (akin to Bernal's cerebral mergings), whose identities will be defined not by geographical location or related political boundaries. Cybernetic communities will literally be 'nowhere', like Morris's *Erewhon*. Dery, for example, reads Gibson's *Neuromancer* as an extended reflection on mind/body dualism as it surfaces in cyberculture:

> The opposition of the dead, heavy flesh ('meat', in compu-slang) and the ethereal body of information — the discorporated self — is one of cyberculture's defining dualisms. The belief that the body is a vestigial appendage no longer needed by late twentieth-century Homo Sapiens — Homo Cyber is not uncommon among obsessive programmers, outlaw hackers, video game junkies, netsurfers cruising electronic bulletin board systems.
>
> (Dery, 1996: 248)

Ideas of virtual reality and cyberspace seem to blur the frontier between internal and external space, creating the illusion that internal and external realities are one and the same, expressing a confusion between some metaphorical idea of inner space and a literal outer space. There appear to be no limits to what can be imagined and acted out and no 'other' to impose restrictions and inhibit what is imagined and done. The exploitation of virtuality becomes a fulfilment of solipsistic and regressive desires.

Heim suggests that belief in such socio-technical fantasies may have real consequences: 'without directly meeting others physically our ethics languishes' (Heim, 1993: 102). Virtual empowerment may entail a 'refusal to recognise the substantive and independent reality of others and to be involved in relations of mutual dependency and responsibility' (Robins, 1996: 14). The selective presentation of ourselves electronically can never fully represent us; our identities are fundamentally bound up with our corporeal life: 'The more we mistake the cyberbodies for ourselves, the more the machine twists ourselves into the prostheses we are wearing' (Heim, 1993: 100).

What seems to be at stake here is the very idea of moral agency. Postmodern accounts in particular have launched an assault on the idea of personhood as a unitary centre of moral decision-making. The concept of the moral agent is held to be ideological, illusory and nostalgic. This I see as a crucial point of convergence between cyber-idealism and postmodernist thinking. The crux of the cyber-idealist position rests on a number of interlocking assumptions concerning the contemporary meaning of identity. First, the self is to be construed in terms of incorporeal conscious (or in some cases unconscious) stuff. Second, in the idea that identity has become no longer stable and continuous but is uncertain and problematic, our ordinary sense of identity is somehow illusory. Third, the idea that the self is fragmented and fractured, so that we can no longer understand our lives in terms of a single, coherent narrative.

The identity of bodiless persons

The notion of identity advocated by proponents of the virtual draws upon the key Cartesian assumption that persons are essentially incorporeal:

> I know that I was a substance the whole essence or nature of which is to
> think, and for its existence there is no need of any place, nor does it
> depend on any material thing: so that this 'me', that is to say, the soul by
> which I am what I am, is entirely distinct from the body, and is even more

easy to know than is the latter: and even if the body were not, the soul
would not cease to be what it is.

(Descartes quoted in Flew, 1986: 91)

Similarly the idea of the fragmented or discontinuous self resonates with the
Humean analysis of personal identity. Hume, however, does not accept
Descartes' talk of 'spiritual substance' but prefers instead to speak of
perceptions of the mind or of ideas and impressions:

> Humes's own self-consciously radical alternative is to urge that, as people
> we are: not allegedly mysteriously and elusive substances which are the
> subjects or havens of Cartesian thoughts; but nothing else but mere
> collections of such entities, supposedly occurring independently.

(*ibid.*)

Thus Hume could

> venture to affirm of the rest of mankind, that they are nothing but a
> bundle or collection of different perceptions, which succeed each other
> with an inconceivable rapidity, and are in a perpetual flux and movement.

(Hume, 1967: 302)

Both positions are fundamentally flawed. The Cartesian mistake is first to
equate people with their souls or minds and then, second, to misconstrue the
words 'souls' and 'minds' as terms for a sort, or sorts, of substance.

Hume's mistake is of similar kind – in the assertion that 'perceptions of the
mind' can be said to be either a loose or separate 'bundle or collection of
different perceptions'. It makes little sense to talk of unowned thoughts or the
'space' occupied by a thought. Why is the talk of disembodied or virtual selves
so erroneous? The error arises from the misconstruction of the word 'person'
and 'person-words'. Flew, for example, points out that

> Both the word 'person' itself and all other person-words – such as the
> personal pronouns and terms like 'butcher' or 'politician', picking out
> members of classes of functionary – are themselves words for members
> of a kind – our own kind – of creatures of flesh and blood.

(Flew, 1986: 91)

This may be demonstrated by reference to the actual ways in which we learn
the meanings of such words. The point is that minds, souls or selves just are
the properties of particular persons. Minds, souls or selves cannot be the

objects of discourse without reference to particular persons' states of consciousness, thoughts and emotions, which are inherently and paradigmatically states of material, flesh and blood creatures. The paradigmatic case for learning to talk about cognitive and affective states is simply the people we meet, and thus 'everyone's paradigms of what persons are are members of our own particular species of flesh and blood organism' (Flew, 1987: 118). Intellectual operations such as believing, remembering, or imagining cannot be explained except by reference to the behaviour of particular persons.

Re-identification and 'just accountability'

People are characteristically those whom we meet in physical space, and our understandings of self and selfhood are constituted by the public language that has evolved to describe this. Talk about 'virtual selves' or 'on-line' selves is to construct souls or minds as if they had some existence apart from the body. As Ryle (1976) demonstrated over half a century ago, to talk of minds as if they were some 'incorporeal substance' distinct from the body is to commit a profound 'category mistake': the two key terms simply do not belong to the same category. Virtual selves cannot be removed from corporeal persons in the same way, and for the same logical reasons, that minds cannot be meaningfully said to be detachable from bodies.

To accept the argument that we are in some sense 'bodiless persons' gives rise to the problem of the continuity, identification and re-identification of such 'bodiless persons'. How is it that we can identify the person at time one as the same person at time two? Such re-identification of 'bodiless persons' is crucial to the idea of accountability. There is, of course, no profound philosophical problem here if it is the case that a person at time one is the same person as at time two on the basis of the former being materially continuous with the latter (Flew, 1987: 100). Just how is it supposed to be possible to identify a bodiless/ virtual person in the first place — logically prior to re-identification? How are 'virtual persons' to be identified in cyberspace except as the electronic projections of their material referent?

The fact that we may talk of transformations in a person's personality logically presupposes that they are the same person; 'different person' is here to be understood in a secondary sense. Difference in this sense is predicated precisely on continuous bodily/material existence. Personal identity and moral agency are then logically predicated on embodiment. The central issue here for moral analysis is that of 'just accountability'. The Platonic-Cartesian or Humean conception of 'the self' encounters the problem of re-identification: our only reference point for understanding what it means to be a person is physical and spatial. Again, how are we supposed to first identify and then re-identify a 'bodiless person' or a 'virtual self' at a different time? Material continuity is personal identity itself. Judicial proceedings rest on witnesses being able to re-identify the culprit in the dock:

> The prisoner in the dock would be conclusively shown to have been the woman who committed the murder if – as could scarcely ever happen – witnesses to that crime had kept the murderer under continuous observation ever since, and are now testifying that the prisoner is indeed the person thus continuously observed.
>
> (Flew, 1987: 100)

The continuity of material, grounded identity is intimately inscribed in notions of rational moral agency. The promise of systems of virtuality which could transform bodily presence into telepresence does not alter the primacy of the corporeal nature of persons. Material continuity constitutes a necessary condition of moral accountability, in the sense that to be accountable for an action requires you to be the same person who committed that action. (It is not obviously a sufficient condition, in that accountability may be mitigated by being unable to do otherwise.)

To return to cyber-idealism: the danger of believing that identity could be disembodied is associated with the idea of entering upon a realm of abstract mental 'mastery' and unlimited technological freedom (unlimited freedom to get what we want, or at least what is deliverable through such technological systems). The illusion is that the ability to use new virtual technologies to bracket out physical presence (either through the omission or simulation of corporeality) frees us from the moral frameworks consistent with our physical identity. The dangers of such beliefs are in their amoral character. There is an apparent suspension of the real, physical self. 'On-line' behaviour can only be dependent on material 'off-line' presence. There can be in fact no such suspension of the real and physical self. Behaviour in cyberspace is contingent upon, and a function of, the physical persons we happen to be. Heim acknowledges this when he writes that

> Being a body constitutes the principle behind our separateness from one another and behind our personal presence. Our bodily existence stands at the forefront of our personal identity and individuality. Both law and morality recognise the physical body as something of a fence, an absolute boundary, establishing and protecting our privacy.
>
> (Heim, 1993: 100)

However, the point apparently so easily obscured in cyber-idealist talk is that personal corporeality and material continuity through time are also inextricably linked to public accountability and moral agency.

Resisting the seductions of fiction

What is evident in much of the literature on virtuality and its radical implications is its origins and reliance on science fiction and fantasy. However, we need to keep clear the distinction between literal space and metaphorical space. The projections of technological futures, such as those imagined by Bernal or latterly the cyber-idealists, are equally fictitious. We should not be seduced by the evocation of fantastic conceptual possibilities: there simply is a categorial difference between fact and fiction (Flew, 1987: 124). Entertaining though conceptual possibilities may be, we must not confuse them with what empirically is the case – the language we do in fact use is based in the everyday, physical world which we do in fact inhabit. It is this world in which our language, and its everyday stock of concepts, has evolved to deal with – including our fundamental moral concepts and ideas of praiseworthy and blameworthy actions.

Cyber-idealist accounts of identity seek to dispense with the conventional paradigms of a life as a life history. The coherence of the self is deconstructed into fragments and the quality of conscious experience is reduced to a succession of loosely connected sensations detached from the body. Such arguments may be used to sustain attitudes which proclaim loss of social meaning and hence retreat from moral engagement; nevertheless, they are false. Baudrillard may celebrate the end of what he calls the 'moral gaze' and 'critical judgementalism', but the simple assertion that something is so does not make it so. As I have sought to show, none of this should daunt us – founded, as it surely is, on the fundamental error of conceiving persons as essentially immaterial or incorporeal substances or potentially virtual inhabitants of cyberspace. Virtuality leaves everything as it is.

Bibliography

Bernal, J. D. (1969) *The World, the Flesh and the Devil: An Enquiry into the Future of the Three Enemies of the Rational Soul*, 2nd edn; 1st edn 1929 (Bloomington: Indiana University Press).

Dery, M. (1996) *Escape Velocity: Cyberculture at the End of the Century* (London: Hodder & Stoughton).

Easlea, B. (1981) *Science and Sexual Oppression: Patriarchy's Confrontation with Women and Nature* (London: Weidenfeld & Nicolson).

Flew, A. (1986) *David Hume: Philosopher of Moral Science* (Oxford: Blackwell).

Flew, A. (1987) *The Logic of Mortality* (Oxford: Blackwell).

Gibson, W. (1995) *Neuromancer* (London: HarperCollins).

Haraway, D. (1990) 'A manifesto for cyborgs: science, technology and socialist feminism in the 1980s', in L. J. Nicholson (ed.), *Feminism/Postmodernism* (London: Routledge), pp. 191–233.

Heim, M. (1993) *Metaphysics of Virtual Reality* (Oxford: Oxford University Press).

Hume, D. (1967) *Treatise of Human Nature Book One* [1739], ed. D. G. C. Macnabb (London: Collins).

Lanier, J. (1990) 'Riding in the giant worm to Saturn: post-symbolic communication in virtual reality', in G. Hattinger *et al.*, *Arts Electronica, 1990, Vol. 2 Virtuelle Welten* (Linz: Veritas-Verlag).

More, M. (1999) 'The Extropian principles: version 3, A transhumanist declaration http://www.extropy.com/extprn3.htm

Nowell-Smith, P. H. (1965) *Ethics* (London: Penguin).

Plant, S. (1993) 'Beyond the screens: film, cyberpunk and cyberfeminism', *Variant*, 14: 16.

Plant, S. (1997) *Zeros and Ones: Digital Women and the New Technoculture* (London: Fourth Estate).

Rheingold, H. (1994) *The Virtual Community: Finding Connection in a Computerized World* (London: Secker and Warburg).

Robins, K. (1996) 'Cyberspace and the world we live in', in J. Dovey (ed.), *Fractal Dreams: New Media in Social Context* (London: Lawrence & Wishart), pp. 1–30.

Rose, H. (1994) *Love, Power and Knowledge: Towards a Feminist Transformation of the Sciences* (Cambridge: Polity Press).

Ryle, G. (1976) *The Concept of Mind*, 1st edn 1949 (Harmondsworth: Penguin).

Springer, C. (1991) 'The pleasure of the interface', *Screen*, 32(3) (Autumn): 303–23.

Squires, J. (1996) 'Fabulous feminist futures and the lure of cyberculture', in J. Dovey (ed.), *Fractal Dreams: New Media in Social Context* (London: Lawrence & Wishart), pp. 194–216.

5

Keeping an eye on them

Control and the visual

ROSA AINLEY

CCTV: prevention or cure?

This chapter will explore the spatial interrelatedness of photography, architecture and social control within the visual and built environment, through a case study of CCTV. Envisaged as a crime preventive and guarantor of safety, CCTV has been widely installed in streets, bus and train stations, shopping centres and all manner of public spaces. Central and local governments and the CCTV industry have boasted that it can reduce crime in any location, but have provided scant proof for its efficacy. CCTV is promoted by law-and-order ideologues as guaranteeing the security of person and property. The presence of a camera is a reminder of the threat of continual observation, though it relies on behind-the-scene personnel to fulfil that promise. It is hyped as *the* technological fix for all urban problems, playing a 'crucial role in the modern fight against crime' (*Observer*, 2 May 1999, p. 2).

It is debatable whether CCTV prevents crime and 'makes' public places safer, or merely displaces problems to other locations, sometimes helping apprehension after the fact. Crime rates embarrass both local and central governments, and they commonly maintain that installing surveillance systems will tackle the problem. However, even where the hardware is operative – and in many case the cameras are empty boxes like so many burglar alarms – CCTV requires an enormous amount of personnel time for it to be effective. The supposed security that CCTV offers is dependent on visual consumption, that there is someone available to watch what it films, interpret the information and then be able to act upon it. It needs to be acknowledged that we cannot control CCTV; we can only present the illusion of control through the ability to watch/consume. The promise of detection/deterrence is rarely fulfilled.

Already the one million cameras said to be installed in the UK is regarded as a conservative guess (*Independent*, 5 May 1999, p. 5). Since 1994 the UK has introduced 585 Home Office-sponsored CCTV schemes and the Home Secretary, Jack Straw, has allocated £150 million for 'crime prevention', of which a good portion is expected to go on purchasing CCTV networks (Institute of Employment Rights, 1998). In London, every person in a public space is said to be captured on camera at least once every five minutes. CCTV is perceived as providing the answer to institutional control over urban and social degeneration.

In the spring of 1999 three nail bombs exploded in London during three consecutive weeks. The first of the three bombs was placed in Brixton, now a thriving and culturally mixed area, but still stereotyped in the media as a black ghetto of London, supposedly rife with muggers and prone to rioting; the second was planted in Brick Lane, an area of east London adjacent to the City that has been home to successive immigrant communities from Huguenot silk weavers to Jews to, currently, Bangladeshis; and the third bomb exploded in Old Compton Street in Soho, the heart of 'Queer Town' and the hub of the commercial gay male scene, killing three people.

The man charged with the crime, David Copeland, was apprehended after police had identified him on CCTV tapes that were taken from each of the three bomb scenes. Press reports suggested that it was a tip-off from the widely televised CCTV footage that led to his arrest. Initially, Copeland was said to be unaligned with any of the British neo-fascist groups such as Combat 18 or the White Wolves, who rushed to claim responsibility; he was later discovered caught on CCTV tape in company that appears to confirm that connection (www.mirror.co.uk, 1999). Other 'target' areas, particularly Southall, with its high Asian population, and Golders Green, a traditionally Jewish area, were still on high alert after the arrest.

The first CCTV system in Britain was launched in 1985 by a local council concerned about street safety, in the slightly unexpected location of Bournemouth, a genteel seaside resort on the south coast of England (Fyfe and Bannister, 1998: 257). Since then the potential arenas for CCTV have rapidly diversified: the first cameras in the capital were installed at Guy's Hospital, where many of the injured people from the Soho bombing were treated. CCTV has become, for some, a factor in business location too. The proprietor of the Glass Bar in Euston, a popular lesbian bar which opened in 1996, found exactly what she was looking for in premises located in one of the listed gatehouses at Euston railway station, in an area containing over 500 CCTV cameras, fulfilling her criteria for customer safety. This is something of an irony when you consider the widely documented movement of lesbians and gay men in search of urban anonymity; an anonymity, moreover, that will paradoxically bring them greater technologically enhanced visibility.

As the surveillance industry booms, so, albeit in a much smaller way, has concern and debate grown around the attendant issues of privacy and civil liberties. There exists as yet no legal or ethical guidelines for the use of CCTV footage: who should be able to watch it; what qualifications and training they might have; to what purpose(s) it might usefully be put; and at what point acceptable desires for security shade dangerously into intrusion. Calls for codes of practice are regular, but command far less media space than the high-profile cases in which CCTV is instrumental in 'solving' crimes, such as the James Bulger murder; less famously, the Earl's Court 'gay serial killer' in west London, who was caught on the system at Charing Cross station; and now London's April bomber too. In May 1999 the *Guardian* reported that law enforcement agencies were seeking to launch a code of practice for undercover surveillance operations (Hopkins, 1999: 11); in June 1999 the Data Protection Act came into force, which included the provision that anyone using a CCTV system will have to report it to the Data Protection Register. It stipulates that recorded material can only be used for crime prevention, but how this law will work in practice remains unclear.

In Britain little political resistance has been mounted against the proliferation of CCTV, but then it would be an unfashionable cause: civil liberties organizations such as Liberty and the Scottish Council for Civil Liberty have argued for a 'balance between the right to privacy and the right to security, rather than actively opposing CCTV' (Fyfe and Bannister, 1998: 260). Since most CCTV systems are privately run, there is no control over the sale or operation of equipment; those who need to be monitored are seemingly always 'them over there', the not-us, the 'non-U'; CCTV plays upon the existing fears of an outer/underclass. Privacy becomes a mutable concept dependent on the status of who it is supposed to protect. Following the death of Diana – a woman with an ambivalent attitude to the camera – an acreage of newsprint was devoted to the importance of maintaining the privacy of the privileged. Ordinary people should, it is intimated, feel grateful for the intrusion of the camera into 'our' space, for there it comes to symbolize protection. In the UK domestic privacy is bought with movement up the ladder of social class. Measured in the property rights of greater home ownership, the socially privileged can move from terrace to semi-detached to detached home, outside of which are increasingly installed private, domestic CCTV systems.

CCTV can be, and has been, used for purposes other than crime prevention. Of the unscrupulous uses to which CCTV footage may be put, extortion to avoid the 'outing' of the apparently heterosexual, or the lesbian or gay man in 'sensitive' employment caught on camera in, say, Old Compton Street, gives a new twist to a nasty old game. Opportunities for sexual and racial harassment; extortion; stalking; checking up on employees' time-keeping, truanting pupils and so on are rife. But its auxiliary uses include the benign too: searching for lost children, and providing a cost-effective means of examining buildings for maintenance requirements. Controversial deployments of CCTV include videotapes that have been made available for viewing by the very tenants whose housing estates are under its watchful eye, and recently a successful prosecution of 'anti-social behaviour', an order brought in under the 1998 Crime and Disorder Act, was supported by the copious taped evidence submitted by vigilant residents living on the same estate. Neighbours in Glossop, Derbyshire, submitted ninety-four videos made over five months to support their case. One of them, Kathy Wilson, commented: 'I've had to install closed circuit television. I'm so frightened. I'm constantly watching my back' (*Guardian*, 14 September 1999, p. 7). The restraining order made against Gary and Fran Tucker for playing loud music elicited this comment: 'This is a very dangerous order,' said Mrs Tucker. 'You don't need as much evidence as in a criminal court' (*ibid.*).

People often believe that they have to relinquish their privacy to be safe from crime: opening up the city to make it a 'safe-for-all' zone has become synonymous with keeping it tightly shut with technological fortification. But this faith in CCTV, shared by many – politicians, urban strategists and broad swathes of the public – is matched by a 'despair at the creation of an Orwellian dystopia' (Fyfe and Bannister, 1998: 256).

Jeremy Bentham and the panopticon

CCTV's watchful hardware eye is usefully compared to another system of surveillance – the panopticon. Panoptic means 'all embracing, in a single view', which sounds considerably more benign than the actual purpose of the structure: an ingenious design, over which the English philosopher Jeremy Bentham (1748–1832) obsessed for twenty years. A panopticon consists of a central tower surrounded by individual compartments – for patients, prisoners, pupils, workers, or any group whose isolation, surveillance and regulation is seen as socially desirable. Through a complex internal structure of screens, blinds and lighting, the inhabitants are unable to see or communicate with each other, nor can they tell whether the inspector, inhabiting the central tower, is observing them. A speaking-tube system allows the inspector to communicate with any inhabitant without any other prisoner being able to hear the content of the exchange. Bentham describes the uses and advantages of the panopticon:

> Morals reformed – health preserved – industry invigorated – instruction
> diffused – public burthens [burdens] lightened – Economy seated, as it

were, upon a rock — the gordian knot of the Poor Laws are not cut, but untied — all by a simple idea in Architecture!

(Bentham, 1995: 31)

His language has the enthusiastic tone of an early form of advertising copy. Since Bentham, who was writing in the late eighteenth century, there have been other ideas in architecture and related disciplines that have, initially at least, set themselves up as utopian solutions to some social 'gordian knot' or other. If we take architecture as a system of representation (Colomina, 1992), the interrelation of the two bears further investigation.

Nowadays, the plan of the panopticon looks quite similar to a late twentieth-century warehouse conversion, or an intriguing amphitheatre structure. Initially, it does not appear sinister until you begin to discover the purpose of all the subdivisions and compartments inside: cells. Michel Foucault's description of the panopticon as a 'laboratory of power' (Foucault, 1979: 202), or Edward Soja's 'concretisation of power applied through architecture' (Soja, 1996: 26), comes considerably closer to conveying something of its purpose, and explains the unease that the contemporary reader feels on consideration of this exercise in social control through solitary confinement. John Ryle, writing in the *Guardian*, describes his visit to a panopticon, built in 1932, on the Isle of Youth, 30 miles south of Cuba, where Castro was once imprisoned, and by whose order it was finally demolished (Ryle, 1996: 3). Ryle mentions the Millbank Penitentiary in London as another example, noting that the prisoners there rioted. Millbank Penitentiary stood on the site now occupied by the Tate Gallery, where people now go mainly to look at artworks. The site, then, remains a building for viewing but has changed from a place of incarceration and surveillance to one of contemplation of an altogether different kind of (classed) gaze.

Bentham's belief in the social force of architecture was perhaps thankfully not borne out in the practice of the working panopticon. There is disagreement about whether a true panopticon ever existed, and therefore whether it may be judged successful or not. Thomas Markus, writing in *Buildings and Power*, asserts that, with the exception of Edinburgh's Bridewell prison (built in 1791), no panopticon has ever been built, rather like Bentham's writings, which are 'frequently cited, rarely read'[1] (Markus, 1993: 145). Whether or not an authentic model has ever existed, it is instructive to revisit the study of an architectural form in the medium of metaphorical imagery. The panopticon has become an image, which we may consider alongside other images, a representation, a spook, a mythical all-seeing power.

Control through categorization and spectacle

In *Discipline and Punish* Foucault makes a distinction between separation and classification as methods of control, in relation to the management of disease and contagion (Foucault, 1979: 195). Whereas people suffering from leprosy were separated from the rest of society in order to maintain its pure and untainted nature, in the case of plague, systems of minute classification and segmentation were used to contain the 'disorder' of the disease. With shades of Freud's notion of dirt being 'matter in the wrong place', he describes plague management as 'a compact model of the disciplinary mechanism' (*ibid.*: 198), and sees the panopticon as the architectural form of this attitude to disciplinarity. This kind of classification/detection – the monitoring of certain categories of citizen which the authorities would prefer were elsewhere – can be carried out by CCTV too. The technology may be new but the principle isn't – Jeremy Bentham made similar claims about the panopticon. The panopticon compartmentalizes the crowd's numerous variables, as Foucault notes. Initially the cruelty of the panopticon – the isolation from society and peers, the constant torture of the random but uncertain gaze – does not seem compatible with Bentham's utilitarianism. But 'punishment is a spectacle' for Bentham (1995: 4), intended as a form of instructive deterrence for the wider, non-transgressive audience.

Enforcing self-vigilance through fear made the idea of the panoptic effective. In his introduction to *The Panopticon Writings*, Miran Bozovic writes that the inspector had to present evidence of the power of his position (in terms of hierarchy and location) only once to a single prisoner to make it proof against the bad behaviour of any of the others (Bentham, 1995: 16). Once this example of the inspector's all-seeing gaze had been displayed, he could then 'peacefully devote himself to his book-keeping' (*ibid.*: 17). If this one-off demonstration by the inspector were truly effective, then there would in fact be no need for the inspector to be present at all. Markus also raises the question of whether the inspector is also trapped within the structure (Markus, 1993: 148). There is a flaw in Bozovic's argument, though: the inmates had no means of finding out what had happened to one another. The question remains of how this knowledge, essential for the functioning of the panopticon model, would come to the inhabitants. Presumably, there is a parallel here with CCTV, in that we have to assume that as a technology it is omnipresent, and fully operational within the urban panorama.

Rather than separating out the *a priori* 'diseased' elements of society, contemporary attitudes to surveillance classify all occupants of public space as potentially 'diseased'. CCTV can be seen as an electronic panopticon, albeit one without spectacle, since everyone is subjected to it.[2] As Edward Soja has suggested: 'every city is a carceral city, a collection of surveillant nodes designed to impose a particular model of conduct and disciplinary adherence on its inhabitants' (Soja, 1996: 29), so the population becomes composed of surveillants, adherents and recalcitrants. The centrality of the panoptic gaze, as distinct from the dispersed nature of CCTV, is directly related to the specular value of each. The wide dispersal of CCTV is said to mirror the fragmentation of contemporary urban life, which is to say that not one transcendent gaze, but *many* gazes sweep the postmodern cityspace. John Ryle describes a continuum from the panopticon as 'the first ancient monument of the age of surveillance' (Ryle, 1996: 3), to the CCTV camera and the monitor, its contemporary manifestation. The gaze of CCTV may be as disembodied as that of the panopticon inspector, but its apparatus can usually be seen as an architectural detail. Sometimes its installers even see fit to install cages around it, against the possibility of vandalism.

Public/private surveillance

In *On Photography* (1977) Susan Sontag explained how the proliferation of photographic equipment and technology has led to a culture of self-surveillance – in domestic sex films for playing in the bedroom, wedding videos, the taping and playback of therapy sessions, conferences, interviews and so on. She anticipated the growth in the use of the camera for public surveillance: 'Our inclination to treat character [appearance] as equivalent to behaviour makes more acceptable a widespread public installation of the mechanized regard from the outside provided by cameras' (Sontag, 1983: 365). She notes that monitoring behaviour is quite a different matter from altering it: 'Social change is replaced by a change in images' (*ibid.:* 366), an idea that seems germane in the so-called 'society of the spectacle'.[3] To illustrate, the Old Compton Street area is now heavily armoured with surveillance hardware, but visibility does not necessarily change homophobic attitudes to gay men and lesbians. As several gay media commentators pointed out after the Soho bomb, the government's ethos is still firmly anchored to the sanctity of the nuclear family unit, and its refusal to legislate in favour of basic civil liberties for lesbians and gay men helps to foster a climate of intolerance, despite post-bomb sound bites to the contrary. The police may have caught the individual bomber, but structural social change remains unachieved; CCTV is misleadingly touted as a panacea, when it's no more than a mirage of social protection, safety, and freedom. The cameras remain in Old Compton Street and in Soho Square, escape from the scrutiny of pervasive homophobia being only an illusion.

Sontag makes a distinction between surveillance and spectacle: 'Cameras define reality in the two ways essential to the workings of an advanced industrial society: as a spectacle (for masses) and as an object of surveillance (for rulers)' (Sontag, 1983: 366). As an older icon of surveillance we might compare them with gargoyles, which although appear to be the master of all they survey from their architectural vantage point are a spectacle which sees nothing. Often found on Gothic churches, they can seem an unsettling contrast to the Christian iconography of the rest of the building. Usually a waterspout, part of a drainage system, a gargoyle's appearance is akin to a piece of iconographic surveillance equipment. Perhaps an early monument to the age of *apparent* surveillance, they are an example of spectacle-as-(non-)surveillance – like the empty CCTV box, the non-functioning security device.[4] The gargoyle *seems* to be able to see into the cloisters, quadrangles, and cornices it faces, perched on its vantage point on the roof gutters, performing as a stone representation of the all-seeing eye of the church. One of God's little sentinels perhaps, extending the sense of his omniscience through this piece of architectural decoration, just as CCTV is an imperfect referent to the omniscience of its various controllers. Gargoyles, though more suggestive of hellish imps and hideous hybrid animals than earthbound mouthpieces of the heavenly father, are functionally similar to the inspector of the panopticon and the CCTV camera/operator. Like the gargoyle, the location of the inspector gives him the opportunity, the reputation, for being able to see all the detainees at any time, even though this is not actually possible. The gargoyle, which appears to be constantly scrutinizing although it can see nothing, is similarly more to do with spectacle than actual vision.

Safety debates

Debates which advocate CCTV on the grounds that it prevents crime respond to the public's perception of danger, rather than the likelihood of danger itself. Perceived threats to safety are different from, though not necessarily less harmful than, 'real' threats. Proponents of CCTV claim that it will create safer environments for women, but there is little discussion about stopping the types of male behaviour in public places that cause women anxiety. An image or illusion of safety can provide a feeling of security, empty rhetoric though it may be. Issues of safety are often subsumed under crime prevention, and security is reduced to a matter of hardware, alarms and ironmongery, of equipment rather than social/discursive transformation.

The concept of 'natural surveillance', as championed by Jane Jacobs in *The Death and Life of Great American Cities* (1961), has been much discussed in debates about how to combat feelings of insecurity through architectural and town planning, especially in relation to residential developments. Natural surveillance results from designing and grouping houses or buildings so that common areas such as courtyards, playgrounds or pathways can be overlooked and monitored by residents. In this way, children may be left to play, apparently unsupervised; outsiders/intruders cannot go unnoticed; vandalism, petty crime and car theft are more likely to be witnessed and so on. The measure of control that, illusory or not, may be gained from this kind of structural design can help to allay fears about safety, by concentrating on the spectre of trouble coming from 'outside'. Neighbourhood Watch schemes run on precisely this principle and – mirroring Foucault's 'leper' model – members of the scheme are deemed pure, while anyone outside is potentially contagious and therefore worthy of suspicion. Supporters of these schemes contend that a heightened community spirit is another benefit. In this context I think 'community' is used as a euphemism for 'territorial' – it is rather the shared fear of losing property that brings people together. The situation may become polarized into a very tribal one that is actually anti-community, anti-society: CCTV is not so much developing inclusivity of social difference as stimulating social cleansing and purification.

The 1980s – that backlash, 'anti-society' decade[5] – saw the popularization of Alice Coleman's (1985) ideas about 'designing out' crime through architectural means.[6] Her thesis was that certain types of design, especially 'unowned' communal spaces such as open green areas and walkways, allowed, even fostered, criminal behaviour, in particular on housing estates which had in earlier decades been seen as the technical solution to the problems of slum clearance, housing and land shortages – just as the panopticon was considered an architectural mechanism for the imposition of forms of behaviour.[7] Her 'solution' involved cutting out communal areas as far as possible and reorganizing the space so that it became individualized territory, which would, so the theory went, then be guarded as private property. This notion of 'defensible space' featured strongly in the work of the housing theorists of the 1980s, exemplified in the work of Oscar Newman, who proposed that if areas – individual gardens instead of green spaces – were 'owned' by individuals, then they would respect rather than damage them.[8] This economic determinism denies the importance of other considerations, ranging from space standards (diminishing) and densities (rising), to the more widely social (such as access to services and existence of facilities) and the plainly economic (availability of regular well-paid employment). By contrast, in the 1990s, housing policy was marked by a focus on the establishment of 'community',[9] and consultation and participation became paramount.

Architecture and control

Attempts at social engineering through the location, layout, design and
proximity of leisure, schooling, childcare, and shopping facilities to housing
developments have been well documented, as have their shortcomings (Boys,
1989). The phrase 'architecture as "congealed ideology"', coined by the team
that authored *Strangely Familiar*, springs to mind here (Borden *et al.*, 1996: 5).
Examples of spatio-social regulation include attempts by local authorities to
prevent children playing on green spaces in public housing developments, and
banning the hanging of washing outdoors. Many of these examples relate to
social housing and often to attempts to contain and control largely low-
income, predominantly working-class populations. What becomes clear is how
the scopic desire designed into the very fabric of our built environment is so
predictable and entrenched in values and form.

At the other end of the social scale, in a fictional example from the USA, the
film *Sliver* (Noyse, 1993) narrates the paranoid regulation of an exclusive
condominium development, filled with high-earning professionals. The owner
of the block, who is able to view all the apartments on his state-of-the-art
surveillance system, plays the role of the panopticon inspector. He punishes
individual tenants for their transgressions, and is represented as an unseen
enforcer. Here, spectacle and surveillance are offered to the same audience, an
audience of one. The owner's mastery of technology is initially part of his
charm, but he becomes more menacing as he assumes the roles of judge and,
literally, executioner. The omnipotence of his gaze focuses and intensifies as
Carly Norris — the frightened, vulnerable, single woman, scared by the stories
of murdered previous tenants — is tempted by the power, dazzled by the
technology, and almost seduced by the attractions of the role of co-voyeur.
'You like to watch, don't you?' the owner asks his erotic target, Norris, played
by Sharon Stone. The viewer is conjoined with the masculine spectatorship
too, voyeuristically enjoying the objectification of Stone, while also, framed
through Barthes' enigmatic code, managing to occupy the position of panoptic
inspector on a voyage of visual discovery. The viewer remains pleasurably
paranoid about technological surveillance, while narrative form renders her/
him safe at the end. Thus, in this movie, as in the more recent *Enemy of the State*
(Dir.: Tony Scott, 1999), the conspiracy convention performs carthartically to
neutralize middle-class anxiety over surveillance.

In a related and similarly gendered manner, modernist architect Le Corbusier
removed Eileen Gray's control over her environment when he painted a mural
Sous les pilotis [10] at her house, E.1027, without her permission. He also built for
himself a wooden shack right behind the house. In a phrase that cannot help
but remind one of the panopticon, Beatriz Colomina writes: 'He occupied and

controlled the site by *overlooking* it, the cabin being little more than an *observation platform*, a sort of *watchdog house*' [my italics]. Not only was Le Corbusier's gaze architecturally imposed – Gray had chosen the site for its inaccessibility – but Gray considered his murals to be vandalism. Colomina quotes Peter Adam: 'It was a rape. A fellow architect, a man she admired, had without her consent defaced her design'[11] (Adam, 1987: 311). But equally important I think is the implicit demand from him that she should organize her living space in a certain way, the attempt to assert control over the space by forcing her to look at his work placed over the top of her design. This kind of violation may be taking the idea that 'architecture is made and remade over and over again each time it is represented through another medium, each time its surroundings change, each time different people experience it' (Borden *et al.*, 1996: 5) into another, and unwelcome, realm.

Summative thoughts

It seems that neither the panopticon nor any of the more modern methods of control, whether social or more personal, through architectural or photo-graphic means, unties any social 'gordian knots'. The costs may be high – a pervasive culture of intrusion in the name of security – and the 'bargain' may not be the entirely good deal it first appears. CCTV has had some widely publicized successes in helping detect criminals, such as the Soho bomber, and currently enjoys a position as panacea to the uncertainties of public space, but there are drawbacks. Bentham's drawing of the panopticon, as a kind of torture chamber based on an illusion, an architectural spectacle, is linked to a realization that its modern manifestations involve turning every public space into a prison-without-walls, and some private spaces into film sets or observation points. Earlier in this chapter I called the panopticon a 'naked exercise in social control'. Perhaps the ubiquity of the CCTV camera, the many forms of attempted architectural coercion, are no more covert, merely lacking the force of presentation (of spectacle) of an impressive and intricate building.

Foucault ends his chapter on panopticism like this: 'Is it surprising that prisons resemble factories, schools, barracks, hospitals, which all resemble prisons?' (Foucault, 1979: 228). We might take this further and add 'housing, shopping complexes, office blocks, public buildings' or, as Bentham classifies it, prisons, houses of industry, workhouses, poorhouses, houses of correction, manufactu-ries, madhouses, lazarettos [ship's storerooms], hospitals, schools, all of which he deemed suited to a panoptic structure. While we may surmise that for Bentham, the spectacle of the panopticon would have alleviated the need for the more pervasively carceral city, many modern commentators believe it is already with

us or at least imminent: 'We should be on our guard that the surveillance city …
does not catch us unarmed, disinterested and incapable' (Charley, 1996: 61).

CCTV is a contemporary manifestation of cure-all solutions for social
problems, in a historical continuum of viewing mechanisms that operate on the
basis of a confusion of fears and illusions over privacy, territory and class.
Ominous new possibilities in this line include digital imaging, tagging (both of
which individualize the mechanism by working on the basis of person, not
place), criminal and 'national security' databases, and smart cards. The
technology is outpacing any monitoring code, and thus there is a danger that
the current moral debates about privacy, tolerance, safety and crime
prevention will be rendered redundant by the context of collapsing socio-
technological spaces. To bring democratic participation back, then, we need to
contest these spaces as determined by social, not technological, imperatives.

Acknowledgements

The author would like to thank Irmi Karl, Pam Fereday, and Jackie Paris (all of
the University of Brighton) for their help on this chapter.

Notes

1. Verso, back cover blurb.
2. See also, the not-so-contemporary *Photographic Surveillance Techniques for Law
   Enforcement Agencies* (Kodak, 1972). The phrase 'law enforcement agencies' now
   means official channels, yet this booklet is plainly aimed at the amateur end of the
   market and struggles to legitimize its seedy, downmarket audience. As with
   CCTV, its approach is technical rather than moral: it offers advice on positioning
   surveillance equipment and how to deal with anger towards it. No moral issues
   are admitted; its stated purpose is 'the observation of *suspected* persons … and to
   record *illegal* activities' [my italics]. The principles of surveillance stated here share
   with the panopticon the same need not to be seen seeing, and also the more
   modern surveillance principle that everyone is under suspicion.
3. The term is Guy Debord's, from *The Society of the Spectacle* (1967), but has now
   become a cliché of postmodernism.
4. A current example would be the case of the notoriously racist murder of black
   British teenager Stephen Lawrence. A CCTV camera was installed by the police to
   monitor the street memorial erected at the site of his death, which was
   consistently vandalized with grafitti of neo-fascist, racist sentiment. No video
   footage recorded the defacement, however, as the police neglected to supply the
   machine with a tape.

5. This was epitomized in Margaret Thatcher's infamous and prophetical statement 'There is no such thing as Society' (*Women's Own*, 31 October 1987).
6. Coleman's ideas were later to fall from favour and then again became fashionable in the early 1990s.
7. Foucault, in *Discipline and Punish* (1979: 216), quotes Julius's description of the panopticon principle as a 'solution of a technical problem' in appearance, but remarks that in fact 'a whole type of society emerges' (N. H. Julius, *Leçons sur les prisons*, 1831, pp. 384–6).
8. See also Newman (1983).
9. An overburdened term, and one often applied euphemistically to under-funded and poorly resourced projects.
10. Also known as *Graffite à Cap Martin* or *Three Women*.
11. It is widely reported that Le Corbusier tacitly accepted credit for E.1027 by *not* crediting Gray for the site of his mural.

Bibliography

Adam, Peter (1987) *Eileen Gray: Architect/Designer* (New York: Harry N. Abrams).

Arts Council (1986) *L'Amour fou: Photography and Surrealism* (London: Arts Council).

Bentham, Jeremy (1995) *The Panopticon Writings*, ed. Miran Bozovic (London: Verso).

Blanchot, Maurice (1982) 'The two versions of the imaginary', in *The Space of Literature* (Lincoln, NE: University of Nebraska Press), pp. 254–71.

Borden, I., Kerr, J., Pivero A., Rendell, J. (eds) (1996) *Strangely Familiar: Narratives of Architecture in the City* (London: Routledge).

Boys, Jos (1989) 'From Alcatraz to the OK Corral: gender and pre-war housing design', in Pat Kirkham and Judy Attfield, *A View from the Interior* (London: The Women's Press), pp. 86–98.

Burrows, Gideon (1999) 'Smile! You're on a police camera', *Pink Paper*, 28 May, p. 8.

Charley, J. (1996) 'Sentences upon architecture', in I. Borden *et al.* (eds), *Strangely Familiar: Narratives of Architecture in the City* (London: Routledge).

Coleman, Alice (1985) *Utopia on Trial: Vision and Reality in Planned Housing* (London: Hilary Shipman).

Colomina, Beatriz (ed.) (1992) *Sexuality and Space* (New York: Princeton Architectural Press).

Foucault, Michel (1979) *Discipline and Punish: The Birth of the Prison* (London: Penguin).

Fyfe, Nicholas and Bannister, Jon (1998) ' "The eyes upon the street": closed-circuit television surveillance and the city', in Nicholas Fyfe, *Images of the Street: Planning, Identity and Control in Public Space* (London and New York: Routledge), pp. 254–67.

hooks, bell (1994) *Outlaw Culture: Resisting Representations* (New York: Routledge).

Hopkins, Nick (1999) 'Police surveillance code welcomed', *Guardian*, 14 May, p. 11.

Institute of Employment Rights (1998) *Surveillance and Privacy at Work* (London: Institute of Employment Rights).

Jacobs, Jane (1961) *The Death and Life of Great American Cities: The Future of Town Planning* (Harmondsworth: Penguin).

Kodak (1972) *Photographic Surveillance Techniques for Law Enforcement Agencies* (New York: Kodak).

Markus, Thomas (1993) *Buildings and Power* (London: Routledge).

Newman, Oscar (1983) *Defensible Space: People Design in the Violent City* (London: AP).

Observer (1999) 'UK leads on cameras to fight crime', 2 May, p. 2.

Orr, Deborah (1999) 'They'll be watching you', *Independent*, 5 May, p. 5.

Ryle, John (1996) 'Gaze of power', *Guardian*, 12 January, p. 3.

Sliver (1993) Dir. Phillip Noyce, UIP, USA.

Soja, E. (1996) 'Heterotopologies', in Sophie Watson and Katherine Gibson (eds), *Postmodern Cities and Spaces* (Oxford: Blackwell), pp. 13–34.

Sontag, Susan (1983) *A Susan Sontag Reader* (London: Penguin).

Ward, David (1999) 'Neighbours told to behave', *Guardian*, 14 September, p. 7.

www.mirror.co.uk (1999) 'Lone wolf theory blown', 25 May.

6

The fortress and the polis

From the postmodern city to cyberspace and back

PAULA E. GEYH

The ordered swirl of houses and streets, from this high angle, sprang at her now with the same unexpected, astonishing clarity as the circuit card had ... there were to both outward patterns a hieroglyphic sense of concealed meaning, of an intent to communicate. There'd seemed no limit to what the printed circuit could have told her (if she had tried to find out); so in her first minute of San Narciso, a revelation also trembled just past the threshold of her understanding.

(Thomas Pynchon, *The Crying of Lot 49*)

One of the most striking recurrent images in contemporary culture is that of the intricate grid of city streets dissolving into the luminous tracery of the computer-generated grid of cyberspace. Prefigured in the passage from Thomas Pynchon's 1966 novel, *The Crying of Lot 49*, which serves as my epigraph here, in which the landscape of the Southern California city of San Narciso evokes for Oedipa Maas, Pynchon's protagonist, the mysterious, 'hieroglyphic' patterns of the printed circuit, this space/information matrix marks a crucial conceptual moment of the computer age. The opening sequence of the Disney film *Tron* (1982), one of the first cinematic attempts to bring the material and the virtual (cyber)world together, features images of computer-generated circuitry dissolving into a shimmering cityscape. The film *Max Headroom* (1986), which became a TV series, similarly insists upon the transposability of real and virtual space, as do, more recently, *Hackers* (1995), *Johnny Mnemonic* (1995), and *The Matrix* (1999).[1] Several of these films feature characters who also shift from the real to the virtual, transforming into simulacra-selves capable of inhabiting the cyberspace or, in the case of *Max Headroom*, the telespace of the television signal. The entire subgenre of science fiction literature that has become known as 'cyberpunk' operates within this space/information matrix and relies on the putative transposability of city- and cyberspace. William Gibson's early novel *Neuromancer* (1984) and Neal Stephenson's more recent *Snow Crash* (1992) are arguably the best-known and most influential representatives of the genre, for reasons that will be discussed at length here. In the wake of such fictional representations, the city/ cyberspace interface (in either sense) has become ubiquitous in advertisements for computer software and services, which, for example, bid you 'Welcome to the City of e' ('A place where more than 10,000 companies from around the corner and across the globe are joined into one seamless, supercharged web of e-commerce').[2] In this chapter, I shall examine what underlies the peculiarly powerful hold of this city/cyberspace interface upon both the popular imagination and the imagination of those who are engaged in the actual construction of cyberspace(s).

The link between urban architecture and information is actually very old. Among the earliest technologies of memory used by the ancient Greek and Roman rhetoricians was the creation of memory palaces.[3] Revived in the Renaissance, this art of memory reached its apotheosis in the memory theatre, envisioned by Giulio Camillo, that was to have contained 'all the things that the human mind can conceive' (Yates, 1966: 132). Similarly, in *Neuromancer*, cyberspace is imagined as the 'graphic representation of data abstracted from the banks of every computer in the human system', ranged across a 'transparent 3-D chessboard extending to infinity' (Gibson, 1984: 51–2). The evocation of the city grid in this description is unmistakable: 'Lines of light ranged in the nonspace of the mind, clusters and constellations of data. Like city lights receding ...' (*ibid.*: 51). When Gibson's hero Case enters cyberspace, he sees computer-generated data analogues of multinational corporate headquarters and governmental agencies in appropriately architectural forms: 'The stepped scarlet pyramid of the Eastern Seaboard Fission Authority burning beyond the green cubes of Mitsubishi Bank of America, and high and very far away ... the spiral arms of military systems, forever beyond his reach' (*ibid.*: 52). It is not surprising that these ideas would influence the theoretical and sometimes even practical designs of cyberspace.

Neuromancer's impact on the theoretical designs of early cyberspace was already the subject of discussion by the time of the First Conference on Cyberspace held at the University of Texas, Austin, in 1990. David Tomas observed that 'Gibson's powerful vision is now beginning to influence the way virtual reality and cyberspace researchers are structuring their research agendas and problematics' (Tomas, 1993: 46).[4] The work of Michael Benedikt, an architect and software design consultant, whose *Cyberspace: First Steps* itself helped to set the terms for cyberspace research and design, is a vivid example of this influence. Benedikt (1991: 149) imagines cyberspace as a 'gigantic ...

and spatially navigable database'. In this three-dimensional space, he proposes, one will be able to access and interact with 'the immense traffic of information that constitutes human enterprise in science, art, business, and culture'. In this new space, 'information-intensive institutions and businesses [will] have a form, identity, and working reality ... quite literally an architecture' (*ibid.*: 123).

But why should they have 'an architecture' in any but the most metaphoric of senses? Why represent data *as* a physical space at all? Numerous theorists and designers argue for the necessity or at least desirability of creating a sort of informational 'mirror world' (as in David Gelernter's *Mirror Worlds*, 1991) of the one we already know. Benedikt is among them: 'We are contemplating the arising shape of a new world,' he opines in *Cyberspace*, 'a world that must, in a multitude of ways begin, at least, as both an extension and a transcription of the world as we know it and have built it thus far' (though his vision of a cybercity, freed from certain material constraints — more on these later — is meant to improve upon the real-world city) (Benedikt, 1991: 23). Such designs build upon our innate conceptual familiarity with 'spatiality', and so are seen as 'anthropic', to use Peter Anders' term, as inherently suited to our thought processes:

> We think with space. Using our mind's ability to dimensionalize information, we reduce complexity to manageable units — objects — of information ... Spatial, anthropic cyberspace links to a pre-linguistic knowledge of the world, a knowledge crucial to our navigation, operation, and communication.
>
> (Anders, 1999: 9–10)

Thus, cyberspace *as* space, is more 'human'. As Alan Wexelblat observes, 'By making data accessible in the form of three-dimensional worlds that are directly present to the senses and to navigation we propose — for the first time — to make the computer adapt to the human' (Wexelblat, 1993: xiv).

Beyond (if not behind) such rationales lie rather mundane frustrations, for instance with the clumsiness of search engines that too often yield a glut of useless information overload. Or, as Slick, one of Gibson's characters in *Mona Lisa Overdrive*, suggests, 'all the data in the world stacked up like one big neon city, so you could cruise around and have a kind of grip on it, visually anyway, because if you didn't, it was too complicated, trying to find your way to a particular piece of data you needed' (Gibson, 1988: 13). Perhaps even more importantly, there is the other-worldly allure of the computer graphic interfaces that we have already experienced in MUDs and MOOs, in video/computer games and simulations (now a very long way from the early days of 'you are in a dark chamber ...' games like *Adventure*), and in emergent forms of sensory feedback virtual reality, although VR will probably only constitute a part of any future cyberspace.

While it is true that we do benefit from the three-dimensional spatial modelling of complex data and systems – for example, in conceptualizing the behaviour of chaotic systems – it is also true that for millennia, humans have transformed three-dimensional phenomena into two-dimensional representations (drawings and charts and graphs) in order to better understand them, in part by reducing the complexity with which their real-world manifestations confront us. This is important to keep in mind when considering what the 'most natural' or optimal organization of future cyberspace might be. It seems important, too, to make a distinction between spatial representations and spatial organizations, between an actual spatial form or topology and a structural(ist?) organization of elements, which is more 'spatial' than 'temporal', in the sense of co-existing together, synchronic (and possibly spatially diagrammed). For example, we can, on the computer screen, virtually move through a cyber space analogously to the way we move through a physical space, say the Bonaventure Hotel in LA, famously considered by Fredric Jameson as a quintessential exemplar of postmodern architecture.[5] But we can also move by using a cursor in a diagram on a TV screen in our room, of, say, different shops in the hotel lobby (perhaps represented by differently coloured circles linked by coloured lines), which does not correspond to the way the shops are arranged in the actual space, but rather to our virtual shopping list (and then, of course, we have the purchased items delivered to our room). It is actually not clear at all that a VR topological 'spatial' organization of cyberspace, whether as a city or any other space, would be either the most useful or desirable one. While the spatial 're-presentation' of the desktop has been fairly successful, there are counter-examples, like Microsoft's graphic BOB interface, that have been spectacular failures. If you know that the URL (i.e. its 'address', in a purely metaphoric sense) of Amazon is www.amazon.com, why surf around some cybercity (or cybermall) hunting for its representational 'location'? Beyond the innate familiarity of cityspaces, there is actually little apparent reason for imitating their architectures at all. As Mitchell points out, 'form and function are not coupled in the same ways in virtual space as they are in real space, so there is no compelling reason to make virtual spaces look like material, gravity-bound ones that stand out there in the weather' (Anders, 1999: xii).

That these visions of cyberspace as cityspace spring from science fiction is perhaps more important than it might initially seem, because it raises the ever-troublesome issue of the 'sci-fi gap' – the gap between what we can imagine or project and what is actually technologically and scientifically possible, now or perhaps ever. Or, as research scientist Meredith Bricken observes, with no small degree of understatement, 'the relationship of existing information technology to virtual world implementation is not entirely clear' (Slouka, 1995: 153). At this point, the computational challenges of creating and sustaining, on an ongoing basis, anything resembling Gibson's or Benedikt's cyberspace seem insurmountable. But much that has seemed impossible in the past has turned out to be possible. For the present, I want to leave aside the (technical) 'possibility' questions and move instead to a more detailed examination of cyberspace, both in its projected and currently existing forms, and the cities, both imagined and actual, that have inspired its dreamers.

A survey of the early visualizations of cyberspace (in *Neuromancer*, *Tron*, etc.) suggests a remarkable connection: they resemble nothing so much as the great modernist 'Cities of Tomorrow', 'Futuramas', and the 'Radiant City' dreams of Le Corbusier and Oscar Niemeyer and their many imitators. It is as if the architects of cyberspace were driven by the same utopian imagination, which, having failed in its real-world incarnations, now sought 'realization' in the ethereal realm of cyberspace. These modernist dreams of rational spaces and 'garden cities', and the eerie, mechanistic logic that underlay them, persist both in the built world we inhabit and, in many ways, in the postmodernist architectural visions that have succeeded, and yet have just as often resurrected as surmounted them. It is this juncture between the physical world, or the physical world as we experience it in our cities (at once both modern and postmodern) at the beginning of the third millennium, and cyberspace (both in its fictional representations and in its current state) that will be examined here. More specifically, I want to explore the underlying spatial logics of these two spaces, cityspace and cyberspace (though each is actually multiple) and the economic and social forces that deploy these logics. I will define in more detail what I mean by 'spatial logics', but essentially they can be understood as the logics of power projected through space and the strategic forms power assumes in urban spaces.

While each city is unique, shaped by its own site, history, economics, and culture, it is possible to identify certain important traits shared by major cities of the industrialized, first world at the beginning of the third millennium. For the sake of this argument, I will speak of 'the postmodern city', for which Los Angeles, a city that is arguably most on the cutting edge of the developments I'll be discussing here, will serve as the primary exemplar. Located at the juncture of East (the Pacific Rim) and West, of South (Mexico and Latin America) and North, of first and third worlds, LA is also probably the best example of the emergent 'world city', with all of the contradictions and collisions that term suggests. It is worth noting that the economy and peculiar ethos of LA are indelibly marked by its proximity to Hollywood and Burbank and their massive entertainment industries; to San Jose and Silicon Valley in the north, the epicentre of computer hard- and software engineering; and, inevitably though perhaps primarily symbolically, Disneyland and the seemingly endless theme parks and 'Disneyfied' spaces it has spawned. The spatial logics at work in LA are also those which tend to be most frequently adopted and extrapolated forward in time in numerous science fiction depictions of future cities. The Ridley Scott film *Blade Runner* (1982) rather famously has served as LA's 'official nightmare' of the future, but there are numerous others as well.

I want to argue here that the virtual landscapes of cyberspace, as the cybercity depicted in both fiction and proposed plans like those of Michael Benedikt, have been profoundly influenced by the underlying – and conflicting – spatial logics (and, to some extent, late-capitalist economic forces) that structure the postmodern city. Essentially, there are two competing visions of the city at present (and perhaps throughout time as well, though there have been many variations of these in the past): *the city as fortress and 'scanscape'*, in which the spatial logics are those of control, containment, exclusion, and surveillance, and *the city as polis*, in which the logics are those of freedom, access, equality, and interchange. The evidence suggests that it is the fortress city that is now nearly everywhere in the ascendancy, while the polis recedes ever further behind us.

Before moving on to the postmodern city, though, I want to return briefly to the modernist city, and to the striking resemblance between the 'grid' upon which so much modernist urban design depended, for example in Le Corbusier's 1925 Plan Voisin for Paris (which is reproduced, as David Harvey points out in *The Condition of Postmodernity* (1989) in the achieved design of Stuyvesant Town in New York City), and the grid depicted in so many representations of cyberspace, including Gibson's *Neuromancer*, *Tron*, Silicon Graphic's 3-D Fusion Information Landscape Prototype (Wexelblat, 1993: 69), Apple's e-World (Mitchell, 1995: 106), and the cyberspace renderings of Daniel Wise and Stan George (Benedikt, 1991: Plates 1–6), etc. As a base for urban design, the grid is ancient, but its imposition upon the metropolitan spaces of Paris and New York, for example, was chiefly a project of the late nineteenth and twentieth centuries – in other words, of the era of modernity, as we understand it now. The imposition of the grid constitutes a Cartesian 'rationalization' of the space of the city, and it facilitates certain municipal functions, among them governance by quarter or precinct, zoning, and taxation.

The city grid also helps to control the movement and circulation of populations (including by containing or excluding them) and, not incidentally, of troops. The broad boulevards of Baron von Haussmann's reconstructed Paris were meant not only to lend a grandeur suitable to the capital of the Second Empire; they were intended to allow for the swift deployment of troops in the event of civil unrest, and to thwart the barricading of or escape through the narrow streets and alleys they erased. In *Speed and Politics* (1987), Paul Virilio sketches the processes by which states historically have extended their power over populations through the creation and regulation of 'transportation vectors', along which travel not just commercial goods but also governmental services and the forces of 'state security'. Commerce and conquest proceed in tandem. If not actually preceded by conquest, the 'opening' of new territories (which might initially serve as a kind of safety valve for restive populations) is always swiftly followed by it, in one form or another. The territory of cyberspace is no exception.

The field on which *Neuromancer*'s data holds are arrayed in cyberspace is peculiarly Cartesian – geometrical, abstract, transcendent: the realm of pure information is composed of 'bright lattices of logic unfolding across that colorless void' (Gibson, 1984: 4), 'lines of light ranged in the nonspace of the mind' (*ibid.*: 51), forming a 'transparent 3-D chessboard extending to infinity' (*ibid.*: 52). Like the city grid it resembles, this must be seen as a form of disciplinary mechanism, a grid creating a striated space allowing simultaneously for intelligibility, surveillance, and control. Here is the successor to the '"cells", "places", and "ranks"' through which, as Michel Foucault observed in *Discipline and Punish*, 'the disciplines create complex spaces that are at once architectural, functional and hierarchical' (Foucault, 1979: 148). Like the drawing up of tables, this ordering of information, the configuration of cyberspace, is 'both a technique of power and a procedure of knowledge'. It is still 'a question of organizing the multiple, of providing oneself with an instrument to cover it and to master it ... a question of imposing upon it an "order"' (*ibid.*: 148). By instituting spatial separations and various types of *cordons sanitaires*, city grids further facilitate both the visual surveillance and supervision of populations. Such goals were explicitly part of numerous modernist proposals for newly colonized cities, among them Le Corbusier's unbuilt Obus projects for Algiers.[6] This logic of 'order' persists into the postmodern era, where it has been augmented by increasingly complex and effective mechanisms of power and discipline.

'In cities like LA, on the bad edge of postmodernity,' urban historian Mike Davis notes, 'one observes an unprecedented tendency to merge urban design, architecture, and the police apparatus into a single, comprehensive security effort' (Davis, 1992: 224). This tendency can be seen (in cities all over the world, as well as in LA) in the astonishing ubiquity of electronic surveillance systems scanning the interiors and exteriors of both private and purportedly public spaces. It is apparent in the increasing privatization of what was formerly public space, in the closing off of public streets, and in the spread of video-surveyed, security-patrolled shopping malls that turn the marketplace inside out, enclosing and privatizing the agora. One observes it in the spread of guarded, walled residential enclaves, and in the architecture of public buildings that implicitly redefine 'public' in highly restrictive ways that amount to a policing of social boundaries. A good example of the latter is Frank Gehry's design for the 'baroquely fortified' Goldwyn Public Library, cited by Davis in his history of LA, *City of Quartz*. The library is surrounded by 'fifteen-foot security walls of stucco-covered concrete block, ... anti-graffiti barricades covered in ceramic tile, ... [a] sunken entrance protected by ten-foot steel stacks, and ... stylized sentry boxes perched precariously on each side' (Davis, 1992: 239). Even those who live outside the confines of the increasingly 'hardening' urban landscapes are likely to be familiar with it from recent American films, with their 'images of carceral inner cities (*Escape from New York*, *Running Man*), high-tech police death squads (*Blade Runner*), sentient buildings (*Die Hard*), urban bantustans (*They Live!*) ... and so on, [that] only extrapolate from actually existing trends' (*ibid.*: 223).

There do not appear to be any public spaces in *Neuromancer*'s cyberspace: the chessboard grids between the corporate and governmental data holds are as empty and devoid of 'street life' as the windswept, video-surveyed glacis that surround the corporate citadels of LA. The hero of *Neuromancer* is an outlaw, a 'cyberspace cowboy' who operates the 'exotic software required to penetrate the bright walls of corporate systems, opening windows into rich fields of data' (Gibson, 1984: 5). Those 'bright walls' are protected by lethal ICE, intrusion countermeasures electronics that detect and dispatch trespassers.

There are, of course, competing versions of cyberspace that model it as a 'consensual public realm', a polis. In *Cyberspace: First Steps*, Michael Benedikt envisions it as a roofless city with a rich street life, a 'three-dimensional field of action and interaction: with recorded and live data, with machines ... and with other people' (Benedikt, 1991: 129). Benedikt's version of cyberspace is a wide-open range for the free play of the intellect: 'Once in cyberspace,' he proposes, 'there may be many ways of getting around, from walking and crawling, to leaping through worm holes, from "bareback" riding or cyberBuick cruising, to floating and flying unencumbered. And there may be just as many alternative modes of action and manipulation' (*ibid.*: 130). Like a good urban planner, Benedikt pays careful attention in his plans to access, both internal and external. His cybercity comes equipped with ports, transit stations, and gateways. On the outside, 'cyberspace processing should be distributed,' he suggests, 'and its communication channels [should be] many and alternative: phone lines, satellite, HDTV, cables, even radio and power lines. The technical aspects of this are daunting ... And, of course,' he adds, 'there are myriad political, economic, and power-related questions involved in this notion of decentralization and redundancy' (*ibid.*: 218). Well, yes. Particularly at a time when Warner buys Time; then Time-Warner buys CNN; then AOL announces it intends to merge with Time-Warner-CNN, and so on.[7]

The development of cyberspace and the infrastructure necessary to support it, like the development of all the related tele-technologies, is an enterprise requiring vast sums of capital — capital on a scale generally available only to governments and mega-corporations. The sheer magnitude of the financial resources necessary to design and build cyberspace would seem to ensure that it will never be — in any sense — free. Benedikt's utopian vision of 'unencumbered' movement through the cybercity is jarringly at odds with his own observation (in a footnote) that 'the dollar-cost of travel to users may be one of the economic engines that drives cyberspace as a money-making enterprise' (*ibid.*: 219).

Benedikt goes on to detail a Midas-like array of 'other sources of income [available] to the owners and maintainers of the system', including:

> outright purchase of real estate in cyberspace, the leasing of such, advertising time and space, connect-time charges to the system and to individual presences, innumerable hardware purchases and upgrades, cabling systems, satellites and so on, access software, endless enhancements to this, etc.; and all this in addition to the value of the information bought and sold as such within the system.
>
> (*ibid.*: 219)

And we shouldn't forget the inevitable security systems to protect one's property (real estate) in the cybercity. The possibilities of 'information capitalism' seem limitless — for the capitalists, that is.[8] Yet the inextricable intertwining of the market and this space suggests that there is little likelihood of any buffering, purely democratic mechanism emerging from or within it.

Neal Stephenson's 1992 depiction of cyberspace (referred to as the 'Metaverse') in *Snow Crash* more closely resembles the exorbitantly hypercapitalist terrain of Benedikt's vision than the somewhat more austere (though also capitalist) version in *Neuromancer*:

> Like any place in Reality, the Street is subject to development ... When Hiro goes into the Metaverse and looks down the street and sees buildings and signs stretching off into the darkness, disappearing over the curve of the globe, he is actually staring at the graphic representations — the user interfaces — of myriad different pieces of software that have been engineered by major corporations. In order to place these things on the Street, they have to get approval from the Global Multimedia Protocol Group, have to buy frontage on the Street,

get zoning approval, obtain permits, bribe inspectors, the whole bit ...
Put a sign or building on the Street, and the hundred million richest,
hippest, best-connected people on earth will see it every day of their
lives.

(Stephenson, 1992: 24–6)

This Street looks like one we've been down before.[9] The privatization of public
space in the postmodern city has its analogue in the commercialization of
cyberspace, and the concomitant emergence of elite databases and subscriber-
only services. This Web-commerce has also brought with it its own
surveillance mechanisms – for example, 'cookies' and 'spiders', which track
Web-users' movements and actions (what they view, read, and buy) in cyberspace.[10] This surveillance usually occurs without the knowledge of the users,
just as many of us proceed about our daily routines unaware of the surveillance
cameras that watch us in convenience stores, at the ATM, in the subway, on
the plaza leading into the company headquarters, etc. Increasingly, all around
us, as Foucault warned, disciplinary mechanisms multiply and swarm; the
panopticon becomes the spatial dominant of the postmodern 'scanscape' of
both the real and virtual realms.

Once the Internet moved beyond being the sole province of the armed
forces, scientists, and academics, it quickly became clear that the new
information class hierarchy was going to look very much like the old property
class hierarchy. Only a few years after Paul Virilio made the observation that
'the society of tomorrow will splinter into two opposing camps: those who
live to the beat of real time of the global city, within the virtual community of
the "haves", and the "have-nots" who survive in the margins of the real space
of local cities', 'tomorrow' seems much like today (Virilio, 1997: 74).

Contemporary concentrations and flows of economic (and, to a very great
extent, political) power can now be effectively traced across the physical
landscape by charting the flow of information. In *Neuromancer*, Gibson
suggested a modelling of this principle, mapping the connections along the
Boston–Atlanta Metropolitan Axis ('the Sprawl'): 'program a map to display
frequency of data exchange every thousand megabytes a single pixel on a very
large screen. Manhattan and Atlanta burn solid white ... At a hundred million
megabytes per second, you begin to make out certain blocks in midtown
Manhattan' (Gibson, 1984: 43). Many such maps, tracking the flow of Internet
traffic via the NFSNET/ANSnet backbone, for example, already exist.[11]

Here the dissolve from cityspace to cyberspace, with which I began, is
reversed. This shift suggests the immense potential power of the abstracted
space of the electronic matrix over the 'material' landscape, which is effectively
deterritorialized through technology that, Virilio notes, juxtaposes 'places and

elements that only yesterday were still distinct and separated by a buffer of distances' (Virilio, 1987: 136). 'The city was the means of mapping out a political space that existed in a given political duration. Now speed – ubiquity, displaces it' (Virilio, 1983: 60).

Cyberspace might be understood as the logical endpoint of a tendency to proximity, 'the single interface between all bodies, all places, all points of the world' that has characterized the historical development of technologies of transportation and information (Virilio, 1983: 62). As a structure, cyberspace approximates the Borgesian Aleph (Borges, 1981), which contains in one point, but without overlap, all spaces. 'With his deck,' Case notes, 'he could reach the Freeside [a city in orbit around the earth] banks as easily as he could reach Atlanta. Travel was a meat thing' (Gibson, 1984: 77). Movement through cyberspace is frictionless and instantaneous: 'Case punched for the Swiss banking sector, feeling a wave of exhilaration as cyberspace shivered, blurred, gelled. The Eastern Seaboard Fission Authority was gone, replaced by the cool geometric intricacy of Zurich commercial banking. He punched again, for Berne' (*ibid.*: 115).

At the same time that the logics transforming the postmodern city are also shaping cyberspace, cyberspace is also, though perhaps still to a lesser degree, restructuring the postmodern landscape. As has already become obvious in the era of 'smart' bombs, such as those deployed by the US in the Gulf War; the Geographical Information System (whose super-detailed mappings of the entire face of the earth are now commercially available); and Echelon, the vast information surveillance system used by the National Security Agency of the US government, the capabilities of computer technologies for exerting a vast, disciplinary control over the spaces of the 'real' world we inhabit are immense. This 'efficacy' of the virtual world within the real can only be further extended by the development of new technologies such as 'smart' houses, appliances, and even clothing that wrap the computer and its virtual spaces ever more closely around us. A recent television advertisement for ADT, an American company selling home security systems, depicts lines of binary code emanating from the wall-mounted control panel, wrapping themselves around the doors, windows, and walls of a suburban house – an image that strongly suggests we are meant to be cosseted, protected, comforted even, by this new 'connectivity'. Yet it seems to me that this cyberization of the world, the creation of an 'augmented' reality, might be dropping yet another veil between us and the real. We create an increasingly complex and entangled mix of the virtual and the real, and the possibilities seem indeed to have 'no limit', as Oedipa sensed. Our task now is to sort out these possibilities between the better and the worse, and to navigate this ever-more mixed (virtual and actual) chaos. But this is, in many ways, what life in the city has always been about.

Notes

1. Stills of depictions of cyberspace from *Tron, Johnny Mnemonic, Hackers* and *The Matrix* may be viewed at *An Atlas of Cyberspaces*. The *Atlas* is also an excellent source for conceptual, historic, and other maps of cyberspaces.

2. From a 2000 print advertisement for mySAP.com — 'a collaborative business environment ... with more than 10,000 companies linked together seamlessly over the Web'.

3. Described in detail by Cicero and Quintilian, the technique involved the imprinting on the memory of a familiar locus or place — usually a large building. The structure of the building itself was a constant, a template. One formed mental images of the things one wished to remember, and then placed the images like furnishings, one by one, into the imaginary building. The first might be left on the threshold, the second affixed to a pillar, the third set in a corner, and so on. When one wished to recall the memory, one would imagine walking through the memory building, retrieving in each place the image left there. Extended feats of memory might require more than one building, perhaps many arrayed along a street or even an entire city.

4. Tomas made this observation in reference to Tim McFadden's 'The structure of cyberspace and the ballistic actors model — an extended abstract', presented at the conference.

5. See Fredric Jameson's article, 'Postmodernism, or the cultural logic of late capitalism' (1984).

6. See Zeynep Celik, 'Cultural intersections: re-visioning architecture and the city in the twentieth century' (1998) for more on this and other features of modernist colonial city design.

7. See Ronald V. Bettig's 'The enclosure of cyberspace' (1997) for an economic analysis of the development of cyberspace.

8. Real-world corporations are equally forthright about the opportunities presented by cyberspace. From an IBM statement, 'The future of computing': 'IBM's view of a "network centric" future is driven by the desire of people and enterprises to connect to other people and enterprises around the world and leverage information using powerful new technologies that transcend distance and time, lower boundaries between markets, cultures and individuals and actually deliver solutions that fulfill the promise of universal connectivity.' (See http://www.ibm.com/IBM/ar95/sv_static/index.html)

9. Stephenson's (1992) novel is also remarkable for its just-a-moment-from-now depiction of postmodern urban spaces, particularly its identical, mass-produced Burbclaves, 'city-state[s] with [their] own constitution[s], a border, laws, cops, everything' (p. 6).

10. Greg Elmer's article, 'Spaces of surveillance: indexicality and solicitation on the Internet' (1997), examines the 'various overlapping, reproductive processes through which the Internet is first mapped through indexical search engines, and then diagnosed, via "spiders" and "cookies," to actively monitor, survey, solicit and subsequently profile users' on-line behavior' (p. 182).

11. See, for example, Terry Harpold's article on such mappings, 'Dark continents: critique of Internet metageographies' (1999) See also *An Atlas of Cyberspaces*.

Bibliography

An Atlas of Cyberspaces (1991) http://www.cybergeography.com/atlas/atlas.html

Anders, Peter (1999) *Envisioning Cyberspace: Designing 3D Electronic Spaces* (New York: McGraw-Hill).

Benedikt, Michael (ed.) (1991) *Cyberspace: First Steps* (Cambridge, MA: MIT Press).

Bettig, Ronald V. (1997) 'The enclosure of cyberspace', *Critical Studies in Mass Communication*, 14: 138–57.

Blade Runner (1982) Dir. Ridley Scott.

Borges, Jorge Luis (1981) 'The Aleph', in Emir Rodriguez Monegal and Alastair Reid (eds), *Borges: A Reader* (New York: E. P. Dutton), pp. 154–65.

Celik, Zeynep (1998) 'Cultural intersections: re-visioning architecture and the city in the twentieth century', in Russell Ferguson (ed.), *At the End of the Century: One Hundred Years of Architecture* (Los Angeles: The Museum of Contemporary Art), pp. 190–227.

Davis, Mike (1992) *City of Quartz: Excavating the Future in Los Angeles* (New York: Vintage Books).

Elmer, Greg (1997) 'Spaces of surveillance: indexicality and solicitation on the Internet', *Critical Studies in Mass Communication*, 14: 182–91.

Foucault, Michel (1997) *Discipline and Punish: The Birth of the Prison*, trans. Alan Sheridan (New York: Vintage Books).

Gelernter, David (1991) *Mirror Worlds or the Day Software Puts the World into a Shoebox: How it Will Happen and What it Will Mean* (New York: Oxford University Press).

Gibson, William (1984) *Neuromancer* (New York: Ace Books).

Gibson, William (1988) *Mona Lisa Overdrive* (New York: Bantam).

Hackers (1995) Dir. Iain Softley.

Harpold, Terry (1999) 'Dark continents: critique of Internet metageographies', *Postmodern Culture*, 9(2) (January). http://muse.jhu.edu/journals/postmodern_culture/v009/9.2harpold.html

Harvey, David (1989) *The Condition of Postmodernity* (Oxford: Blackwell).

Jameson, Fredric (1984) 'Postmodernism, or the cultural logic of late capitalism', *New Left Review*, 146: 53–92.

Johnny Mnemonic (1995) Dir. Robert Longo.

The Matrix (1999) Dirs Wachowski Brothers.

Max Headroom (1986) Dir. Rocky Morton.

Mitchell, William J. (1995) *City of Bits: Space, Place, and the Infobahn* (Cambridge, MA: MIT Press).

Pynchon, Thomas (1966) *The Crying of Lot 49* (Philadelphia: J.B. Lippincott; New York: Bantam edition, 1967).

Slouka, Mark (1995) *War of the Worlds: Cyberspace and the Assault on Reality* (New York: Basic Books).

Stephenson, Neal (1992) *Snow Crash* (New York: Bantam).

Tomas, David (1993) 'Old rituals for new space: rites de passage and William Gibson's cultural model of cyberspace', in Michael Benedikt (ed.), *Cyberspace: First Steps* (Cambridge: MIT Press), pp. 31–48.

Tron (1982) Dir. Steven Lisberger.

Virilio, Paul (1983) *Pure War*, trans. Mark Polizzotti. Foreign Agent Series (New York: Semiotext(e)).

Virilio, Paul (1987) *Speed and Politics: An Essay on Dromology*, trans. Mark Polizzotti (New York: Semiotext(e)).

Virilio, Paul (1997) *Open Sky*, trans. Julie Rose (New York: Verso).

Wexelblat, Alan (ed.) (1993) *Virtual Reality: Applications and Explorations* (Cambridge, MA: Academic Press Professional).

Yates, Frances A. (1966) *The Art of Memory* (Chicago: University of Chicago Press).

7

Studying feminist e-spaces

Introducing transnational/post-colonial concerns

RADHIKA GAJJALA

Technological, discursive and symbolic artefacts re-present and contribute to the shaping of the socio-cultural realities of individuals and communities. These everyday realities are presuppositionally and ontologically spatial (Soja, 1996: 46). Human and 'post-human' subjects inscribe selves and are themselves inscribed within digital domains (Hayles, 1998). In fact, several subject positions are possible through the multiple inscriptions of self. Subjects thus inscribed are both digitally and materially embodied, appearing and disappearing within social spaces characterized by various unequal power relations. Different social realities – digital and material, virtual and real – produce variations of an embodied subject framed by hegemonic ideologies and discourses. The virtual environments within which subjects interact on-line are structured by the symbolic and technological realities of cyberspace (Holmes, 1997: 11). These realities of cyberspace, in turn, are produced in negotiation with hegemonic ideologies and structures of power. Virtual subjects communicate and interact within epistemological and ontological structures embedded in material reality. On-line interactions, and the human subjects produced in interaction with the new mediating technologies, cannot be discussed in isolation from the cultural, social, political and economic contexts within which emerging technologies and new forms of communication operate. The illusion that virtual existence is separate from real life is a result of mainstream celebratory discourses about new technologies and virtual reality, which are rooted in the Cartesian mind/body binary (see Benedikt, 1991; Markley, 1996).

It is this interaction between virtual and real, mind and body that is of interest to several cyberfeminist scholars such as Katherine Hayles, Donna Harraway, Anne Balsamo, and Alluquerre Roseanne Stone. They and others have written about cyborg subjectivities and post-human embodiment, engaging with the philosophy and politics of knowledge-production in relation to science and technology studies. A majority of feminist scholarship that specifically examines the Internet as a site for socio-cultural interaction has produced a rhetoric of empowerment, stressing increased access to communities and relationships, gender anonymity, and experimentation with multiple selves (Turkle, 1995; Stone, 1992). Elsewhere this scholarship has deployed a rhetoric of victimization, chronicling instances of women being harassed, flamed, or ignored on-line (Spender, 1995). Both theoretical and empirical treatments that approach the study of electronic culture and practices from feminist perspectives have begun to question not merely whether or not virtual communities for women exist, but what fosters or inhibits their development into genuinely empowering e-spaces for women. In attempting to draw connections between material and virtual practices, some of these same feminist cyberscholars are also attempting to go beyond the boundaries implicit in much of the utopian rhetoric surrounding on-line existence. Cyberfeminist scholars are insisting on questioning the critical and material contexts that underlie virtual communities, on-line identities and cybercultures. For many of them it is not enough to ask if virtual communities exist; instead they ask under what material, discursive, socio-economic, political and cultural conditions on-line communities have developed (for example, Harcourt, 1999). Studies have begun to examine the rules and protocol for participation and interaction, asking when and how these networks for interaction become dialogic; they explore biases that are implicit in the way on-line networks are organized, and analyse to what extent on-line democracy is active. For instance, Laura Agustin, in her article entitled 'They speak, but who listens?', argues that questions relating to the 'right' to communicate and access the Internet need to be carefully examined and that the theoretical frameworks from within which we are asked to view the information economy as democratic need to be challenged:

> Some of those excluded from much of mainstream societies *want* to include themselves in this new technology, whatever it turns out to be. They see themselves as protagonists of the revolution. But what of those who are excluded and who see nothing (so far) about this new technology to attract them or who do not know it exists? Should they be forced to be included, if being included could 'help' them (acquire useful information, tell their stories, and educate others)?
>
> (Agustin, 1999: 152)

Earlier mainstream often celebratory discourses concerning digital technologies continue to circulate in academic and popular forums. These are 'largely unchallenged discourses of the metaphysics of cyberspace' (Markley, 1996), produced by writers such as Michael Benedikt and Nicholas Negroponte and visible in recent works such as *Net Gain* by John Hagel III and Arthur Armstrong (1997). These suggest that on-line interaction and virtual existence provide possibilities for 'going beyond' some of the binaries manifested within the structures of modern society while erasing the complexities of negotiating unequal power relations. However, an examination of much of the available literature on the topic of cyber-interaction reveals the existence of binary modes of thought that arise from a history of knowledge-production that is still very much rooted in positivist research paradigms, developmentalist narratives of linear progress, and objective science. Virtual/real, mind/body, self/other, global/local, digital/analogue, masculine/feminine are some of the most obvious binary oppositions visible in much of the rhetoric surrounding cyberspace and the use of on-line technologies.

Feminists writing about the Internet negotiate theoretical binaries in various ways. Sometimes they unintentionally reproduce the binaries, which prevents the understanding of communication which falls outside of such framings. For example, it is apparent that most analyses of the gendered nature of communication via e-spaces rely to a large extent on an examination of the 'women-centredness' or 'women friendliness' of e-spaces (Herring, 1996; Spender, 1995; Warnick, 1999; Youngs, 1999). Often, the studies contrast women-centred e-spaces with male-dominated spaces in which women are perceived as subject to harassment and various forms of textual violence (Gilbert, 1996; Dibbell, 1993). Cyberfeminist researchers can also assume that silence on-line implies a general lack of off-line voice and power, thus conflating 'power' with having a visible presence on-line and being adept at using digital technologies.[1] As Warnick points out, the '"unconnected" in the present' are negatively equated with the '"illiterate" of the past' (Warnick, 1999: 5). The unit of analysis in such studies tends to remain a universal category 'Woman' as constructed within hegemonic Westernized, urban feminist discourses. These discourses regarding the construction of Woman rely too much on a 'single-theme analysis' where the category 'Woman' can be separated from other intersecting categories of lived experience such as race, class, caste, age, sexuality and geographical location. It is presumed that each of these categories is autonomous. Yet, as Norma Alarcon points out using De Beavoir, such analyses ignore the fact that

> one 'becomes a woman' in ways that are more complex than in simple opposition to men. In cultures in which 'asymmetric race and class relations are a central organizing principle of society,' one may also 'become a woman' in opposition to other women.
>
> (Alarcon, 1990: 361, as cited in Dhaliwal, 1996: 46)

Even as identity issues on the Internet are discussed in relation to race (Tal, 1996; Nakamura, 1995), and in relation to the imbalances of access between the 'North' and the 'South', the Internet haves and have-nots (Harcourt, 1999), feminist critiques of digital existence continue to privilege the aforementioned single-themed analysis. Furthermore, while research concerning racial identity, women and technology, women and development and globalization is currently being produced in various fields of study, very few available studies of Internet interaction have engaged extensively with theoretical analyses that implicitly or explicitly critique the developmentalism embedded in linear narrative of Eurocentric, Anglo-American progress.[2] As Robert Markley asserts:

> The blind spot of many critiques of virtual technologies lies in their linked rhetoric of progress as natural and inevitable, and their acceptance of the view that we are living in revolutionary times in which technology can intervene in our subjectivity in ways undreamt of prior to the late twentieth century.
>
> (Markley, 1996: 439)

This blind spot prevails in many studies related to the Internet and women. This, in spite of the fact that theoretical work by scholars like Donna Haraway (1992, 1994), Katherine Hayles (1998), Arturo Escobar (1999) and Sandra Harding (1998) provides a point of entry into such theoretical examinations of cyberculture by highlighting concerns regarding the situatedness of theory and practice (Gajjala, 1999).

This framing of e-spaces in relation to gender easily falls into the stereotypical Woman = Other system that inhibits the expression of any 'Other' behaviours. As Judith Butler (1993) argues, in modern (Westernized, urban, bourgeois) societies, we learn to perform maleness or femaleness, masculinity or femininity. Our consciousness is subjected to a 'tyranny of gender', which holds us prisoner to a two-category (binary) system of gender (Danet, 1998). The research strategy frequently adopted is to 'identify the feminine through a strategy of exclusion from the masculine' (Butler 1993: 126). In these instances, notions of 'feminine' and 'masculine' often have their roots in received notions of middle-class Anglo-American socio-cultural etiquette. Theoretical analyses that merely examine and/or celebrate the difference between male and female subjects without acknowledging that the men and women they are observing are actually situated within diverse cultural locations focus only on processes of identification with specific forms of gendered difference. They fail to account for the fact that the process of identification with a single identity that relies heavily on a single theme requires a simultaneous dis-identification and rejection of other kinds of identities and behaviours. 'Other'[3] women entering these women-centred e-spaces are required to reshape and reconstruct their identities and discursive modes of expression to conform to a certain specific notion of 'Woman' in order to be able to participate within such on-line forums. Thus, even within these social spaces, 'the subject is constituted through the force of exclusion and abjection, one which produces a constitutive outside to the subject, an abjected outside' (Butler, 1993: 3). The (implicit) exclusion and rejection of dissent within the regulatory norms for what is perceived as democratic/ dialogic exchange ironically succeed in inhibiting a more intense level of democratic or dialogic mode of interaction. The problem, then, is how to maintain an atmosphere of interaction, which acknowledges (sometimes violent) dissent as within and not outside of dialogue. As Butler further points out, 'it may be that the persistence of *dis*-identification is equally crucial to the rearticulation of democratic contestation' (*ibid.*).

On-line social spaces inhabit various configurations, scales and hybrid forms of the 'global' and 'local' (glocal).[4] In the formation of these digital 'glocalities', framed by unequal power relations between the local and the global, several locales are marginalized. My project here is to urge the importance of examining various interconnections between women's use of the Internet and the subjectivities forged on-line within a climate of 'glocalization' (Dirlik, 1998; Escobar, 1999). In examining these interconnections, we might ask what 'voices' emerge within different socio-spatial technological configurations and where the silenced voices are shifted to. As we produce theories and practices within virtual (academic) matrices, I suggest that we also attempt to map the routes that theory travels hand in hand with practices. Thus we may begin to better understand how virtual practices impinge upon, enhance or disrupt analogue material realities.

Mapping the intersections of theory and practice leads us to sites of political practice, where even seemingly unlikely coalitions are formed in the interest of collective goals. For example, as digital technologies and the Internet increasingly assume primary importance in facilitating the expansion of multinational corporate markets, not only is there a resulting 'denationaliza-tion' of corporate power but there is also an increased mobilization of women's labour within the world economy. As more women are mobilized as part of the labour force and forced or lured into social spaces unfamiliar to them that are governed by rules set in place prior to their entry into these sites, there is a 'reorganization of oppositional movements and constituencies against capital that articulate themselves in terms and relations other than the "national" — notably, movements of women of color and third-world-women' (Lowe, 1996: 103). From these transnational and post-colonial formations there can emerge collaborations and coalitions that lead to action based on common goals. Individual subjects that form a part of such coalitions can view themselves as heterogeneous and political subjects who resist the binarism implicit in a unitary construction of agency/subjecthood. Rather than focus on differences as meaning 'essentialist differences that are insurmountable for the formations of coalitions or for solidarity with various struggles', the agents that form such transnational coalitions focus on providing constant critiques of 'power relations that structure global economic [and cultural] flows' (Grewal and Kaplan, 1994: 234). They can view themselves as subjects-in-process instead of complete, unified agents with essential qualities that flag their sameness and/or difference.

The controversies and discussions that emerge at the intersection of transnational feminism and post-colonial theory engage different transnational struggles and practices that do not rely on identifications based on single, autonomous and exclusionary themes, but seek to understand the different historical and political configurations of power that operate within specific contexts, searching for points of entry into common struggles against oppressive hegemonies. I argue that a post-colonial feminist perspective to the study of on-line spaces might better allow us to understand subjectivity and political practice on-line. I wish to introduce some concerns to the general body of work that is being produced about communicating within e-space and to open some issues up for further discussion.[5] To this end, I will use Susan Herring's study of women-centred spaces as a critique of such single-theme analyses of women's communication within electronic spaces.

Susan Herring (1996) discusses the masculinist construction of netiquette in relation to the different styles of postings that men and women adopt within certain women-centred spaces. According to Herring, women-centred e-spaces are seen as more empowering to women than e-spaces that are dominated by male styles of posting. It is assumed that women-centred e-spaces not only focus topically on issues that apparently speak directly to women's experiences in the private and the public sphere but would ideally also encourage a style of posting that is 'woman-friendly'. I would argue, however, that not only is the construction of netiquette 'masculinist', it is also class-specific even in the construction of feminist netiquette based on the different styles of posting exhibited by men and women.

In her work, Susan Herring examines some specific women-centred e-spaces. She observes that, within these e-spaces, women's posts generally tend to be supportive and inviting of friendly responses from other members of the list. She observes that women in these spaces attempt to be inclusive, while at the same time they make conscious efforts not to be intrusive and arrogant by posting lengthy diatribes to lists. Men, according to Herring, tend to be more inflammatory, neutral or adversarial in the way they post. Often, their posts are lengthy and can be interpreted as arrogant. While adversariality is the discursive norm on male-dominated lists, women-centred lists tend to focus on support/attenuation. She claims that

> women and men appeal to different − and partially incompatible − systems of values both as the rational foundation of their posting behavior and in interpreting and evaluating the behavior of others online. These values correspond to differences in posting style, and are evident as well in official netiquette guidelines, where the general bias in favor of values preferred by men has practical consequences for how comfortable women feel in mainstream electronic forums.
>
> (Herring, 1996: 115)

The idea that men and women have different ways of knowing, communicating and even interacting on-line has its source in feminist socio-feminist linguistics and a further body of feminist literature that focuses on women's ways of knowing and the 'ethic of care' (Gilligan, 1977, 1982; Gilligan and Attanucci, 1988). The ethic of care is discussed in opposition to the ethic of justice. According to the proponents of this argument, women's socio-cultural upbringing encourages an ethic of care, whereas men's experiences and socio-cultural upbringing encourage the formation of an ethic of justice. Critics of this viewpoint have cautioned against the danger that such an argument might reinforce essentialist notions of difference between men and women (Mednick, 1989; Pollitt, 1992; Steiner, 1989). Susan Herring, however, suggests that we should be wary of dismissing theories that talk of women's 'different voice' by arguing it reproduces essentialist notions of male/female difference. 'Quite to the contrary,' she writes, 'differences that reproduce patterns of dominance must be named and understood, lest inequality be perpetuated and recreated through the uncritical acting out of familiar scripts' (Herring, 1996: 117). However, the complexity of the patterns of dominance manifested in various configurations of gender, class and geographical power relations are not being 'named', when all we focus on is the naming of two 'different voices' of male and female. There are other logics of difference that contribute to the various posting styles on-line, and there is a different kind of essentialism at work when styles of posting are characterized as just typically female or male. As Barbara Warnick points out, 'hierarchies embed themselves in the constructs of gender, race, profession, religion and personal interest' (Warnick, 1999: 5). The hierarchy embedded in the construction of male and female ways of communicating suggests that women cannot function effectively within contentious on-line e-spaces. The notion of a universalized Woman's Way can lead to an on-line tyranny of essentialized femaleness which excludes complex 'Othered' female *and* male voices.

Certain types of specific non-confrontational, passive behaviours expected of women within polite Westernized societies are characterized as feminine postings that are 'supportive' (Herring, 1996) and 'inviting' (Warnick, 1999); an essentially positive value is attributed to these types of behaviour. Correspondingly, types of behaviours that appear confrontational or even just indignant are characterized as typically masculine styles that are 'adversarial', 'neutral' and 'arrogant' (Herring, 1996); a negative value is attributed to such behaviours. The possibility of constructive conflict risks being suppressed and/or disapproved of in women-centred e-spaces. 'Civility' and netiquette are defined within very Westernized and urban bourgeois terms and contexts, while the speaking and silencing of women from various races, classes, castes and geographical locations continues to be governed by a 'benevolence' that is nonetheless hierarchical, in that it 'allows' or disallows the Other's speech. Awaiting the patronage of this benevolent tyranny, the Other is either 'empowered', 'given voice to' or silenced within these e-spaces. In digital spheres as elsewhere in real life, the only experience of 'woman-ness' to be acknowledged is the kind allowed by dominant and universalized definitions of what it means to be a woman in heterosexual, Westernized, middle-class socio-cultural spaces.

How, then, are dislocations and dis-identifications performed on-line? I suggest that this question may lead to a richer understanding of the complex role that gender, race, class, age, sexuality and geographical location play in how we communicate on-line. Herring, like most feminist scholars, struggles with the binary framing that positions women as either victim or victor. I suggest that an examination of strategic relocation of the cybercitizen, through the subject's dis-identifications and refusals, is necessary. Perhaps the 'subaltern' would rather not speak from within, but relocate her subjectivity through dis-identifications that enable her to be heard, even if unpleasantly. Thus her 'speech' might come in the form of resistant silences or 'adversarial' flames.[6]

Often 'women-centred' analyses implicitly locate essentialized and universalized women's and men's ways of knowing, being and communicating as the primary categories for the understanding of silence, voice and aggression within on-line contexts. In these instances, race, class and geographical location are suggested as mere secondary add-on categories. In order to understand if poorer women living under unequal economic, social and cultural power relations are indeed being empowered by technology, we need to engage in analyses that take into consideration all the complexities involved in 'conceptualizations of identity, opposition, consciousness and voice' (Dhaliwal, 1996: 43).

Discursive, digital identity-formations are situated within the Anglo-American hegemony of the Internet. The digital (post)colonial subject is formed within this language, medium and rhetoric in ways similar and dissimilar to the formation of the colonized subject that Fanon refers to in his work on *Black Skin, White Masks* (1967). Fanon argues that encounters between the colonized and the colonizers produce contradictory subjects who are at once fluent in and antagonistic to dominant culture and language. Extending his analysis of colonial narratives and subject formation, Lisa Lowe articulates a theory of 'immigrant acts' in relation to Asian Americans in the United States. She examines '"cultural institutions" of subject formation in order to consider the alternative forms of subjectivity and history whose emergences are obscured by ... dominant forms' (Lowe, 1996: 98). Extending Lowe's analysis to digital (post)colonial spaces, we can observe implications for the emergence of alternative forms of subjectivity in on-line women-centred spaces, and argue that these alternative emergences are obscured by the binary (either/or) framings of cyberculture. Current research surrounding cyberculture and cyberfeminism in turn 'legitimates particular forms and subjects of history and subjugates or erases others' (*ibid.*).

On e-mail discussion lists, web-based and usenet bulletin boards as well as synchronous text-based e-spaces like 'MOOs' and 'MUDs', interactive computer-mediated communication between two or more people is composed of a socio-cultural cyberspatial environment through clusters of interpersonal exchanges (Holeton, 1998). In these instances, on-line interactions are both subjects-in-process and texts frozen in time within cyberspatial archives (Gajjala, 1999). Digital subjects emerge within clusters of interactive exchange within the broader social, political, cultural and economic framing of cyberspace. Further, each cluster of interpersonal exchange is a communicative event that provides insights into aspects of the participants' prismatic selves. Therefore, within such discursive/digital settings, rather than asking the question 'who speaks?', it would be better to ask what kind of subject emerges.

Having said that, I must emphasize that the digital subjects that emerge at the intersection of these clusters of interpersonal computer-mediated exchanges are nonetheless discursive reproductions of real-life societies and imagined communities. In spite of the illusion that there is only pure text and no human form from which the cybertext emanates, we have not all dispersed into virtual reality. We are not disembodied beings, and even when we are interacting within virtual communities, we are still very much part of those economies and hierarchies that are maintained within 'real' hegemonic structures.

Thus, in addition to asking and examining what kind of subject emerges within these digital contexts, we need to ask what kind of hierarchies (visible and invisible) are embedded within each cluster of interaction and how this contributes to the formation of an Internet culture that marginalizes a majority of the population in the world today – the 'Information Rich' versus the 'Information Poor'.

We need an examination of the locations and dislocations of contradictory subjects that emerge (even if barely 'visible') through the fluency and antagonisms of prolific participation, flaming and lurking within so-called woman-centred on-line discussion contexts. This could lead to a better understanding of the socio-cultural, political and economic (whether they be 'post' colonial, 'post' modern or 'neo' colonial) framings of social spaces on-line. We would also need to open up issues for further consideration by problematizing some of the assumptions made in relation to women and the Internet. The notion of women-centredness that is used in relation to on-line communication is not a 'universal' notion, but is culturally specific to Westernized, materially privileged women. We should further problematize the celebratory rhetoric concerning the Internet, and open up some claims for further discussion and analysis in the interests of trying to compose a cyberspatial environment that might potentially provide a democratic global forum for communication and self re-presentations, particularly for those who are marginalized. A body of intellectual work on 'race', ethnicity and class already exists, but it needs to be critically appropriated and deployed to on-line (con)texts and computer-mediated public discourse and interpersonal interaction, in order to avoid the pitfalls of universal claim-making.

Acknowledgements

I wish to acknowledge Dr Kris Blair for her advice and guidance in formulating the ideas for this chapter, Dr Sally Munt for her patient comments on several drafts of this work and Philippa Hudson for her editorial work. In addition, I wish to thank members of the women-writing-culture list, sa-cyborgs list and third-world-women list for increasing my understanding of issues discussed in this chapter. Finally, thanks must also go to the Spoon Collective, who carry out the technical and maintenance work required to run the lists on `lists.village.virginia.edu.server`.

Notes

1. See, for example, discussions of gender perspectives at
   http://commposite.uqam.ca/videaz/wg/genderen.html

2. For example, a few of the contributions to the collection entitled *Women on the Internet* by Wendy Harcourt (1999).

3. I am using the concept of 'Other' in terms of various configurations of social class/caste, cultural and geographical location, race, sexuality, age and so on. It is to be noted that I do not consider any of these variables of 'Otherness' to be the only forms of Otherness, nor do I consider these variables to be autonomous or universal signifiers of Otherness.

4. Arif Dirlik (1998) and Erik Swyngedouw (1997) use the term 'glocal' to refer to the interdependence and hybridity of local and global.

5. If any reader wishes to dialogue with me, I am happy to engage with these discussions further on-line. My e-mail address is rad@cyberdiva.org

6. See Gajjala (1999) for an account/discussion of possible 'resistance' in the form of refusal and/or silence within a virtual community of South Asian women.

Bibliography

Alarcon, Norma (1990) 'The theoretical subjects of "This Bridge Called My Back" and Anglo-American feminism', in Gloria Anzaldua (ed.), *Making Waves, Making Soul: Haciendo Caras* (San Francisco: Aunt Lute Books), p. 361.

Agustin, Laura (1999) 'They speak, but who listens?', in Wendy Harcourt (ed.), *Women on the Internet: Creating New Cultures in Cyberspace* (London: Zed Press), pp. 149–55.

Benedikt, Michael (ed.) (1991) *Cyberspace: First Steps* (Cambridge, MA: MIT Press).

Butler, J. (1993) *Bodies that Matter: On the Discursive Limits of 'Sex'* (New York: Routledge).

Danet, B. (1998) 'Text as mask', in Steven Jones (ed.), *Cybersociety 2.0: Revisiting Computer-Mediated and Communication and Community* (Thousand Oaks, CA: Sage), pp. 129–58.

Dhaliwal, A. (1996) 'Can the subaltern vote? Radical democracy, discourses of representation and rights, and questions of race', in David Trend (ed.), *Radical Democracy* (New York: Routledge) pp. 42–61.

Dibbell, J. (1993) 'A rape in cyberspace', *Village Voice*, 21 December, pp. 36–42.

Dirlik, A. (1998) 'Globalism and the politics of place', *Development*, 41(2): 7–13.

Escobar, A. (1999) 'Gender, place and networks: apolitical ecology of cyberculture', in Wendy Harcourt (ed.), *Women on the Internet: Creating New Cultures in Cyberspace* (London: Zed Press), pp. 31–54.

Fanon, F. (1967) *Black Skin, White Masks*, trans. Charles Lam Markmann (New York: Grove Press).

Gajjala, R. (1999) 'Cyborg-diaspora: virtual imagined community', *Cybersociology: Magazine for Social-Scientific Researchers of Cyberspace*, 6 (August).

Gilbert, P. (1996) 'On space, sex and stalkers', in *Women and Performance: A Journal of Feminist Theory*, 1(17): 125–50.

Gilligan, C. (1977) 'Concepts of self and morality', *Harvard Educational Review*, 47(4): 481–517.

Gilligan, C. (1982) *In a Different Voice* (Cambridge, MA: Harvard University Press).

Gilligan, C. and Attanucci, Jane (1988) 'Two moral orientations', in Carol Gilligan, Janie Victoria Ward, Jill McLean Taylor (eds), *Mapping the Moral Domain* (Cambridge: Harvard University Press), pp. 73–86.

Grewal, Inderpal and Kaplan, Caren (1994) *Scattered Hegemonies: Postmodernity and Transnational Feminist Practices* (Minneapolis: University of Minnesota Press).

Hagel John, III, and Armstrong, Arthur (1997) *Net Gain: Expanding Markets through Virtual Communities* (Boston: Harvard Business School Press).

Haraway, Donna (1992) 'The promises of monsters: a regenerative politics for inappropriate/d others', in Lawrence Grossberg, Cary Nelson and Paula Treichler (eds), *Cultural Studies* (New York and London: Routledge), pp. 295–337.

Haraway, Donna (1994) 'Manifesto for cyborgs: science, technology, and socialist feminism in the 1980s', in Nancy Fraser (ed.), *Feminism/Postmodernism* (New York: Routledge), pp. 190–233.

Harcourt, W. (ed.) (1999) *Women on the Internet: Creating New Cultures in Cyberspace* (London: Zed Press).

Harding, S. (1998) *Is Science Multicultural? Postcolonialisms, Feminisms and Epistemologies* (Bloomington and Indianapolis: Indiana University Press).

Hayles, K. (1998) *How We Became Posthuman: Virtual Bodies in Cybernetics, Literature, and Informatics* (Chicago: University of Chicago Press).

Herring, S. (1996) 'Posting in a different voice: gender and ethics in CMC', in Charles Ess (ed.), *Philosophical Perspectives in Computer Mediated Communication* (New York: SUNY Press), pp. 115–45.

Holeton, R. (1998) *Composing Cyberspace: Identity, Community, and Knowledge in the Electronic Age* (Boston: McGraw-Hill).

Holmes, David (1997) *Virtual Politics: Identity and Community in Cyberspace* (Gold Coast Campus: Griffith University).

Lowe, L. (1996) *Immigrant Acts* (Durham and London: Duke University Press).

Markley, R. (1996) *Virtual Realities and Their Discontents* (Baltimore: Johns Hopkins University).

Mednick, Martha T. (1989) 'On the politics of psychological constructs: stop the bandwagon, I want to get off', *American Psychologist*, 44(8): 118–23.

Nakamura, L. (1995) 'Race in/for cyberspace: identity tourism and racial passing on the Internet', in *Works and Days 25/26*, 13(1/2): 181–94.

Pollitt, Katha (1992) 'Are women morally superior to men?', *The Nation*, 28 December, pp. 799–807.

Soja, Edward (1996) *Thirdspace: Journeys to Los Angeles and Other Real-and-Imagined Places* (Massachusetts: Blackwell).

Spender, D. (1995) *Nattering on the net: women, power and cyberspace* (North Melbourne, Australia: Spinifex).

Steiner, Linda (1989) 'Feminist theorizing and communication ethics', *Communication*, 12: 157–73.

Stone, Allucquerre R. (1992) 'Virtual systems', in J. Crary and S. Kwinter (eds), *Incorporations* (New York: Zone), pp. 608–25.

Swyngedouw, Eric (1997) 'Neither global nor local: "glocalization" and the politics of scale', in Kevin R. Cox (ed.), *Spaces of Globalization: Reasserting the Power of the Local* (New York: Guilford Press).

Tal, K. (1996) 'The unbearable whiteness of being: African American critical theory and cyberculture', *Wired*, October.

Turkle, S. (1995) *Life on the Screen: Identity in the Age of the Internet* (New York: Simon & Schuster).

Warnick, B. (1999) 'Masculinizing the feminine: inviting women on line 1997', *Critical Studies in Mass Communication*, 16(1): 1–19.

Youngs, Gillian (1999) 'Virtual voices: real lives', in Wendy Harcourt (ed.), *Women on the Internet: Creating New Cultures in Cyberspace* (London: Zed Press).

Part II

Smart Spaces

Strategies and tactics in new media technologies

8

Smart spaces @ The Final Frontier

ZOË SOFOULIS

It seems appropriate that a collection about new technological spaces would include a *Star Trek* chapter. Not only were Trekkies (*Star Trek* fans) early occupants of the new technological spaces of bulletin boards, discussion lists and the World Wide Web, but more generally the study of fictional popular cultural forms like the *Star Trek* television series and films is relevant for the appreciation of computer culture. This is because so much popular discourse around computers is rarely purely technical, and is frequently science fictional, constantly sliding between the capabilities of present-day machines and fantasies about what they will be like in the future. The *Star Trek* television world is arguably of particular interest because its audiences over the past thirty years include people who almost by definition have an active interest in stories that explore the implications of science and technology in human lives. *Star Trek* has undoubtedly been influential in shaping some of the high technologies we now live with – not because the series writers and designers were somehow prescient, but because they, on the one hand, have tapped into existing and projected future trends in technologies, and on the other, their creations have been taken as inspiration by the computer geeks and techno-nerds who ultimately design the real equipment. A cordless phone in my office looks very much like a *Star Trek* communicator; I use a laptop computer whose portability, smallness, shape and colour conform very closely to the computer consoles featured on *Star Trek* long before they were available in real life. However, my rationale for the investigations and interpretations made here will not rest on the proof of direct connections between *Star Trek* and technological design (which might be shown through a sociological study), but on a more simple and general claim that the world of *Star Trek* is not as futuristic as we might like to think, in so far as it presents, fantasizes, idealizes and helps create cultural formations and obsessions that are part of cultural reality in the late twentieth century.

This chapter looks at some of the implications of new forms of technological space by examining examples of what I shall call 'smart spaces' drawn mainly from the television series *Star Trek: The Next Generation*, which was produced in the late 1980s and early 1990s at Paramount Studios, Los Angeles. The technological spaces considered here are the Starship *Enterprise* as a whole, its command bridge, and the holodeck. These fictional smart spaces could be said to represent different models and uses of computers and computerized spaces:

- The ship as a whole suggests ubiquitous computing as a part of technological cocoons like shopping malls or 'smart houses'.
- The bridge is the site for playing out the top-down militaristic command-control model of computer power.
- The holodeck invokes the entertainment uses of computers for games and simulations.

Cultural fantasies and anxieties about these real-world spaces can be mapped in terms of the disasters that befall their fictional counterparts in various episodes of the series.

But before examining some examples from *Star Trek*, let us briefly survey a number of sources for ideas that contribute to the notion of smart space.

Smart spaces

A key source for the idea of smart space comes from science fiction itself, especially fantasies about computers which have been associated both with outer space and with the inner space of the mind, such as in the 1968 film *2001: A Space Odyssey*, which featured a demonic computer and images of space travel popularly linked to psychedelic, drug-enhanced journeys of consciousness (especially in the Star Gate sequence). *Star Trek* is a significant part of a broader cultural apparatus that glamorizes extraterrestrialism, manufacturing dreams of outer space that is full of worlds to explore and lifeforms to encounter, when in fact most of space is empty, dark, practically heatless, and unreachable by humans. Extraterrestrialism is a convenient fiction for capitalist enterprise, in that it can allay anxieties about the destruction of planet Earth with a vision of off-world abundance. Outer space has become a sacred space to technoculture, depicted as both origin and destiny of life – and of technology.

The association between extraterrestrialism and futuristic fantasies about computers is part of my cultural heritage as an Australian baby boomer. My first sight of computers and a demonstration of their powers came from television footage of the IBMs at NASA control centres during the space race in the 1960s. At that time many film and television audiences in the northern hemisphere had already seen fictional examples of powerful computers in outer space, such as HAL in *2001* and the ubiquitous voice-activated computer on board the original *Enterprise* of *Star Trek*, broadcast in the USA from September 1966 to March 1969. But in my southern homeland, these fictions arrived *after* the real thing, making it hard for me subsequently to tell the difference between science fiction and high-tech reality: the high-tech world is already a science fiction, a world remade into a futuristic and off-world projection of itself. This confusion was only exacerbated when NASA named one of its space shuttles *Enterprise*, after the *Star Trek* ships.

As the use of personal computers spread in the 1980s, covers for magazines like *Omni* and advertisements for computers and peripherals used images that associated outer space with computer space, human brain space and fertile womb space, each of these being frequently represented by a grid of thin, often blue, lines stretching across a dark space, and sometimes formed by a grid of city or suburban street lights, or shots of skyscrapers with regular square windows. This was the imagery William Gibson distilled into literary form in his descriptions of what has become known as 'cyberspace', and which at the time I called 'Jupiter Space' (Sofia, 1984, 1993, 1998). In the notion of cyber-space the emphasis is on the fusion of human consciousness with the field formed by the information matrix of the computer network. My term puts the emphasis more on the links between computers and outer space and comes from the scene in *2001* where the astronaut floats embryo-like in the womb-red interior of the ship's computer HAL and removes his logic circuits. A pre-recorded videotape announces that the ship is in 'Jupiter Space', alluding to the god Jupiter (the Greek Zeus), who gave birth to Athena from his brain, to the brain-womb of HAL in which the astronaut floats, and to the outer space surrounding the planet Jupiter where the astronaut later transforms into an Earth-sized foetus. This ancient metaphor of the pregnant masculine brain-womb – the masculine matrix – is a prototype for high-tech images of 'smart space': the human (especially male) brain or the computer's memory banks, and by extension other male-controlled spaces for invention (the laboratory, the studio, the workshop), and eventually the entire terrestrial and extraterrestrial universe, are mythologized as the container and producer of brain children in Jupiter Space imagery. This kind of smart space can be thought of as a technically rationalized yet fantasy-governed site of a fertility denied male bodies by nature (Sofia, 1993, 1999).

The brain-womb metaphor and the computer itself are, I would argue, extremely significant models of intelligence-based generativity in cyberculture, especially in the 1980s, but they are not the only kinds of smart spaces of interest here. From what other sources can we arrive at an idea of space that is intelligent, agentic, and productive? Certainly not from mainstream Western metaphysics, which aside from the brain-womb fantasy usually represents space as passive, dumb, empty and feminine (Irigaray, 1985; Grosz, 1995; Best, 1995; Sofia, 2000). Woman's body is seen as a mere vessel or space to be inhabited by a transcendent masculine ego; in narratives this body is not usually an actor but the plot space to be traversed and conquered by the (male) hero (de Lauretis, 1984: 139–43). Space does attract more interesting attention in a countervailing Western tradition of immanence, which has only this century gained more prominence through biological and mathematical studies and simulations of natural patterns and system dynamics (morphology and morphogenesis; theories of catastrophes, chaos and complexity), which seem to suggest that space has a certain structure. In my layperson's understanding of chaos theory, iterative equations involving irreal numbers (such as the square root of minus one) are used to generate mathematical simulations of aspects of the structure of real space. This structure – which includes fractional or partial dimensions and intensities such as strange attractors, chreods, or morphogenetic fields – gives space and spaces particular 'grains', both constraining and permitting flows of matter and the development of physical forms (Waddington, 1977; Lewin, 1993). These ideas imply that at a very real level, space exhibits pattern and agency, which can be considered forms of mind or intelligence (Bateson, 1972, 1979): forms emerge the way they do, not simply because some transcendent mind or set of codes commands them to, but out of real interactions between matter and space. Thus, while physics and mathematics explore many different kinds of sophisticated and counter-intuitive spaces, phenomenologically in the real world space is always in a sense still experienced as it was by the ancients as *res extensa*, embodied space-filling stuff, inextricable from the matter it not only contains but shapes.

The notion of space as immanently intelligent may be found in the work of Gregory Bateson and later biologists, theorists and philosophers interested in cybernetic and ecological approaches to the understanding of evolution and adaptation (e.g. Oyama, 1985). Bateson (1972) elaborated the idea that an entity (whether that be an organism, a schizophrenic person, a mind, or a nation) cannot be understood in isolation from its context (a habitat, a family, an environment, international relations). In evolutionary and ecological terms, the unit of survival is not the organism, the line or species, but 'the flexible organism-in-its-environment' (Bateson, 1972: 451). Moreover, Bateson contends that 'The mental world – the mind – the world of information processing – is not limited by the skin' (*ibid.*: 454): information, pattern and intelligence pass through a circuit that is not confined to the deliberations of the intending ego or *cogito*, but can be found in the changing patterns of mutual adaptation and co-adaptation undergone within and by the organism–environment ensemble. This idea questions the separability of human, site and intelligence, as illustrated in Bateson's example of a blind man using a cane:

> The stick is a pathway along which transforms of difference are being transmitted. The way to delineate the system is to draw the limiting line in such a way that you do not cut any of these pathways in ways which leave things inexplicable. If what you are trying to explain is a given piece of behaviour, such as the locomotion of the blind man, then ... you will need the street, the stick, the man, the street, the stick, and so on, round and round.
>
> (*ibid.*: 459)

Another angle on space as both constitutive and smart comes from Winnicottian psychoanalysis and the tradition of intersubjectivist psychoanalysis that has grown from it (for example, Stern, 1985). The infant's subjectivity itself is not ready-made, but emerges from the interpersonal field set up between it and its mother: 'two subjects who together create an intersubjectivity through which the infant is created as an individual subject' (Ogden, 1992: 619). Winnicott's statement 'There's no such thing as an infant' makes the point that the infant has no existence apart from the maternal environment which sustains it; without this it would die (Winnicott, 1960: 39 fn; Ogden, 1992: 620). The baby moves from its first nurturing interuterine space to the 'facilitating environment' provided by the mother, who also comes to serve as a container into which the infant projects feelings it cannot deal with by itself. The infant relies on the maternal caretaker to be sensitive to its needs, and to undertake various physical, emotional and intellectual labours to ensure that its world is ordered, regulated, comfortable and sustaining. Within the domain of what Winnicott (1971) called 'potential space', a space for imagination and experimentation, the infant plays with 'transitional objects' as negotiations between its inner fantasy world and the outer world of social and technical reality, exploring its emergent autonomy within a safe domain under the watchful eye, though not complete control, of the maternal caretaker. So it is not simply that we are 'shaped' by these early spatial contexts: we cannot even come into human being without them, without the presence of an ordered, sheltering and intersubjective space within which we can emerge and exist as regulated body and social person. Space continues to play a constitutive role in the formation, maintenance and reformation of adult subjectivity. As Foucault teaches us, the subject continues to be formed through the ordering of bodies, behaviours and interpersonal relations in certain kinds of spaces and intersubjective fields.

Actor Network Theory (or ANT, as it is known within social studies of science) is an approach to the study of the construction of scientific and technological objects which has some kinship with object-relations or intersubjectivist theory, as well as with Batesonian notions of mind embedded in a broader ecological circuit. It looks at the emergence of the artefact from within a network or assemblage of human and non-human agents that exchange properties. Like the Winnicottian transitional object, which straddles the border of inner and outer worlds, the technoscientific object is also a liminal entity, a 'material-semiotic object' or agent (Haraway, 1991: Part 3), which represents the contingent outcome of negotiations between its own material properties and capacities, and those claims and designs made on it by other actors in the network. As Haraway develops this idea, such objects map or embody 'universes of knowledge, practice and power' (Haraway, 1997: 11) and act as 'nodes' or 'stem cells' from which 'sticky threads lead to every nook and cranny of the world' (*ibid.*: 129). ANT examines how boundaries are drawn between humans and non-human or technological entities, and how agency and competence are delegated among them (Bijker and Law, 1992). Bruno Latour argues that 'anthropomorphism' is a two-way process: its etymology can 'mean either that which *has* human shape or that which *gives shape* to humans' (Latour, 1992: 235). Designers of technological artefacts define actors with specific tastes, competencies, prejudices, etc., and a design attempts to predetermine settings for the users of technology: 'Thus like a film script, technical objects define a framework of action together with the actors and the space in which they are supposed to act' (Akrich, 1992: 208). Although space is here acknowledged as a construction, the *mise en scène*, it is still something *in* which action takes place. But a central idea I want to pursue in the rest of this chapter is whether we can consider technologically shaped and technologically shaping space as an actor in its own right.

So now let us board the Starship *Enterprise* for a study tour of this science fictional smart space, informed by the above ideas, and aided along the way by philosopher of technology Don Ihde (1990), whose programme in the phenomenology of technics offers a useful framework for analysis of the relations between humans, technologies, and the worlds they share and co-create.

The ship

The great paradox about exploring 'The Final Frontier' is that amid the vastness of the universe, the space of most immediate concern is a much more bounded technology of containment: the voyagers are basically confined inside a sealed transport vehicle – 'Spam in a can', as one of the early US astronauts put it.

The Starship *Enterprise* is a giant technological container, a complex ensemble of various kinds of technologies (engines, weapons and shield systems, internal and external sensors and communications, life-support systems, replicators, etc.); it is internally differentiated into many other compartments (the bridge, engineering, sick bay, living quarters, the holodecks) and includes other transport technologies (shuttles, transporters, turbolifts). The ship is run along the military lines of Star Fleet and the behaviour on board is an idealization of elite military and professional communities, with highly competent crew members who require minimal supervision.

A Titanic catastrophe may result if this 'technological cocoon' (Ihde, 1990: 110) fails in its job of containment, and *Star Trek* narratives regularly express anxiety about disruptions to the boundaries between inside and outside. Characteristic disasters revolve around containment, such as loss of shields (force fields protecting the ship), hull breaches (always on decks away from the regular sets) and 'intruder alerts', while down in engineering the regular threat is a loss of the containment field for the matter/anti-matter reaction in the warp core (the ship's main engine); there are also disasters of supply, such as loss of power and the ship's enforced reliance on auxiliary sources, threatened or imminent failure of life-support systems, failure or malfunctioning of replicators; and related problems of mobility, when the ship is unable to move or move fast enough, through loss of functioning engines or controls, or occasionally because it is caught in some force field or tractor beam.

As a mobile life-supporting microworld, the ship is primarily in what Ihde (1990) would call background relations with its crew: it is a technology inhabited as a world, and is akin to real-world enclosing technospaces such as office blocks, airports, shopping malls,[1] 'smart' houses and apartment blocks. Like these technoworlds, which characteristically emit a background hum from appliances, utilities and automatic equipment, climate-control systems, power generators, etc., the *Enterprise* emits a background drone which is usually heard in corridors and is louder and more bassy down in engineering. This noise is overlain with a variety of higher-pitched electronic sounds emitted from various consoles, screens and monitors and on the bridge, in the sick bay, and parts of engineering. Just as the screens and monitors in the sick bay report on the 'life signs' emitted by organs of the ill or injured, the screens on the bridge and in engineering display the ship's multiple 'life signs' in glowing arrays of graphic and textual data. In these parts of the ship, hermeneutic technics are emphasized: the displays are texts to be interpreted and acted upon, in the faith that these reporting technologies are giving complete and accurate information.

The *Enterprise* is not only a background for the drama, but a key actor in it. Important to the television series are the ship's relations of what Ihde would call alterity with its crew and perhaps especially its captain, who is in a sense 'married' to it. In one kind of alterity relation, the human relates to the technology as though it were a person, a rival or a collaborator. Giving particular sharpness to the sense of the ship as a character and a 'smart space' is the way it is anthropomorphized through a talking computer which crew members can access from anywhere on board. Indeed it is difficult to distinguish the ship from its ubiquitous computer system, and we occasionally get computer point-of-view shots (e.g. in 'The Defector'). The ship is given a specifically feminine personification in the third season episode 'Booby Trap', where in order to help solve a problem, Geordi and the computer create a holodeck simulation of Leah Brahms, one of the ship's designers. Geordi falls in love with the simulation, but when they inevitably part, she assures him that 'I am with you every day, Geordi. Every time you're looking at this ship, you're looking at me. Every time you touch it, it's me.'

Another kind of alterity relation concerns itself with the technical details of the apparatus itself, something which a certain subclass of fans finds utterly absorbing, aided by detailed technical manuals for various versions of the *Enterprise*. Special features of the ship and its technical constraints are provided as incidental details, or figure in suspenseful moments in the narrative: Can Scotty (in the original series) repair the dilithium crystal chamber before it goes critical? Can Geordi maintain the warp core containment field? These episodes cumulatively depict the ship as an entity with its own unique properties and limits.

However, when the ship is not the subject of a love interest or a technical crisis, the role it plays is not a fully personable character, but more like the original 'smart space': good old Mum, that familiar, taken-for-granted space-provider and nurturer, the 'environment mother' whose eyes and ears seem to be everywhere, keeping tabs on the whereabouts and life signs of its crew. The mother ship is always available to answer questions and provide meals; it unobtrusively manages itself as well as sustaining the assorted lifeforms that inhabit it. The ship's computer is the repository of huge databanks about human and extraterrestrial life, the universe and practically everything. As Picard points out in the episode 'Emergence', those databanks are also the repository of various details about the crews' lives, serving as the ship's memory. In this sense, the large, knowing ship functions to the humans like the mother of infancy who is a container or repository of the feelings and experiences we project into her (Ogden, 1992). [2] We are regularly put in a position of possible identification with this databank mother through the opening device of a shot of the ship in space accompanied by a voiceover, usually the Captain's, making a log entry about the current situation, simultaneously addressing the computer and the television audience.

In sum, the starship as a whole can be thought of as an agentic and knowing container with various maternal qualities, especially life support, that is formed in an ensemble with a huge array of other technologies and systems. It also at times, as we shall see in a later example, reaches its technical limits and appears as a difficult, intractable and obstinate creature that can't be controlled or hurried: more like an infant than a mother. While the ship does exist in and as the background for crew activity, it is also frequently personified or rendered as an active agent in the drama; thus it could be considered in what Ihde would call a 'horizonal' instance of technological relations, in this case a hybrid of background and alterity: the ship is both a space or world and an actor in it.

The bridge

In analysing which aspects of *Star Trek* gave me fannish thrills, I discovered I felt a frisson of excitement whenever I heard those particular electronic chirrups and beeps, the background machinic rumbles and electronic hums, and other ambient noises signalling that most familiar technospace of the *Enterprise*: the bridge.[3] Although the entire ship is a smart space, the bridge of the *Enterprise* is a high-density node where all parts of this actor network come together, and where its various competencies and 'life signs' are displayed and co-ordinated.

In Ihde's terms, the main relations here are of hermeneutic technics: the walls of the bridge are studded with screens of constantly changing graphic displays and bleeping monitor lights – all so many texts to be interpreted. The faith here is that these reporting technologies are giving complete and accurate information. Our attention is regularly focused on one or the other of these displays, as someone (usually Geordi or Data) explains some technical issue and the ship computer responds to their voiced commands to retrieve information, to enhance, repeat, slow down, run a diagnostic, etc. (similar displays are found in engineering). For the most part, though, the technical features of the bridge remain in the background, along with a number of crew, whose backs are to the camera as they work at their consoles deciphering the data.

Centrally placed on the bridge is the captain's chair, from which the ship and its crew are commanded, and to which they feed data and reports. All it takes is Captain Picard's imperative 'Make it so!' and the command is turned into action. The Captain's marriage to the ship is quite a traditional one: she may be smart, but what he says goes.

Perhaps the most powerfully seductive fantasy *Star Trek* regularly affords its viewers (or at least this viewer) is of sharing the instant access to and mastery of space, technologies and people possessed by the occupant of that chair. This is the power of the C^3I: the bridge is a condensed expression of the military-industrial principles of command, control, communication, intelligence/information which are exerted over the crew, the ship and indeed the galaxy. The egoistic fantasy attached to this kind of smart space is of being at the convergence of all kinds of technological systems, taking in complete, relevant information about them and the situation as a whole, and moreover, being able to command these systems and keep everything under control. This is of course the military fantasy, whose connections with the command-control microworlds of computing have been ably examined by Paul North Edwards (1990, 1996). It is also the fantasy of ultimate access to information promised by the personal computer revolution. The other side of this fantasy is anxiety about not being in control, and not surprisingly the main disaster characteristic of the bridge is that control is lost – control may be re-routed to somewhere other than the bridge, command codes are overridden, or something or someone else takes control of the ship from within or without. Related or consequent disruptions include commands that don't work – the Captain says 'make it so' and nothing happens (as in 'Remember Me'), as well as communications failures and insufficient or false information.

The pleasures – and vulnerabilities – of the C^3I are of course no longer confined to the military, or a fictional future, but have already 'trickled down' into the technologies in the world of twentieth-century *Star Trek* viewers, such as in air, road, rail or naval traffic control rooms; or in security and monitoring stations in nuclear power plants, factories, offices or stores; as well as computer-accessed databases, networked communication and information systems, voice-activated interfaces, computer-aided design and graphics programs, elaborately simulated air, space and war games (as well as real wars programmed to resemble special effects shows). The power of the C^3I and the fantasy of instant access and control is also 'quoted' in such mundane technologies as the hand-held remote control by which viewers operate the TV and VCR while watching shows like *Star Trek* in their living rooms. Military technologies of simulations have become part of the world of entertainment, and indeed larger games halls (such as *Intencity* in Parramatta, visited as part of a cultural studies field trip with my students) boast of the military origins of their flight simulators, and of how military and commercial pilots like to come and play the elaborate simulations, which involve being taken through a military-style induction and briefing about the mission before suiting up and strapping into highly realistic airplane cockpits. Here, in *Star Trek* terms, the functions and logic of the bridge and the holodeck become hard to distinguish.

The holodeck

On the bridge, the entire ship's resources of power, material, people and information are available on command in a hierarchical chain of decision-making and action. But on the holodeck, the ship's resources, especially its psychological and cultural databanks, are frequently marshalled to serve the purposes of play and daydreaming. The holodeck is a suite of rooms whose interiors can be programmed to holographically display seemingly real and material spaces, landscapes, objects, and characters. These can be used for training and exercise purposes, for sheer escape, romantic trysts, erotic adventures (a speciality in those attached to the bar on *Deep Space Nine*), or for group games, costume dramas and cultural/religious rituals. In its resting state, the holodeck is simply a black-walled room lined by a grid (matrix) of yellow lines.

Like museums, shopping malls, and amusement or theme parks, as well as domestic technologies of broadcast and cable television, and now the World Wide Web, the holodeck embodies the fantasy of a space that contains other worlds — which was an early fantasy of Jaron Lanier, one of the mavens of virtual reality (Rheingold, 1992: Ch. 7). Its real-world referents include domestic spaces like the bedroom, living room or games room — sites of consumption of television and increasingly inhabited in young boys' leisure pursuits of video or computer games, and the above-mentioned flight simulators and other technological assemblages used for training and entertainment, providing ever more realistic and 'real-time' interactive simulations of characters, spaces, and props (including weapons). The computer power of the *Enterprise* allows a quantum leap from late twentieth-century two-dimensional representations of three-dimensional spaces (as in video and computer games) operated by joystick or data glove and relying on the imaginative inhabiting of the virtual space, to three-dimensional interactive simulations in which real bodies can wander around and interact with characters both virtual and real. Just like computer and video games, the holodeck characters and scenes can be set to various degrees of strength and difficulty, though normally safety protocols prevent any serious injury to the crew.

Stories set on the holodeck provide viewers with a break from the regular sets and costumes and are entertaining to fans in part because of their meta-televisuality. Just like television scenes, holodeck scenarios may be programmed, directed and modified to use different actors and spaces. Holodeck simulations where the regular crew put on special costumes to take part in a 'play within the play' do not so much reinforce the 'reality' of the crew in their normal roles as remind us that the crew members too are *already* actors within a TV costume drama set in the twenty-third century.

The meta-televisuality of the holodeck was brought out particularly acutely in an episode titled 'Worst Case Scenario' near the end of *Star Trek: Voyager*'s third season, where the crew get involved in playing, then rescripting, an unfinished holonovel of a mutiny on *Voyager* featuring all the regular crew, and secretly written by the security officer Tuvok as a training exercise. In support of the crew's involvement in this diversion Captain Janeway makes a speech about the importance of entertainment, culture and the arts, which resonates directly with the viewer's own experience of watching *Star Trek* as entertainment. Various versions of the mutiny scenario are played out, and characters comment and criticize the way their scripts have been written, much as real actors would do with actual *Star Trek* scripts. Then the scenario turns dangerous once Tuvok gets in to finish the story, because the Maquis saboteur Seska has completed the scenario in a way that puts the safety protocols off-line and threatens to kill Tuvok and Paris who is assisting him. 'Who says *deus ex machina* is outmoded?' Janeway remarks, as she frantically scrambles to rewrite Seska's narrative and script helpful events and tools into the story to save the two members of the crew.

In psychoanalytic terms, the holodeck corresponds to the inner world, the world of unconscious, dreaming and fantasy; and to potential space, where inner and outer worlds are negotiated. Both actual and imagined actors and events are translated into the realm of the virtual, and it is sometimes difficult to tell where your own brain ends and computer space begins; hard to know whether you are truly interacting with something outside yourself, or whether it is mostly in your imagination, just a one-sided techno-toss (Robins, 1996). These *Star Trek* microworlds of entertainment arouse similar cultural anxieties to those expressed in cyberfiction and set off by the obsessive practices of proverbial nerds, hackers, *otaku*, etc.: namely, the fear of the breakdown of boundaries between real and virtual. Will simulations prove too real? Failure of the safety protocols is one of the regular holodeck malfunctions. Will people become more isolated, and start neglecting their friends and jobs in favour of addictive devotion to playing in simulated microworlds where they are confident and in control (as does Barclay in 'Hollow Pursuits'; see also Turkle, 1996)? Computer sex may be better than the real thing and men regularly fall in love (or intrigue) with holodeck women. More worryingly, some threatening entity can emerge from the holodeck to become too real and competent, as in the episode 'Elementary, Dear Data', where a new artificial intelligence called Moriarty is created, who possesses dangerous powers to control the ship, and who is subsequently frozen into virtual storage.

Case study: 'Emergence'

A fascinating episode from *The Next Generation*'s seventh series entitled 'Emergence' is of interest for the way it explicitly mobilizes the ship as a smart as well as a fertile space. First the *Orient Express* appears in the middle of a holodeck program of Shakespeare's *The Tempest*, and the holodeck cannot be shut down. Geordi and Data find the ship is growing silicon-based nodes connecting sensors, warp engines, and other ship's systems. The ship has independently set itself on course for a star that emits a particular kind of energy particle. Meanwhile on the holodeck train are characters from a variety of programs in some quite bizarre and dreamlike scenes. A knight in armour is cutting a chain of paper dolls, some people are seated at a table making a jigsaw puzzle of an image that resembles the mysterious circuits. The train's engineer anxiously warns the crew that the other characters are trying to hijack the train, and is promptly shot dead by a gangster, who takes a brick the engineer was carrying. Later, at a stop called Keystone City, Deanna and Data watch the gangster place this brick into a gap in a wall of similar bricks. This is followed by the appearance in Cargo Bay 5 of a glowing three-dimensional crystalline version of the circuit, which appears to be emitting life signs. Evidently the ship's replicators combined with the transporters to help create the crystalline being.

Comparing the structures of the human cortex, his own artificial 'positronic' brain, and the pattern of nodes around the ship and centred on Holodeck 3, Data hypothesizes that the *Enterprise* is forming a neural net and becoming conscious of itself. He delivers a mini-lecture about emergence as a property of complex systems, and consciousness as an emergent phenomenon. The crew go on to compare the ship with a biological organism, which 'sees with its sensors, talks with communication systems', and, says Dr Crusher, 'in a sense it almost reproduces with its replicators'. The ship's emergent intelligence was 'like an infant, acting on impulse, trying to figure itself out as it goes', and the only experiences it could draw on were the holodeck programs and databanks. As ship's Counsellor Deanna Troi puts it, the holodeck was 'like an imagination'. The scenes of a puzzle being put together, a foundation being laid (keystone) and the chain of paper dolls were all images of something being constructed. The holodeck characters represented various systems: the engineer was the navigational system, a gunslinger the weapons system, the armoured knight the shields. The Captain proposes that this emergent intelligent entity deserves respect, and advises the crew to co-operate with the holodeck characters. The crew help provide a source of energy particles for the crystalline being to live on, and it floats off the cargo-bay floor in a show of light and transports itself into outer space. All traces of the emergent intelligence vanish from the ship and the holodeck scenario disappears.

   The unusual events in this story are interesting for what they reveal about the normal relationships and distinctions between the ship, the bridge, the holodeck, and the crew. The ship, as the crew here realize, is itself like a complex organism. However, normally its systems function in relative independence of each other, and are co-ordinated via the crew in a chain of command with Captain 'Make it so!' Picard at the peak. When the ship starts making its own connections, it gains increasing control and co-ordination over its own functions. Control of the ship passes from the bridge to the holodeck, where an alternative model of ship's governance is represented in the actor network of characters on the train. This is a more chaotic and 'bottom-up' model of agency, which is not embedded in a single unified self. Instead it is a heterogeneous aggregation of selves − human, non-human, real and virtual − with incomplete knowledges, competing claims, and different contributions to make towards a course of action that is not fully planned or understood in advance. Instead of a military logic of precise control, the ship deploys a metaphoric logic to formulate its intentions and conceive of action plans as it lurches awkwardly and step by step towards its fuzzy reproductive goals. In this way it probably behaves more like normal 'enterprises' do, with their various stakeholders not precisely in accord with each other, bungling their way through various contingencies, but managing to produce something anyway.

   Data questions the Captain about the risk he had taken in letting the *Enterprise* complete its generative task. This was a valid question, since at one point it was apparent that the ship was ready to compromise human life support in order to grow its crystal baby. If writers with more cyberpunk sensibilities, such as Pat Cadigan or William Gibson, had been given free rein with the script, the ship's intelligence, once formed, would likely have continued to exist, and Data's question could have been the occasion for a speech celebrating the post-human. Instead Picard replies:

> The intelligence that was formed on the *Enterprise* didn't just come out of the ship's systems, it came from us, from our mission records, our personal logs, holodeck programs − our fantasies. Now if our experiences with the *Enterprise* have been honourable, can't we trust that the sum of those experiences would be the same?

Is this speech yet another assertion of *Star Trek*'s humanistic philosophy: even the ship's unnatural extraterrestrial creation will carry the noble human spirit onwards into the stars? Maybe. A more interesting reading is that Picard is neither humanist nor post-humanist but Latourian (Latour, 1993, 1994): he appreciates that both humans and non-humans are *socio-technical* hybrids; there cannot be a 'post-human', because technologies cannot exist without societies or socialities (and vice versa). There are instead greater or lesser extended or complex networks of human and non-human actors who mutually shape – and we might say contain – each other. Along with the holodeck characters, the various ship's systems, the crew and their computer logs are actors enlisted into the network to create the new entity, which will inevitably be partly human.

At a more mythic/psychoanalytic level, we could interpret Picard's speech as a rationalization of the investment he might have in the new entity: a sense of proud and protective paternity for the offspring of the mother ship to whom he is (Oedipally?) wedded. Although the story entertains some quite recent theories about emergence and complexity, they are ultimately in the service of the standard science fiction fertility fantasy: a brain – or a smart technospace – produces an extraterrestrial baby – it is *2001* again. There are two emergences in 'Emergence': first, an imaginative intelligence is emergent from the ship's neural net and from the 'potential space' of the holodeck. Then this intelligence devotes all its resources to creating another entity, its brainchild, which takes off into outer space. As Data remarks, 'it appears that the purpose of the ship's emergent intelligence was to bring new life into being'. So often it is in science fiction culture that the highest resources of technology and intellect are devoted to developing new and unnatural ways of reproduction, especially through a combination of man, technologies, and 'facilitating environments' that don't involve women, except perhaps as invisible maintenance workers (e.g. Frankenstein and his 'workshop of filthy creation'; a bloke and his shed; a captain and his ship). Even though the ship, as I have suggested, functions generally as a maternal 'smart space' that looks after its crew, in this episode the ship plays an unusually active role in the drama, and its own fertile intelligence is represented as infantile and almost instinctual, while Picard and the crew become 'mothers' or 'midwives' of this infant's creation of its own offspring. A mother ship with a fully mature intellect would perhaps be too dangerous a challenge to Picard's command. More to the point, as respondents to spoken versions of this chapter have pointed out, *Star Trek* would in that event morph into *Blake's 7* or *Red Dwarf*, or even *The Hitchhiker's Guide to the Galaxy*: it would no longer be *Star Trek*.

This episode is in an Ihdean sense 'horizonal', in so far as the distinctions between the ship, the bridge, the holodeck, and the real and the virtual break down; information is communicated in ambiguous ways, control is uncertain, and the 'identity' of the ship is fragmented into a network of actors. The holodeck becomes the seat of consciousness for the ship itself and provides an alternative model of ship's governance to the normal hierarchical chain of command. I have suggested that Captain Picard tolerates these extremes of disruption to the ship's command because of his investment in the dream of the fertility of the high-tech matrix. However, one of the effects of this episode, and hopefully also of my own investigations of smart space, is to encourage us to rethink our understanding of technological spaces like the *Enterprise*: they may look like systems commanded from the top down, but they might also be working as a network or ensemble of actors, building goals, selves, and destinies from the bottom up in the messy contingencies – or what Pickering (1995) calls 'the mangle' – of productive practice. Moreover, as my general line of argument suggests, even when the ship's emergent wilful and self-centred intelligence disappears along with its progeny, and it reverts to playing its normal role of the background container-mum function, it is still very much a smart space, whose unheralded labours continue to sustain, provide, shelter and collaborate with the humans (and non-humans) inhabiting it.

Notes

1. On the mother ship/mother shop connection, see Sofia (1996).
2. Fans might appreciate another dimension of the ship's maternal character from knowing that the ship's voice in many of the original *Star Trek* episodes, and in *Star Trek: The Next Generation*, was played by Majel Barrett, who also occasionally appears as Lwaxana, the mother of ship's Counsellor Deanna Troi, and who by being in real life the wife (and now widow) of Gene Roddenberry, creator of the series, is in a certain sense the 'mother' of *Star Trek*.
3. As the editor, Sally Munt, pointed out in a comment on this manuscript, noise is a primary indicator of the mother's presence for the foetus, who cannot see its maternal container.

Filmography

2001: A Space Odyssey (1968). Directed by Stanley Kubrick, story by Stanley Kubrick and Arthur C. Clarke. Star Gate sequence by Douglas Trumbull.

'Booby Trap' (1989) *Star Trek: The Next Generation*, episode 154. Directed by Gabrielle Beaumont, story by Michael Wagner and Ron Roman, teleplay by Ron Roman, Michael Piller and Richard Davies. Los Angeles: Paramount Pictures.

'The Defector' (1990) *Star Trek: The Next Generation*, episode 158. Directed by Robert Scheerer, written by Ronald D. Moore. Los Angeles: Paramount Pictures.

'Elementary, Dear Data' (1988) *Star Trek: The Next Generation*, episode 129. Directed by Ron Bowman, written by Brian Alan Lane. Los Angeles: Paramount Pictures.

'Emergence' (1994) *Star Trek: The Next Generation*, episode 275. Directed by Cliff Bole, story by Brannon Braga, teleplay by Joe Menosky. Los Angeles: Paramount Pictures.

'Hollow Pursuits' (1990) *Star Trek: The Next Generation*, episode 169. Directed by Cliff Bole, written by Sally Caves. Los Angeles: Paramount Pictures.

'Remember Me' (1990) *Star Trek: The Next Generation*, episode 179. Directed by Cliff Bole, written by Lee Sheldon. Los Angeles: Paramount Pictures.

'Worst Case Scenario' (1997) *Star Trek: Voyager*, episode 66. Directed by Alex Singer, written by Kenneth Biller. Los Angeles: Paramount Pictures.

Bibliography

Akrich, Madeleine (1992) 'The de-scription of technical objects', in Wiebe E. Bijker and John Law (eds), *Shaping Technology/Building Society: Studies in Sociotechnical Change* (Cambridge, MA: MIT Press), pp. 204–24.

Bateson, Gregory (1972) *Steps to an Ecology of Mind* (New York: Ballantine/Random House).

Bateson, Gregory (1979) *Mind and Nature: A Necessary Unity* (New York: Dutton).

Best, Sue (1995) 'Sexualizing space', in Elizabeth Grosz and Elspeth Probyn (eds), *Sexy Bodies* (London and New York: Routledge), pp. 181–94.

Bijker, Wiebe E. and Law, John (eds) (1992) *Shaping Technology/Building Society: Studies in Sociotechnical Change* (Cambridge, MA: MIT Press).

de Lauretis, Teresa (1984) *Alice Doesn't: Feminism, Semiotics, Cinema* (Bloomington: Indiana University Press).

Edwards, Paul North (1990) 'The army and the microworld: computers and the politics of gender identity', *Signs*, 16(1): 102–27.

Edwards, Paul North (1996) *The Closed World: Computers and the Politics of Discourse in Cold War America* (Cambridge, MA: MIT Press).

Grosz, Elizabeth (1995) *Space, Time and Perversion: Essays on the Politics of Bodies* (St Leonard's, NSW: Allen and Unwin/Routledge).

Haraway, Donna (1991) *Simians, Cyborgs, and Women: The Reinvention of Nature* (New York: Routledge).

Haraway, Donna (1997) *Modest_Witness@Second_Millennium. FemaleMan©_Meets _OncoMouse™* (New York: Routledge).

Ihde, Don (1990) *Technology and the Lifeworld* (Bloomington: Indiana University Press).

Irigaray, Luce (1985) *Speculum of the Other Woman*, trans. G. C. Gill (Ithaca, NY: Cornell University Press).

Latour, Bruno (1992) 'Where are the missing masses? The sociology of a few mundane artifacts', in Wiebe E. Bijker and John Law (eds), *Shaping Technology/Building Society: Studies in Sociotechnical Change* (Cambridge, MA: MIT Press), pp. 225–64.

Latour, Bruno (1993) *We Have Never Been Modern*, trans. Catherine Porter (Cambridge, MA: Harvard University Press).

Latour, Bruno (1994) 'Pragmatogonies', *American Behavioural Scientist*, 37(6) (May): 791–808.

Lewin, Roger (1993) *Complexity: Life on the Edge of Chaos* (London: Phoenix Press).

Nemecek, Larry (1992) *The Star Trek: The Next Generation Companion* (New York: Pocket Books/Simon & Schuster).

Ogden, Thomas H. (1992) 'The dialectically constituted/decentred subject of psychoanalysis. II. The contributions of Klein and Winnicott', *IJP*, 73: 613–26.

Oyama, Susan (1995) *The Ontogeny of Information* (Cambridge: Cambridge University Press).

Pickering, Andrew (1995) *The Mangle of Practice: Time, Agency, Science* (Chicago: University of Chicago Press).

Rheingold, Howard (1992) *Virtual Reality* (London: Mandarin).

Robins, Kevin (1996) 'Cyberspace and the world we live in', in Mike Featherstone and Roger Burrows (eds), *Cyberspace, Cyberbodies, Cyberpunk: Cultures of Technological Embodiment* (London: Sage), pp. 135–55.

Sofia, Zoë (1984) 'Exterminating fetuses: abortion, disarmament, and the sexo-semiotics of extraterrestrialism', *Diacritics*, 14(2) (Summer): 47–59.

Sofia, Zoë (1993) *Whose Second Self? Gender and (Ir)Rationality in Computer Culture* (Geelong: Deakin University Press).

Sofia, Zoë (1996) 'Spacing out in the mother shop', in Stephanie Holt and Maryanne Lynch (eds), *Motherlode* (Melbourne: Sybylla Press).

Sofia, Zoë (1998) 'The mythic machine: gendered irrationalities and computer culture', in Hank Bromley and Michael W. Apple (eds), *Education/Technology/Power: Educational Computing as a Social Practice* (Albany, NY: SUNY Press), pp. 29–51.

Sofia, Zoë (1999) 'Virtual corporeality: a feminist view', in Jenny Wolmark (ed.), *Cybersexualities* (Edinburgh: Edinburgh University Press), pp. 55–68.

Sofia, Zoë (2000) 'Container technologies', *Hypatia*, 15(2): 181–201.

Stern, Daniel (1985) *The Interpersonal World of the Infant: A View from Psychoanalysis and Developmental Psychology* (New York: Basic Books).

Turkle, Sherry (1996) *Life on Screen: Identity in the Age of the Internet* (London: Weidenfeld & Nicolson).

Waddington, C. H. (1977) *Tools for Thought* (St Albans: Paladin).

Winnicott, D. W. (1960) 'The theory of the parent–infant relationship', in Winnicott (1965), *The Maturational Processes and the Facilitating Environment* (New York: International University Press), pp. 179–92.

Winnicott, D. W. (1971) *Playing and Reality* (London: Routledge).

9

Virtually out there

Strategies, tactics and affective spaces in on-line fandom

MATTHEW HILLS

This chapter is concerned with how fan activities have been reconstructed by new media technologies, taking the Internet newsgroup as its focus. I will argue that Internet newsgroups — which offer constant and near-immediate access to virtual fan communities — constitute a novel 'affective space' for fans. I will further argue that the work of Michel de Certeau (1988) on 'strategies' and 'tactics', work which has been centrally important within theories of media fandom, cannot be readily applied to the affective space of on-line fandom (Jenkins, 1992; Mikulak, 1998). I will therefore outline how the affective space of the fan newsgroup supports and sustains a *community of imagination*[1] which is distinct from Benedict Anderson's (1991) concept of the seemingly affectless 'imagined community'. Anderson's work deals with the phenomenon of nationalism, considering how 'the nation' has been constructed as a community despite the fact that its inhabitants will never meet more than a minuscule fraction of their 'fellows'. I will argue that work on nationalism has been unhelpfully and inaccurately applied to on-line communities. To illustrate this, I will refer to postings to the US-oriented newsgroup alt.tv.X-Files.[2]

What is meant by the 'affective space' of the newsgroup? By referring to affect I am drawing on a body of work which has theorized how popular culture matters to people, especially fans of certain texts or icons (Grossberg, 1992a, 1992b). Affect is a way of referring to emotion, although as Grossberg points out, affect is distinct from libidinal attachments or desire. Armon-Jones (1991) also comes to the same conclusions as Grossberg, noting that affect is not always linked to an object, but can act as a mood or a disposition which colours one's perceptions. As Grossberg puts it: 'Libidinal affect ... is always focused on an object (whether real or imaginary), while nonlibidinal affect (affect for short) is dispersed into the entire context of daily life' (Grossberg, 1992a: 81).

What is important about affect is that it draws attention to a dimension of fandom which cannot be reduced to models of psychoanalytic desire. This affective dimension nevertheless indicates an 'attachment' on the part of the fan. Fan affect is both mapped onto a set of texts, and continues to act as a disposition rather than a 'desire' (see Grossberg, 1992b: 56–7 on 'mattering maps'). Fans care intensely about their objects of fandom, and it is this that distinguishes the fan newsgroup's 'community of imagination' from Anderson's seemingly affectless 'imagined community'. Focusing on affect rather than theories of pleasure allows us to consider the specific emotional colourations and relationships of fandom, without placing these fan–text and fan–fan affective relationships within a transhistorical psychoanalytic narrative.

The importance of the newsgroup as a virtual fan community is that it allows continual access to fandom's affective realm: a 'space' in which what matters to the fan can be taken for granted as being of shared significance. Newsgroups are unlike fan conventions, which are restricted to specific times and places, and which therefore function as ritually bounded spaces separated off from fans' everyday lives. The fan convention, involving embodied face-to-face fan contact and an increased intensity of fan sentiment, might be described using Durkheim's account of religious ritual:

> If collective life ... rises to a certain intensity, that is so because it brings about a state of effervescence that alters the conditions of psychic activity. The ... passions [become] more intense, the sensations more powerful ... In short, upon the real world where profane life is lived, [the participant] superimposes another that, in a sense, exists only in his thought, but one to which he ascribes a higher kind of dignity than he ascribes to the real world of profane life.
>
> (Durkheim, 1995: 386)

By sustaining a form of 'collective effervescence' the ritual of such fan gatherings allows the fan's values and affective experiences to be reaffirmed. This recharging and reinforcing of fan sentiments also sustains a separation of 'fan' identity from non-fan identity (Jenkins, 1992). The newsgroup, I would suggest, performs a similar function for fans – affirming their 'mattering maps' and passions – but it does so on demand, and hence without the ritualistic boundaries of the face-to-face convention.

Fans can often access newsgroups at work, and can post or lurk as and when the impulse takes them. Displaying one's fan identity to like-minded individuals therefore provides an ongoing possibility for sociality rather than operating as a ritually bounded experience. Newsgroups erode the sacred/profane separation which underpins fan cultural identity by allowing fan expression and fan identity to leak out into, and potentially permeate, the fan's everyday life. Like the anthropologically coded spaces referred to by Lefebvre, newsgroups are marked by affect; they are signposts to fannish ways of feeling: 'Space thus acquires symbolic value. Symbols, on this view, always imply an emotional investment, an affective charge ... which is so to speak deposited at a particular place and thereafter "represented" for the benefit of everyone else' (Lefebvre, 1991: 141). Being marked by affect, fan newsgroups display forms of social hierarchy which do not directly correspond to forms of cultural or economic capital. Instead, it is typically *proximity* to the object of fandom which secures status for posters and regulars (MacDonald, 1998). If, as Brooker notes, 'fandom is built around love', then the question I want to explore here is how this 'love' is channelled, reinforced and reconstituted by the availability of ongoing fan speculation and interpretation when 'the textual archives of ... *The X-Files* are augmented almost every week with a new and instantly canonical episode' which can be explored and negotiated by on-line fans (Brooker, 1999: 52; Clerc, 1996).

Spatial practices have been central to theories of fandom, not least through applications of the work of Michel de Certeau such as Henry Jenkins' *Textual Poachers* (1992). De Certeau distinguishes between 'strategies' and 'tactics' as follows: 'strategies are able to produce, tabulate and impose ... spaces ... whereas tactics can only use, manipulate, and divert these spaces' (de Certeau, 1988: 30). Strategies represent, as de Certeau indicates, a '*triumph of place over time*' (*ibid.*: 36, original italics). This strategic control is also described as 'a mastery of places through sight' (*ibid.*). Strategies are powerful precisely because they are able to define and oversee autonomous spaces which can be reproduced and sustained over time. Tactics, by contrast, have no autonomous or 'proper' spaces of their own. The tactic is defined according to its ability to 'make use of the cracks that particular conjunctions open in the surveillance of the proprietary powers. It poaches in them' (*ibid.*: 37). Tactics are the art of the weak, the art of those who 'make do' by using the materials of popular culture.

Jenkins has examined fan practices as instances of tactical poaching, and Mikulak has extended this thesis to the uses which on-line fans have made of Warner Brothers' animated characters (Jenkins, 1992; Mikulak, 1998). However, whereas fanzines can be physically restricted to small networks of fan producer-consumers, on-line fan spaces are potentially accessible to far greater numbers of fans. Fan newsgroups, in particular, are readily accessible, and unlike listservers require neither subscription nor 'insider' knowledge in order to locate them (MacDonald, 1998). As an affective space in which fan sentiment can be shared, mirrored and reaffirmed, the fan newsgroup counters de Certeau's argument that consumers have no place of their own, and no space in which to respond to the texts of popular culture: 'the steadily increasing expansion of these systems [television, urban development, commerce] no longer leaves "consumers" any *place* in which they can indicate what they *make* or *do* with the products of these systems' (de Certeau, 1988: xii). Newsgroups, and the wider proliferation of on-line fan sites, reconfigure textual 'poaching' as an activity which possesses a space of its own, a space which is neither consistently nor rigorously subjected to the intellectual property rights of copyright owners. As such, the surveillance of proprietary power is curtailed. Whereas de Certeau writes vaguely of 'particular conjunctions' which can temporarily crack open the panoptic surveillance of the powerful, the newsgroup represents not merely a 'conjunction' but part of a novel techno-sociality which has unfolded a range of persistent rather than fleeting possibilities. This, then, deconstructs the opposition of 'fixed' space versus 'slices' of time which de Certeau presupposes. These possibilities reveal that de Certeau's splitting of space and time cannot be sustained in the face of electronically enabled affective spaces, since the proper space of the 'powerful' depends on the production of material spaces. The newsgroup, however, spatializes affect and produces space metaphorically, morally and emotionally rather than materially. Space is no longer simply physical; *contra* de Certeau's objectivist account it is no longer the fortress of a controlling and all-seeing 'strategy'. Instead it is reconfigured as predominantly affective. Affective space is not merely about where fans are; it is also about how fans feel about their objects of attachment. All of which obliges us to rethink what we mean by 'community' when we consider the term 'virtual community'.

On-line spaces and sentiments: from 'imagined community' to community of imagination

Recent discussions of virtual community have attempted to counter the socially transformative claims which have been made on behalf of computer-mediated communication, as well as more extreme claims that cyberspace can do away with the geographical differences which currently determine subjectivity and self-identity (Rheingold, 1994; Mitchell, 1995). Cultural critics have stressed the need to relate developments in cyberspace back to 'embodied' politics and fantasies (Robins, 1997: 195). The typical structure of newsgroups — formed purely on the basis of common interest or elective affinity — has also led to criticism on the basis of their narrow focus:

'A community is more than a bunch of people distributed in all 24 time zones, sitting in their dens and pounding away on keyboards about the latest news in alt.music.indigogirls. That's not a community; it's a fan club. Newsgroups, mailing lists, chat rooms – call them what you will – the Internet's virtual communities are not communities in almost any sense of the word. A community is people who have greater things in common than a fascination with a narrowly defined topic.'

(Snyder, quoted in Mitra, 1997: 56)

'Virtual community' has been addressed as a metaphor to be applied with caution, and as a postmodern simulation of solidarity which is in fact fundamentally asocial (McLaughlin *et al.*, 1995: 102; Robins, 1995: 150). It has also been considered as a deconstructive turn which reveals the 'virtuality' at the heart of any 'real' community and as a form of intimate communication, the quality of which is constantly threatened by newsgroup or listserver population growth (Poster, 1995: 90; Watson, 1997: 108–10). Some theorists have celebrated 'virtual community' as a space of actual dialogue as opposed to the editorially restricted dialogues of magazine and newspaper letters pages (MacKinnon, 1995: 117). Its fiercest critics, meanwhile, have described the notion of on-line community as a spurious falsehood (Lockard, 1997: 225).

Even within pro- and anti- positions on 'virtual community', though, one organizing concept remains common, and that is the significance of the imagination within the cultural processes under examination. Benedict Anderson's famous formulation, that of the 'imagined community', has been central to much of the literature in this field. Anderson's work has been more or less simplistically transferred to cyberspace, with theorists emphasizing that since virtual communities are disembodied and lack face-to-face contact, then they must be closer to processes of imagination than more physically or geographically grounded 'communities'. More nuanced and subtle work has focused on developing Anderson's observation that we cannot simply separate communities into categories, thereby concluding that some are 'real' and some are supposedly 'false'. Instead, Anderson suggests, communities need to be approached not as real or imagined, but in terms of how they are imagined. Some communities may imagine themselves through geographical similarities, others through religious observances, and others again through common interests. No type of imagined community is any less real than the alternatives (compare Smith, cited in Rheingold, 1994: 64, with Anderson, 1991: 6). Examining alt.folklore.urban and its practice of trolling,[3] Michele Tepper concludes that

we can distinguish the AFU community as one that imagines itself as predicated on the production and transmission of information ... Trolling takes this mastery [over information] to a meta-level, demonstrating one's ability to play with information, to feel so confident of one's

mastery of a body of information and of the intellectual skills necessary
for managing it that one can pretend not to have mastery while still
managing to signal that one's show of ignorance is a joke ...

(Tepper, 1997: 47–8)

Following this lead, we might consider the 'style' in which the community
of alt.tv.X-Files imagines itself.[4] For Anderson, the 'imagined community' is based on a simultaneous movement through clock/calendrical time of a
body of people (typically the nation) who consume information simultaneously, and imagine their compatriots involved in a similar undertaking.
Anderson makes the point that nevertheless

an idea of *simultaneity* is wholly alien to our own [consciousness] ...
What has come to take the place of the medieval conception of
simultaneity-along-time is, to borrow ... from Benjamin, an idea of
'homogeneous, empty time', in which simultaneity is ... transverse, cross-
time, marked not by prefiguring and fulfillment, but by temporal
coincidence, and measured by clock and calendar.

(Anderson, 1991: 24)

The kind of imagining characteristic of the nation is therefore one of pseudo-
simultaneity, the assumption being that thousands of anonymous, unseen and
unknown individuals are watching the same television programme at the
same time. Simultaneity is merely nominal within Anderson's schema.
Alt.tv.X-Files undoubtedly continues superficially to represent a form
of empty clocked and calendrical time (postings have a date line which
records not only the day and month, but also the time of posting in hours,
minutes and seconds GMT). The asynchronous posting of threads clustered
around issues and information derived either from the originating text or
from secondary texts such as magazines like *TV Guide* may also be taken to
indicate the 'temporal coincidence' of patterns of media consumption. And
yet, what is clearly altered by alt.tv.X-Files is the place of imagination
within this process: given that one can read the interpretations of a number
of regular posters, the space for imaginative projection of 'community' is
supplanted. Lurkers and posters to alt.tv.X-Files need no longer
imagine their fellows viewing the same material; the availability of the fan
audience displaces this imagined space with the density of its own meta-text
of speculative commentary which circulates around *The X-Files'* own ongoing
narrative.

Although a sense of 'homogeneous, empty time' lingers, this emptiness is
disavowed by the heterogeneous 'filling in' of the newsgroup's postings, in

which the diegesis of the originating text is supplemented, extended and reworked through fan criticism, commentary and, where necessary, the reconstruction of continuity lapses (Zizek, 1997: 155). Anderson refers to the reading of daily newspapers as a 'mass ceremony', asking 'what more vivid figure for the secular, historically clocked, imagined community can be envisioned?' (Anderson, 1991: 35). His example does not readily fit the *niche ceremony* enacted on alt.tv.X-Files, a ceremony in which pure coincidence is overwritten both by interaction between fans on the basis of their common media consumption, and through the overarching metanarrative of fan-text attachment which converts 'empty, homogeneous' time into an experiential time of expectation, delay, anticipation and frustration. This is not to argue that community ceases altogether to be imagined according to the principles outlined by Anderson, given that the entire audience for *The X-Files* cannot be encountered or become self-present on-line. Furthermore, alt.tv.X-Files continues to define itself relationally against specific interest groups such as OBSSE (The Order of Blessed Saint Scully the Enigmatic):

> drscully ... wrote:
> the website is OK but having it plastered all over the newsgroups ... is a bit much. This stuff even shows up on aol. If I wanted to read the OBBSE stuff I'd subscribe for the newsletter or go to the page. But I'm not in OBBSE or whatever and I am still subjected to its ramblings ...
> (atx, 18 May 1997)

Fans posting to atx also seek to define themselves against other fan groups and their implied or assumed activities:

> come on kids ... it's a great show ... don't stoop to trekkie levels.
> 'Ooooo I think that Picard is sexier then Spock' ... Just discuss the show and stuff you would like to see happen. I love the show and I hate to see crap like 'Ooooo ... John Cusack would be a great replacement' ... I feel better that I have vented. And yes I hate Star Trek.
> (Captain Angst, atx, 15 May 1997)

Alt.tv.X-Files imagines itself as predicated on the intensive reproduction of *The X-Files* transmission schedule which, in turn, allows for the production of extra-textual information and self-reflexively 'paranoid' speculations. Yet this is not merely a 'style' of imagining which rests comfortably within a repertoire of different styles; it is actually a style which differs from the parameters established by Anderson in two crucial respects:

time is no longer purely 'homogeneous and empty' in spite of appearances to
the contrary, and the role of the imagination is neither as clearly definable nor
locatable as it is in Anderson's work.

Rather than addressing `alt.tv.X-Files` as an imagined community, then,
I believe that it may be more adequately considered as a 'community of
imagination'. This is a community which, rather than merely imagining itself as
co-existent in clocked time, constitutes itself precisely through a common
affective engagement, and thereby through a common respect for a popular
cultural representational space, for as Winnicott has observed: 'We can share a
respect for illusory experience, and if we wish we may collect together on the
basis of the similarity of our illusory experiences. This is a natural root of
grouping among human beings' (Winnicott, 1974: 3). Winnicott's work is
useful here, because he has a distinctive notion of imaginative space. Rather
than 'the imagination' being merely subjective and akin to daydreaming or any
other such fantasizing which might be contrasted to 'objective' reality,
Winnicott does not view imaginative activity as somehow secondary or
unreal. For Winnicott, imaginative activity lies at the root of cultural
experience; indeed he describes imagination as occupying a distinctive 'third
area' between subjectivity and objectivity. It is this imaginative third area or
space which provides the location for cultural activity[5] (Winnicott, 1974: 121).

`Alt.tv.X-Files` offers one instance in which similar imaginative
experiences form the basis of group identity. This common respect for
imaginative material determines the particular narratives which remain
constitutive of the group: narratives of anticipation and speculation, narratives
of information, dissemination and status, narratives of detection, and narratives
of conspiracy. The 'community of imagination' is less interested in imagining
itself as a community *per se*, than in constantly confronting and refining the
relationships between individual fans and the text as object of fandom. That is
to say, the imagined relationship between fan and text will tend to take
precedence over relationships between fans.

The coincidence which defines the 'community of imagination' occurs on a
different level to that which defines the imagined community. Rather than a
coincidence in the temporality of information and consumption (the 'mass
ceremony'), the defining coincidence here is affective. Unlike imagined
communities, which can function in a mechanical and taken-for-granted
fashion, being re-secured for as long as their routines and repetitions ground
their narratives of commonality, the community of imagination constantly
threatens to fragment. Routine and repetition do not afford the same
protective weight, exactly because this is a community based on the
assumption that its respondents can experience a common affective tie and
not merely a common, immediately visible instance of media consumption.

Such a development moves beyond the routinized visibility attested to by Anderson: 'the newspaper reader, observing exact replicas of his own paper being consumed by his subway, barbershop or residential neighbours, is continually reassured that the imagined world is visibly rooted in everyday life' (Anderson, 1991: 35–6).

What if one does seek the fan community as 'visibly rooted in everyday life'? Merely observing a fellow reader does not suffice as evidence of a common affective tie. How can we ascertain that a meaningfully shared affective experience has occurred? What underpins alt.tv.X-Files and its proliferation of postings and 'communications' is the possibility that the 'community of imagination' may only ever consist of people attempting to speak their affects and passions, their mimetic 'identifications', across and between one another without any significant form of contact.

The community of imagination therefore acts as a specific defence against the possible 'otherness' or even 'alien-ness' of the inexplicable intensity and emotionality of fandom (Harrington and Bielby, 1995). Reassuringly, by going on-line this intense but somehow almost inarticulate fan experience can be endlessly replicated, and the affect involved can be displaced through a circuit of mimesis, such that the self rebounds against its own unspeakable identifications:

> This first emotional tie to another, which is also the unrepresentable event of my 'own' birth, can never be remembered, never be recalled to memory. This is also why it can never be 'dissolved', as Freud would have it. But (and this is what happens all the time, if it happens) it can be repeated – for example, in hypnotic trance, or in the oblivion of the transference.
>
> (Borch-Jacobsen, 1993: 61)

Borch-Jacobsen's instances of mimetic 'suggestibility' repeat the moment at which the ego constituted its very self out of an affective opening to the 'suggestion' of another. Posting and lurking on alt.tv.X-Files may not obviously resemble either hypnosis or the psychoanalytic transference, but posters and lurkers may nonetheless participate in processes of identification, mimesis and affect which outrun the subject's capacity for satisfactory self-articulation, self-explanation and self-justification. The fan-text affective attachment tends, therefore, to be presented via self-reflexive and humorous analogies:

> OK … it's early Friday morning and I am slightly inebriated. My hands are shaking, my heart is pounding. I have what many would call a

sickness. I am insanely obsessed. I hope to NEVER be cured. Here among the similarly afflicted I am comfortable with my illness. I can step forward and proudly say 'My name is Piper and I am a philoholic'. Please let my addiction forever flourish, and please oh please oh please let Sunday come as fast as lightning. OK what are the other 11 steps?

(Piper Maru, atx, 16 May 1997)

`Alt.tv.X-Files` needs to be addressed not as a point of theoretical explication, but as a social and historical context which allows for a specific form of mediated fan-text relationship. Where the fan impersonator transforms an affective relationship through a form of 'writing on the body', and where attending fan conventions converts affect into a form of 'pilgrimage' narrative, the `alt.tv.X-Files` newsgroupers pursue a further form of specific affective processing via the newsgroup (Hills, 1999). The originating text and its affective impact upon the fan are legitimated in this instance through the ever-present affirmation of the affective relationship itself:

BBSs [Bulletin Board Services] ... *create a space where only the fan identity is relevant; fans' mattering maps converge* in a space that both celebrates and validates their knowledge. This is enormously gratifying for fans who would not otherwise have access to a large, articulate, readily available, and informed community of like-minded viewers.

(Harrington and Bielby, 1995: 167–8, my emphasis)

Although Harrington and Bielby sometimes approach a fan-based 'uses and gratifications' perspective – separating different forms of fan expression according to how they meet the perceived needs of differing fan groups, and suggesting on the basis of questionnaire data that BBSs replace 'traditional fan activities' for those who habitually use them, rather than redefining what it means to be a 'fan' – their detailed perception of cyberspace and its difference remains useful, since they do emphasize the centrality of affect and emotion within the construction of fan identities. However, despite ultimately concluding that the 'experience and emotion of a viewer's subjective engagement with the narrative is the business of collective sharing at the sites through which fans communicate' (Harrington and Bielby, 1995: 186), Harrington and Bielby focus on the circulation of information and the attribution of status in their examination of BBS users. Affect is not sufficiently theorized in this movement. Clearly it makes good sense to analyse fan postings in terms of the hierarchies of knowledge and information which they represent and enact, and Henry Jenkins' work is the clearest example of this approach. However, Jenkins' informational bias replicates an emphasis on the rational and cognitive processes of fan 'mastery' (Jenkins, 1995). To perceive information technology primarily as a technology of information flow is to neglect the affective dimensions and intensifications which can accompany this process. Alt.tv.X-Files does not only celebrate and validate the fan's knowledge, it also mirrors the fan's attachment back to him/herself, revalidating this affective experience:

> You watch the *X-Files* with other people? Am I the only one who refuses to let people be with me when the *X-Files* is on? What do you do if they talk while it's on? Don't you have like a special place where you sit? Special *X-Files* watching clothing that you wear?
>
> (camgib, atx, 18 May 1997)

I have argued that it is vital to consider fandom through the lens of affect, and that on-line fandom's novelty lies in its constant availability as a source of reinforcement and legitimation of fan affect. Functioning as a community of imagination rather than as an imagined community, I have suggested that the fan newsgroup poses a challenge to the narrative of de Certeau's work on strategies and tactics, arising from his separation of 'proper' space and the space-less consumer-as-poacher. As an affective space in which caring for, and about, the object of fandom constitutes the most significant communal claim, the fan newsgroup resembles an ongoing and never-ending fan convention (Porter, 1999). It is thus a 'space' in which common sentiment can migrate from a fixed or ritualistic point, moving out into the fan's practice of everyday life via the newsgroup's constant availability.

And yet the newsgroup's availability cannot be simply celebrated as a utopian achievement of fan identity. Its affective space remains tied to a commodity-text, and atx therefore remains bound to the schedules and *The X-Files'* US transmission dates and times. While creating difficulties for the spatial emphasis of de Certeau's work, atx also intensifies links between the temporalities and rhythms of fandom and 'the framework of prescribed ... temporal modes of schedules' (de Certeau, 1988: 34). The sharing of affective fan experience is always to hand, always virtually out there, but this has positive and negative implications for de Certeau's work. Atx *both* provides an affective space which contests producers' 'proper' space, *and* simultaneously occupies the rhythms of the commodity-text ever more extensively: 'stressing the "situatedness" of those using the internet, the "places" in virtual reality ... are no longer just "out there". They become articulated with reality' (Slevin, 2000: 72).

Notes

1. Throughout this chapter I have deliberately chosen to refer to a 'community of imagination' rather than a 'community of *the* imagination'. The syntax of the latter implies that imagination can be thought of as a definite article, and can therefore be located as an objective or subjective state. However, the implication of the phrase 'community of imagination' is two-fold; first, that imagination is conceptualized as an *affective process* which underpins the formation and fragility of any such community, and second, that this process is conceptualized as belonging distinctively *between* 'objective' and 'subjective' spaces (Winnicott 1974).

2. Abbreviated on some occasions to 'atx', a term used by newsgroup members. The fact that this newsgroup is US-oriented (with postings referring to episodes transmitted in the USA) indicates that on-line communities are not inevitably cut adrift from off-line geographies and spaces.

3. 'Trolling' is the practice of posting deliberately and comically incorrect information, then waiting to see how many irate posters or 'newbies' (new users) will create and sustain a thread based around the correction of this original posting. All these posters are then 'trollees'; people who fail to realize that by offering a correction – and thereby supposedly demonstrating their superiority to the first poster – they are actually being hoodwinked, and are therefore victims of the troll's informational practical joke.

4. Alt.tv.X-Files also supports a culture in which 'trolling' is considered a valid way of demonstrating informational expertise while incriminating 'newbies'. One newsgroup regular discussed a repeated episode as if it continued on from a season finale, while another reviewed an invented 'new' episode.

5. This should not be taken to imply that all cultural activities are similarly powerful affective spaces. One of the difficulties with Winnicott's model is that it appears to view affect as being evenly dispersed across cultural activities. I am arguing here that any such notion of a 'level playing field' of cultural activities is mistaken, and that affective spaces are precisely those areas (emotional rather than strictly geographical, but not entirely separable from geographical space) where fans' affect is the most significant marker of community.

Bibliography

Anderson, B. (1991) *Imagined Communities: Reflections on the Origin and Spread of Nationalism* (London: Verso).

Armon-Jones, C. (1991) *Varieties of Affect* (Toronto: University of Toronto Press).

Borch-Jacobsen, M. (1993) *The Emotional Tie: Psychoanalysis, Mimesis and Affect* (Stanford, CA: Stanford University Press).

Brooker, W. (1999) 'Internet fandom and the continuing narratives of *Star Wars, Blade Runner* and *Alien*', in A. Kuhn (ed.), *Alien Zone II: The Spaces of Science Fiction Cinema* (London: Verso), pp. 50–72.

Clerc, S. (1996) 'DDEB, GATB, MPPB, and Ratboy: *The X-Files'* media fandom, on-line and off', in D. Lavery, A. Hague and M. Cartwright (eds), *Deny All Knowledge: Reading the* X-Files (London: Faber & Faber), pp. 36–51.

de Certeau, M. (1988) *The Practice of Everyday Life* (London: University of California Press).

Durkheim, E. (1995) *The Elementary Forms of Religious Life,* trans. and intro. K. E. Fields (New York: The Free Press).

Grossberg, L. (1992a) *We gotta get out of this place* (London: Routledge).

Grossberg, L. (1992b) 'Is there a fan in the house?: the affective sensibility of fandom' in L. A. Lewis (ed.), *The Adoring Audience* (London: Routledge), pp. 50–65.

Harrington, C. L. and Bielby, D. (1995) *Soap Fans: Pursuing Pleasure and Making Meaning in Everyday Life* (Philadelphia: Temple University Press).

Hills, M. (1999) 'Dialectic of value: the sociology and psychoanalysis of cult media', unpublished PhD dissertation, University of Sussex.

Jenkins, H. (1992) *Textual Poachers: Television Fans and Participatory Cultures* (London: Routledge).

Jenkins, H. (1995) ' "Do you enjoy making the rest of us feel stupid?": alt.tv. twinpeaks, the trickster author and viewer mastery', in D. Lavery (ed.), *Full of Secrets: Critical Approaches to* Twin Peaks (Detroit: Wayne State University Press), pp. 51–69.

Lefebvre, H. (1991) *The Production of Space* (Oxford: Blackwell).

Lockard, J. (1997) 'Progressive politics, electronic individualism and the myth of virtual community', in D. Porter (ed.), *Internet Culture* (London: Routledge), pp. 219–31.

MacDonald, A. (1998) 'Uncertain utopia: science fiction media fandom and computer mediated communication', in C. Harris and A. Alexander (eds), *Theorizing Fandom: Fans, Subculture and Identity* (New Jersey: Hampton Press), pp. 131–52.

MacKinnon, R. C. (1995) 'Searching for the leviathan in Usenet', in S. G. Jones (ed.), *Cybersociety: Computer-Mediated Communication and Community* (London: Sage), pp. 112–37.

McLaughlin, M. L., Osborne, K. K., Smith, C. B. (1995) 'Standards of conduct on Usenet', in S. G. Jones (ed.), *Cybersociety: Computer-Mediated Communication and Community* (London: Sage), pp. 90–111.

Mikulak, B. (1998) 'Fans versus Time-Warner: who owns Looney Tunes?', in K. S. Sandler (ed.), *Reading the Rabbit: Explorations in Warner Bros. Animation* (New Brunswick, NJ, and London: Rutgers University Press), pp. 193–208.

Mitchell, W. J. (1995) *City of Bits: Space, Place, and the Infobahn* (Cambridge, MA: MIT Press).

Mitra, A. (1997) 'Virtual commonality: looking for India on the Internet', in S. G. Jones (ed.), *Virtual Culture: Identity and Communication in Cybersociety* (London: Sage), pp. 55–79.

Porter, Jennifer (1999) 'To boldly go: *Star Trek* convention attendance as pilgrimage', in J. E. Porter and D. L. McLaren (eds), Star Trek *and Sacred Ground: Explorations of* Star Trek, *Religion and American Culture* (Albany: State University of New York Press), pp. 245–70.

Poster, M. (1995) 'Postmodern virtualities', in M. Featherstone and R. Burrows (eds), *Cyberspace, Cyberbodies, Cyberpunk: Cultures of Technological Embodiment* (London: Sage), pp. 79–95.

Rheingold, H. (1994) *The Virtual Community: Finding Connection in a Computerized World* (London: Secker and Warburg).

Robins, K. (1995) 'Cyberspace and the world we live in', in M. Featherstone and R. Burrows (eds), *Cyberspace, Cyberbodies, Cyberpunk: Cultures of Technological Embodiment* (London: Sage), pp. 135–55.

Robins, K. (1997) 'The new communications geography and the politics of optimism', *Soundings*, 5 (Spring): 191–202.

Slevin, J. (2000) *The Internet and Society* (Cambridge: Polity Press).

Tepper, M. (1997) 'Usenet communities and the cultural politics of information', in D. Porter (ed.), *Internet Culture* (London: Routledge), pp. 39–54.

Watson, N. (1997) 'Why we argue about virtual community: a case study of the phish.net fan community', in S. G. Jones (ed.), *Virtual Culture: Identity and Communication in Cybersociety* (London: Sage), pp. 102–32.

Winnicott, D. W. (1974) *Playing and Reality* (London: Penguin).

Zizek, S. (1997) *The Plague of Fantasies* (London: Verso).

10

Fresh Kill

Information technologies as sites of resistance

AYLISH WOOD

Fresh Kill (1994, Shu Lea Cheang; USA) is a distinctive video-feature. It is visually striking, with a strong use of deep tones of red, green and blue. Its range of references is broad – from melodrama to minimalism and cybertech to Borges; from formalistic shots to commercial break-ins. The editing crosscuts between an array of different narrative events creating a complex and occasionally disorienting progression.[1] It is passionate, humorous and, at times, cold. As the director, Shu Lea Cheang, describes it:

> There was a certain political agenda we wanted to deal with, in terms of media and environmental racism. That environmental racism was manifested in the transport of industrial toxic waste to Third World countries. Right from the beginning, we made a parallel between the waste and the dumping of garbage TV programs into Third World countries. Basically, once that was constructed, it seemed like we kept on making parallels. You have First World/Third World, then you have New York/Staten Island, and even within New York City you have 'Tent City' (a makeshift community of homeless people) as a kind of garbage dump. We set up a bunch of characters with the intention of trying to reverse stereotypes. Right from the beginning we wanted to have this Asian hacker, who was also this really quiet sushi chef, a lesbian couple ... There were all these pre-set characters we wanted to put into the landscape (ellipsis in original).[2]

My interest in *Fresh Kill* arises from the ways in which the narrative elements discussed in the above quotation – pollution, waste and dumping, the control of media technologies, and the characters – are arranged in relation to one another. In an analysis located in contemporary spatial theories and postmodern theories of narrative, I will argue that *Fresh Kill* is organized around a series of distinct spatial groupings, with connections established through a variety of media technologies used by the various characters within the text. The terms 'spatial' and 'space' will be used here in two ways. First, in the sense of how the social spaces of the film are depicted and how these operate within the narrative movements of the text. Second, the spatial is used to show how physically disconnected spaces are brought into connection with each other through the mediation of media technologies. In *Fresh Kill* the making and unmaking of these connections involves a series of political strategies in relation to pollution; it is the means by which the opposing groups come into conflict with one another, and resist the operations of one another.

'The way you deal with cinematic space seems much less about the use of space as a fixed territorial reference than a fluid way of exploring it'[3]

Throughout the 1990s 'space' became a key term in a variety of critical discourses, including postmodernism, cultural geography, and architecture. This chapter is concerned with the definition of space used to refer to cultural/ social spaces in which, as Edward Soja puts it, 'social relations are simultaneously and conflictually space-forming and space contingent' (Soja, 1989: 126). To put it another way, a space that is both rendered by and that activates the social relations occurring in a given space. This space is a politicized one in the sense that the social relations constitute, and are constituted by, the dynamic operations of race, class, sexuality, and gender.[4] As Doreen Massey has argued:

> It [the spatial] is a way of thinking in terms of the ever-shifting geometry of social/power relations, and it forces into view the real multiplicities of space-time ... The spatial is both open to, and a necessary element in, politics in the broadest sense of the word.
>
> (Massey, 1994: 4)

While much of the work in these fields has referred to spaces that are inhabited on a day-to-day basis by animals, plants and a whole variety of fabrications, mobile and immobile, this chapter is concerned with the textual spaces of *Fresh Kill*. This textual spatiality can be thought through in (at least) two distinct ways. First, the ways in which a distinct location within the narrative is constructed by a visualization of the space as 'space-forming and space contingent'. Second, how the text is organized into a narrative space that is not fixed to a resolution, but one that is more fluid, contingent on the connections made across different elements of the story.

'What's a computer hack like you doing in a fish joint?' (Miguel)

Taking first the visualization of space, while *Fresh Kill* revolves around an apparently distinct set of groups, shown in distinct locations, there are points of overlap that enable an analysis of the 'global' spatial relations of the text. One of these occurs almost at the beginning of the video-feature and introduces several of the central characters. The sequence focuses on the Naga Saki sushi bar, the space of which is defined by different but intersecting sets of social relations. For the owner and staff this is a workplace, primarily an economic relation. But this economic relation does not fully define the characters – the chef, Jiannbin Liu, is also a computer hacker, and the waiters, Claire and Miguel, are also a musician and a writer respectively. For the patrons of the café, the location is an extension of work, a place to celebrate by eating the concept fish dishes; the speciality dish is the lips of the Yamakazoo, an expensive fish with succulent lips that is given the alternative name of 'sucking fish'. In a long tracking sequence these different uses of the café become clear. As the camera moves from the workers preparing and serving food into the body of the café, it discloses the multi-ethnic groups of smartly dressed people talking about work (the music industry, the art scene, and the stockmarket), doing work or just talking. Through the use of a single uncut shot the café emerges as a multi-functional space.

This single shot suggests a relatively discrete location, an effect that is repeated in the *mise-en-scène*. The depths of the café space are dark, while the work and eating spaces are given an immediacy through the use of strong colours and lighting. Shelves of back-lit, deep-blue bottles mark the food preparation area; Claire, who is serving food, wears a red costume; and bold orange fishes hang above her, just around head height. Inside each tabletop is a source of illumination that throws light onto the faces of the figures sitting above it. Such a technique combines to focus attention on the activities within the space, obscuring not only the margins but also the outside. Definitions of space, however, are concerned with what is absent as much as with what is present in a given space, as Doreen Massey argues:

> But the particular mix of social relations which are thus part of what defines the uniqueness of any place is by no means all included within that place itself. Importantly, it includes relations which stretch beyond –

the global as part of what constitutes the local, the outside as part of the inside. Such a view of place challenges any possibility of claims to internal histories or to timeless identities.

(Massey, 1994: 5)

Massey here is pointing to the often-invisible contingencies that define spaces, those relations that have an effect upon a space but are not visible within it. In the sequence discussed above, even as it tends to focus on the activities inside Naga Saki there are cuts to the outside, gesturing to the influencing relations invisible within the café space itself. The outside scene depicted is that of the fish market, where the owner buys the increasingly hard-to-find sucking fish that her regulars are willing to pay 'top dollars' for. The contingencies of the café space are indicated in economic terms of supply and demand; in the need for a wealthy clientele and a source for the exotic fish.

'230 cans, 200 missing cats. What does it prove?' (Mimi)

In addition to theories of the formulation of socio-political space, my analysis draws on ideas about narrative space. In terms of the history of filmmaking, especially Hollywood film, narrative space is periodized into distinct eras – primitive, classical and post-classical narrative space (Bordwell *et al.*, 1985). In the classical text a narrative typically takes place in a specific unified time and space. Conventionally, the space of the narrative is a coherent and continuous one, excepting those sequences that deliberately break with this to depict a psychotic/nightmare/drugged experience. The space seen within the frame makes sense within the generic demands of the story-world, and functions as part of the progress of the narrative, cueing the spectator to particular events, things or characters. This classical organization of time and space is understood to limit the spectator's point of view, to keep it in line with the major narrative enigma, the solving of a murder, the finding of the lost item and so forth.

So-called non-classical narrative may, though not necessarily, break with this convention through an expansion of the perceived space. By different means – variations include shifts in focus, reframing camera movements, references to or visualizations of the frame itself – the act of framing by the technology of the camera, film or video, and the consequent control of the visual field, is drawn attention to. Through the act of drawing attention to the processes of enframing, the perceived space is expanded into what is excluded by the frame as well as what is included within it. This expansion may loosen the connection between the space of the narrative and the linearity of the narrative. While this is never an absolute separation, it nonetheless provides alternative movements within the narrative, enabling connections between elements which have only oblique relationships with the direction of progress towards the end of the text, which may or may not entail a resolution (Gibson, 1996). Such a re-conceptualization of narrative space avoids the hierarchical positioning of characters and events imposed by viewing them only in relation to the resolution.

This is especially useful when analysing a text such as *Fresh Kill*, which has an ensemble cast and series of events that bear only a tentative connection to the resolution. In *Fresh Kill*, however, it is not simply the framing of scenes around a particular image that draws attention to the action of enframing, to the potential closing off of a location or the limitation of the visual and/or imaginative spaces of the viewer. Instead, it is in the presentation of the different spaces as separate but connectable that the spatial constructions of the narrative are revealed. The social spaces of *Fresh Kill* are initially dislocated – they include the Naga Saki, Los Gatos (a village on the Pacific Coast), Jiannbin's home, Claire, Shareen and Honey's home. Each of these spaces is distinct, but they also intersect with each other enabling an expanded narrative space. For instance, Claire (who waits table at the Naga Saki), Shareen and Honey (Claire's daughter) form a family unit. This family is described in terms of the lesbian relationship between Claire and Shareen, the domestic relationship between Claire, Shareen and Honey, as well as the location of where they live, and what they do for work and play. It is also described through a series of extensions beyond that discrete location to Mimi (Claire's mother) and Clayton (Shareen's father). These extensions enable another story about extended family relations. Also, Claire, Shareen and Honey's space is expanded through the video-feature's theme of pollution. Honey is contaminated by the gifts of Yamakazoo from Jiannbin, who works with Claire as the chef at Naga Saki. As this acts to solidify the theme of pollution, it also expands the potential narrative spaces with which the viewer imaginatively interacts. In an equivalent way to the contemporary theorization of cultural and social space, the narrative space becomes multiple and less fixed.

**'Now ... what about this fishy incident in the town of Los Gatos ...
Zap ... I wonder about the sushi apparition in the legendary
Naga Saki in New York City' (Miguel)**

These words spoken by Miguel, a friend of Jiannbin, draw attention to the trail of pollution that runs through *Fresh Kill*, a trail that is also the focus of this analysis. As a central theme of *Fresh Kill*, pollution features in different ways within the video – the trash barge taking New York City's waste ('17 tonnes a day') to the Staten Island landfill site, the eponymous Fresh Kill; a barge of toxic chemical waste seeking a docking site in Africa; disintegrating H-bombs in the ocean; the illegal dumping of radioactive waste in the Pacific fishing waters off the US coast. Less toxically, Shareen's work is based around clearance and the redistribution of people's excess furniture and televisions. Pollution, as well as being an event within *Fresh Kill*, creates a linking device between the different groups of the film – Claire, Shareen, Honey; Jiannbin and Miguel; Mimi; the African Unity Network; GX; Stuart Sterling. As I have already suggested, each of these groups occupies a distinct narrative location, and in some cases a separate physical space. As the activities of these groups come together, a space of action is created within the narrative. However, this space is not one constituted by the practices of people within a particular location; rather, its existence is constituted and mediated by moments of connectivity across the locations through technologies such as the Internet, radio, and television.

These moments of connectivity can be likened to the assemblages of Deleuze and Guattari (Deleuze and Guattari, 1987; Deleuze, 1990). For them, assemblages are the processes by which various configurations of linked components function in an intersection with each other, a process that can be both productive and disruptive. Any such process involves a territorialization; this is a double movement where something accumulates meanings (re-territorialization), but does so co-extensively with a de-territorialization where the same thing is disinvested of meanings. The organization of a territory is characterized by such a double movement. An example in *Fresh Kill* is the green economy; this can be conceived of as a territory, a specific thing defined by the production and sale of goods in accordance with green politics. Within the video-feature one of the characters, Stuart Sterling, opens a 'green product' shop. Since he is clearly represented in *Fresh Kill* as an exploitative stockmarket trader, Sterling's appropriation of the green economy causes it to lose some of its associations with non-exploitative practices, and in the same gesture accumulate associations with profit-making. An assemblage is an extension of this process, and can be thought of as constituted by an intensification of these processes around a particular site through a multiplicity of intersections of such territorializations.

In *Fresh Kill* one such complex assemblage operates around the marketplace. Although never visible within the text, the marketplace is primarily constituted through representative figures from two distinct groupings. Roger Bailey, the director of the transnational company GX, represents the first grouping. GX is depicted within *Fresh Kill* through a series of montage sequences that indicate the extent of its influence. The company is shown to be involved with nuclear power production, media news production, telecommunications, pet food and breakfast cereals. These montages of GX are not simply present to provide narrative details for the external spectators of the video-feature *Fresh Kill*, they also appear to the internal audience as a series of advertisements, usually seen framed within one of the many television sets that feature within the video. In each montage sequence, an image of modern technologies is followed by Roger Bailey holding the Earth cupped in his hands to the mantra of 'we care'. Each of these sections is preceded by a word pairing: ENERGY = POWER; POWER = SECURITY; SECURITY = CONTROL; CONTROL = FREEDOM; FREEDOM = INTEREST; INTEREST = PROGRESS; PROGRESS = GREED; GREED = GREEN. These advertisements are examples of media technologies being mobilized to mediate GX's message to the public within the story-world of *Fresh Kill*. The economic effectiveness of this media campaign can be gauged through a second group of characters associated with Stuart Sterling, an aptly named stock trader first encountered in the Naga Saki. As dealers and traders on the stockmarket who talk about nothing but share prices, they act as indices for the success of GX. The intersections of these two groups provide one of the dimensions of the space in question in this discussion: if GX is successful in its marketing operations then Sterling will tell his friends to buy their shares. Taken together, the GX/Sterling interconnection displays the profit-making orientation of the marketplace.

A further dimension of the marketplace assemblage is suggested through the news reports that form a part of the video-feature's narrative. Initially, the connections between the newscast events and the marketplace are not particularly apparent; however, it becomes evident that the media technologies are another site at which the different dimensions of the text come into contact with one another. Towards the beginning of the video, the mainstream newscasting corporation ACC (American Communications Corporation) reports pollution events from around the globe. These include a rotting H-bomb off the coast of Japan, serious pollution of fishing waters off the coast of California, and a barge of toxic waste seeking a port off the coast of Africa. The interweaving of these newscasts into the story-world of *Fresh Kill* implicitly attaches the different acts of pollution to one another, and also forms connections between global pollution and the more local pollution on Staten Island. Each circumstance of pollution is initially isolated, but when mobilized by different characters and connected by the media technologies, a larger political space is created.

These kinds of connections and mobilizations, and their disclosure of complex relationships between social practices and technoscience, have been explored through science-technology studies.[5] While the majority of the theoretical work has concentrated on practices, it is not inappropriate to extend the model into the critical analysis of representations of technoscience. In science-technology studies, Actor Network Theory (ANT) has emerged as a significant means of engagement with the complex relationships between social practices and science and technology. Through ANT, science and technology is conceived of in terms of complex sets of processes and practices that intersect with each other in the production of knowledge or things. The forms of technologies and knowledge are contingent on a diverse set of decisions that encompass the 'how and why' behind the objects that are constructed.[6] In addition to thinking through the events leading to a product, ANT enables an analysis of technologies whereby they are not simply determined by their apparent functionality, but also according to a complex interrelationship between location *and* functionality. This moves away from a linear perspective in which functionality is the sole determinant of social uses, towards a framework in which the technological and the social space in which it is located both undergo some degree of compromise. Such a framework overlaps with the critique of linearity in both theories of space and postmodern theories of narrative. In contemporary spatial theory, there is no simple relation between space and the social — the spatial evolves through a negotiation between the two. Likewise, the processes of fictional narratives are not simply tied to the linear development of the plot; they emerge through an expansion into dimensions that have a more oblique relationship with linearity.

Within *Fresh Kill* the complex connections and mobilizations that establish relationships between social practices and technoscience evolve around media technologies. Returning to the case of ACC, when the newscasting corporation first appears in *Fresh Kill* it presents a series of stories exploring the problem of pollution. Once ACC is acquired by GX, an event that alters the territorialization of ACC, there ensues a new alignment across the spatial organization of groups and technologies. ACC's broadcasts are, through their association with GX, reoriented towards the power field of the economic interests of GX. The conflict of interests between 'independent' newscasting and the controlling company is made explicit through the character Peter Finn. Finn, an award-winning journalist, chases up the story of sea pollution off the coast of California, but he dies in a helicopter crash. Finn's motivation for his news chase is ambiguous: the narrative implies it is the desire for another award. Speaking on an audio link-up he says, referring to the spill in Los Gatos, 'It's too big to kill Jack ... two minutes ... another Emmy ... fuck GX.' Whatever the case, Finn's desire in this instance can be interpreted as overlapping with those of the anti-pollution groups, forming an unintentional coalition of interests.[7]

A further counterpoint to the mainstream newscasting corporation is public access television. Mimi Mayakovsky, Claire's mother, runs the programme

Yours Truly Mimi, which solicits calls from the public, providing yet another site of technological interaction. At the outset of the video-feature the concerns about pollution expressed in Mimi's programme are local ones relating to the Staten Island landfill site. Throughout the text's duration, they expand to include the question of Los Gatos (the village affected by offshore pollution), once that source of contamination begins to impinge on the lives of the people in Manhattan and Staten Island through the poisoned fish. The contingency of this dimension of space is made clear when Mimi's programme is taken off air. Again, the controlling power of GX is exerted in an attempt to orient public opinion towards their perspective, a reaction against the activist groups that question their authority.

The media technologies in *Fresh Kill* are, then, put into motion by each of the dimensions of the virtual nexus that assemble in the interplay of resistances. By resistances here, I do not simply mean the more conventionally understood opposition between a dominant and subversive position; rather, resistance is used to mean the countering movements made by either the domineering or the subservient. These movements are a part of the spatial organization of relationships between social practices and technoscience. Such a model has the benefit of perceiving social/spatial relations as never simply progressive or repressive, but as an interplay or negotiation between the two. From this perspective resistance does not simply mean a radical form of action against a dominating force (whether that be economic, military, textual, cultural, or political); rather, resistance is an opposition, something which can be radical, but can equally be reactionary. This definition implies an ongoingness in which movements of resistance are unstable and dynamic, and in process through a particular assemblage. From such a perspective, the media technologies are not simply allied to either an oppressive dimension or one that seeks to resist such oppression; they can be mobilized by *all* groups. To a certain extent, these media technologies function in a similar way to a cyborg. They can be understood as mediating the relationships between individuals/groups, in the sense that they do not simply operate as a vehicle with which to deliver a message, but become a constituent feature of how that message is conceived and delivered. This notion of cyborg is drawing on Donna Haraway's highly influential essay 'A manifesto for cyborgs'. In this Haraway states:

> Cyborg imagery ... means refusing an anti-science metaphysics, a demonology of technology, and so means embracing the skilful task of reconstructing the boundaries of daily life, in partial connection with others, in communication with all our parts. It is not just that science and technology are possible means of great human satisfaction, as well as a matrix of complex dominations. Cyborg imagery can suggest a way out

of the maze of dualisms in which we have explained our bodies and our tools to ourselves.

(Haraway, 1991: 181)

This reading of *Fresh Kill*, through its attempts to articulate the multi-dimensional relationship between humans and technologies, moves beyond a simple set of dualisms. In doing so, it touches on an aspect of Haraway's cyborg which is sometimes overlooked in the theoretical gestures towards the cyborg as site of political renewal (though not by Haraway herself). That is, the cyborg is open to appropriation by anyone who has the means (financial, technological or imaginative), whatever their alignment with radical or conservative positions. Like the technologies of *Fresh Kill*, the cyborg has the potential to be constructive, instructive and/or destructive.

'Are the radiant fish an omen of the Second Coming?' (Miguel)

As I have indicated, pollution is a linking device in *Fresh Kill* that brings together the narrative spaces of different groups via the mediation of media technologies. A further series of connections is created through the subplot of chemical dumping, one that poisons the sea water off Los Gatos. This causes both the death of fish and the evacuation of the village community whose fragile economy is dependent on fishing. A connection is made between this event and the contamination of Sea Wonder pet food. Sea Wonder, along with ACC, has been bought out by GX, establishing an association between GX and the dumping of waste. This connection is strengthened by the information that Jiannbin hacks from GX's system; information that reveals GX's prior knowledge of the contamination of the sea water. The tainted pet food, however, is not the only site through which the contamination of the sea impinges on the citizens in *Fresh Kill*. The prestige fish, the Yamakazoo, is also a source of contamination visualized through a strange green glow that emanates from it – '*verde*, the colour of death'.[8] Initially seen only briefly on the fish themselves, the Day-Glo hue illuminates the faces of the people who eat the fish – in particular, Stuart Sterling and Honey Mayakovsky. This green glow, a manifestation of the contamination of the prestige fish, also serves to link this fish with the more mundane piscine cat food fodder, a visual reminder of the extent to which contamination can spread, as cats begin to glow green across the city.

Once the strange green glow is noted within the community, the different dimensions discussed above come together to form a central component of the narrative. When the green cats go missing, presumably abducted by GX in an attempt to hide the evidence, a media campaign ensues. ACC tells stories about the evacuation of Los Gatos; Mimi's public access show, which has already been campaigning about the landfill site, begins a campaign about the green cats and their sudden disappearance. GX also makes use of television to attempt a damage-limitation strategy. Television is utilized here to create a virtual space of negotiation around the effects of pollution. The effectiveness of the media campaign is rendered through scenes in which tins of Sea Wonder are removed from supermarket shelves, and the discussions of money loss on the stockmarket due to the consequent fall in share prices.

'Freaky, are you there?' (e-mail message)

The Internet also features as a technology in *Fresh Kill*, though it is less prevalent than television. Jiannbin Lui possesses a computer system that gives him access to the Internet. A hacker, his skills are displayed when he breaks into an on-line shopping site. These skills are later deployed when Jiannbin hacks into GX's system and steals information from their 'Central Data' store. In addition to the interaction between Jiannbin and GX over the Internet, a global connection is created through the deployment of this technology in the form of messages from the African Unity Network (AUN). The AUN creates another dimension in the space around pollution as it sends activist messages around the global communication networks concerning the dumping of waste in Africa by Western countries. Not only does the AUN make use of the Internet but it also deploys satellite technology when it breaks into the transmission of newscasts from ACC.

The technologies of telecommunications and the Internet can be understood as giving substance to an assemblage, through which the expansionist designs of transglobal corporations such as GX can be intersected by oppositional group(s). In themselves, these groups cannot be said to cause the space of negotiation; however, with the additional components of technology, a 'cyborg' space is created as the humans and technologies operate together.[9] Technology is not simply a medium by which a message is delivered; it makes possible the negotiation.

'Why are we still dumping?' (Stuart Sterling)

The territories occupied by the spatial organizations of the anti-pollution groups/GX/communication technologies cannot be contained within a discrete space. This can be understood through reading both Massey, and Deleuze and Guattari. For Massey, space is contingent, defined by things which are both present and absent; 'it includes relations which stretch beyond' the local towards the global (Massey, 1994: 5). This space is always unstable, the presences and absences shifting, creating new spatializations. In Deleuze and Guattari, territories, or territorializations, are conceived of in a similar way:

> A territory borrows from all the milieus; it bites into them, seizes them bodily (although it remains vulnerable to intrusions). It is built from aspects or portions of milieus. It itself has an exterior milieu, an interior milieu, an intermediary milieu, and an annexed milieu. It has the interior zone of a residence or shelter, the exterior zone of its domain, more or less retractable limits or membranes, intermediary or even neutralized zones, and energy reserves or annexes.
>
> (Deleuze and Guattari, 1987: 314)

In *Fresh Kill* the space of negotiation is a shifting one, the processes of territorialization give an account of what is included/excluded in the space, which is at the same time also a moving on. GX may be damaged by the anti-pollution grouping, who by implication are therefore triumphant, and indeed there is a celebration as the AUN prevents a shipment of cat food fertilizer, presumably one that glows green. However, this is only one moment, and the ongoing processes at play in *Fresh Kill* can be seen through Stuart Sterling. His character begins the narrative associated with the economic benefits derived from the market strategies of GX, and ends the film associated with the economic benefits derived from the green economy. His turning point can be seen when he asks, 'Why are we still dumping?' In *Fresh Kill* a cynical view is taken of this transition. Stuart Sterling is presented as exploiting the green economy, as much as he had exploited the stockmarket. Initially a part of the GX dimension of the spatial organization of the virtual nexus, he shifts territories, or his shift in orientation territorializes another dimension, one that is constituted by the components of the green economy. Since one of Stuart Sterling's primary functions is defined through his successful financial activities, there is in the end little difference between the green economy and the stockmarket. As Sterling says: 'The Earth's worth saving, but there's no excuse not for making a profit.'

'Our special tonight is farm-grown Virginia catfish fed on soya beans and absolutely toxin free' (Claire)

Spaces in *Fresh Kill*, whether they be virtual ones or otherwise, are open spatio-temporal organizations that undergo constant macro and micro transitions.

The spaces created through, and at the intersections of, groups, individuals and technologies, have multiple meanings.[10] In *Fresh Kill*, each negotiation has the potential for expansion, yet at the same time is limited by its intersection with other dimensions that may be economic, political, exploitative, or regenerative. Technologically enhanced resistances, when spatialized in this way, reveal their contingencies. Actions cease to be events that gain meanings from a single site (groups or individuals); instead they are only components in a complex negotiation. Such a perspective has implications for political action: a radical act can only ever be contingent. This is not to say that action is then futile, rather that progress is a complex balance of events and effects constantly in transition.

Notes

1. In an interview about *Fresh Kill* with Lawrence Chua, Shu Lea Cheang discusses this aspect of the editing: 'I tell people if they are too confused, they should think about it as someone switching TV channels behind your back. At the same time, people have been finding that it's not passive viewing ... You have to work on it to get that story.' Shu Lea Cheang and Jessica Hagedorn, interviewed by Lawrence Chua, http://www.echonyc.com/~freshkill/interview.html.
2. *Ibid.*
3. Lawrence Chua discussing *Fresh Kill, ibid.*
4. The dynamic operations of race, class, sexuality, and gender are discussed in Massey (1994) and Bell and Valentine (1995).
5. Useful introductions to debates in this field include Latour (1987); *Science Technology and Human Values* (1995); Bingham (1996); Hinchcliffe (1996); and Law and Hassard (1999).
6. In the collection of essays, *Actor Network Theory and After* (1999), John Law and John Hassard re-emphasize the dynamism of the processes of thinking about technoscience. They express the concern that ANT has itself become prone to a form of stasis when it is unreflectively put into play around a technoscientific system.
7. In a narrative strand that is never resolved, one of many within the video, when Finn dies in the helicopter crash there is an implicit suggestion that this may not have been an accident, adding to the idea that GX is a thoroughly corrupt company.
8. Miguel makes this statement in the sequence in which his reading of Jorge Luis Borges' *Dreamtigers* is intercut with Jiannbin's reading of GX's confidential report on the contamination of the fish life off the coast of Los Gatos. An association between green and death/life is a theme found in the writing of Federico Garcia Lorca, from whose work Miguel also recites throughout the video.
9. In terms of the narrative of *Fresh Kill*, the theme of technology also creates a link

between the separate narrative events that occur around each of the separate groups that feature within the video. While the link does not necessarily reinstall a coherent linearity to this reading of the narrative, it does provide one (of several) means of progressing through it.
10. The play on the title of the video-feature echoes this. *Kill* means stream in Dutch; that this is stated within the video expands the potential meanings of the conjugation of *Kill* with *Fresh*. Fresh stream and fresh kill have an irony in a video-feature about water pollution.

Bibliography

Bell, David and Valentine, Gill (eds) (1995) *Mapping Desire: Geographies of Sexualities* (London: Routledge).

Bingham, Nick (1996) 'Objections: from technological determinism towards geographies of relations', *Environment and Planning D: Society and Space*, 14: 636–57.

Bordwell, David, Staiger, Janet and Thompson, Kristin (1985) *The Classical Hollywood Cinema: Film Style and Mode of Production to 1960* (London: Routledge & Kegan Paul).

Deleuze, Gilles (1990) *Negotiations: 1972–1990* (New York: Columbia University Press).

Deleuze, Gilles and Guattari, Félix (1987) *A Thousand Plateaus: Capitalism and Schizophrenia* (Minneapolis and London: University of Minnesota Press).

Gibson, Andrew (1996) *Towards a Postmodern Theory of Narrative* (1996) (Edinburgh: Edinburgh University Press).

Haraway, Donna (1991) 'A manifesto for cyborgs: science, technology, and socialist-feminism in the late twentieth century', in *Simians, Cyborgs, and Women: The Reinvention of Nature* (London: Free Association Books), pp. 149–81.

Hinchcliffe, Steve (1996) 'Technology, power and space – the means and ends of geographies of technology', *Environment and Planning D: Society and Space*, 14: 659–82.

Latour, Bruno (1987) *Science in Action: How to Follow Scientists and Engineers through Society* (Milton Keynes: Open University Press).

Law, John and Hassard, John (eds) (1999) *Actor Network Theory and After* (Oxford: Blackwell).

Massey, Doreen (1994) *Space, Place and Gender* (Cambridge: Polity Press).

Science Technology and Human Values (1995) 20(3) (Special Issue: Feminist and Constructivist Perspectives on New Technology).

Soja, Edward (1989) *Postmodern Geographies: The Reassertion of Space in Critical Social Theory* (London: Verso).

11

Revolting bodies

The resignification of fat in cyberspace

KATHLEEN LEBESCO

Judith Butler writes that 'all social systems are vulnerable at their margins, and
... all margins are accordingly considered dangerous' (Butler, 1990: 132). The
fat body, when read as disgusting, has been pushed to the margins of Western
culture, but the resources of abjection[1] there make the fat body, performed as
subversive, quite threatening to comfortably held ideas about the social,
political, and economic entitlement of those people currently ascribed as
natural, beautiful, and healthy. This chapter focuses on a community of bodies
which have failed to materialize – which haven't been constructed as bodies –
and examines their attempts to qualify as bodies that matter through the use of
technology.

The primary purpose of this study is to investigate the embodied experience
of fatness in spaces between subjectivity and subjection on various Internet
newsgroups and listservers. I examine how fat people are simultaneously
constructed as *subjects,* with the power to make choices about their bodies and
the meanings written on their bodies (despite their choices being ultimately
deemed 'bad' or 'unhealthy'), and are *subjected to* fat oppression (or lack of will,
depending on whom you ask). My ultimate goal in looking at the
resignification of fat through technology is to change the terrain of
relationships around fat, rather than to 'celebrate or condemn particular
political subjects' (Mann, 1994: 27). My analysis will investigate the varied
positions of agency of members of fat-related groups in an attempt to
understand the contestatory nature of political struggle over – and social
transformation of – the meaning of fat.

The Internet is posed as a forum for political work, a 'subaltern
counterpublic' (Fraser, 1992), which has the potential to create new rules for
identity membership, due to the erasure of the physical on text-based sites.

The context of the on-line communication about fat under investigation here is quite interesting historically: the two groups I examine, FD and FAS, have been around since 1994 and 1995, not long after mainstream awareness of the Internet boomed with the information revolution of the early 1990s. FAS (discussions for anyone pro-fat) was founded in 1994 when a subset of users on a diet newsgroup splintered off into their own group after responding to self-loathing posts by talking about size acceptance, and FD (discussions about fat for pro-fat, pro-lesbian women) was founded in the summer of 1995.[2] The conversations on both sites are set against a mainstream backdrop of contempt for fat, with public ridicule of fat people claimed by many to be the last socially-sanctioned-but-politically-incorrect form of humour. Diet and fitness industries are currently multi-billion dollar enterprises, and an estimated 20 to 40 per cent of adults in the USA are engaged in dieting behaviours (NIH, 1993: 765), seeking the slender, muscled body that is the choice signifier of health, beauty, and nature in today's society.

The physical setting of the on-line discussion groups presents an invisible, text-only space for representing the fat body. My investigation is limited to a listserver and a newsgroup, each of which is marked by the exchange of words rather than pictures (with few exceptions). Members of the FD listserver belong to a moderated community, where the moderator functions mostly to screen out self-identified men, and occasionally to remind subscribers of the group's charter. Participants on the FAS newsgroup may choose to indulge in or ignore postings from anyone, fat positive or not, as the discussions are public. In one crucial difference, a large percentage of FD participants hail from the same large West Coast city, and often engage with one another in fat-related activities outside of the list, while for most members of FAS, the newsgroup constitutes their only contact with such like-minded others.

It is difficult to ascertain exactly how many people belong to each group, because of the possibility that a large number of participants prefer simply to read the postings of others rather than to post their own stories. Officially, according to the list wrangler, between 200 and 300 people subscribed to FD during my study (8 March 1997). However, at any given time, the number of 'posting' participants on FD might range from twenty to fifty, depending on the level of interest in the topics being discussed at the time. I have observed that following periods of intense conflict, when the number of daily postings increases dramatically, a significant number of participants de-affiliate from the list (though some of them return to the fold later). Since the mechanics of a newsgroup are different, with public postings and no subscription requirement, it is impossible to know how many silent participants there are. Still, on any given day, one can expect between fifteen and seventy-five posts on the FAS bulletin board.

While many of the members of both groups have been transient or silent over the years, each site has a core of dedicated participants who must be noted for their ability to shape and sustain a large amount of fat-related conversation. Participants on both sites have remarked that a large number of these key subscribers have graduate degrees and appear to work both early and late, judging by what they reveal about themselves and when they post.[3] Another set of individuals must also be recognized as key players on both sites, though their contributions are neither frequent nor consistent: the provocateurs, or flamers. These are people whose presence at their respective site is usually short-lived and is marked by some sense of antagonism towards either the group in general or towards some perspective represented by one or more of the group members.

The two groups were established with slightly different mission statements, and thus the activities which occur on each site differ relative to the boundaries established by these statements. In both cases, though, the central activity is conversation that represents positive attitudes towards fat. These conversations take on any number of forms: from banter about where to buy speciality clothing and equipment, to discussions about the relationship of embodiment to sexuality, to exchanges of support for other participants facing discrimination from employers or medical doctors. Occasionally, the sites are used as advertising space for upcoming events of interest to many of the participants, such as a fat women's swim night or a play party; of course, given the wide geographic dispersal of group members, such postings provide useful information to only a relatively small number of nearby participants. Still, the existence of such postings indicates the extent to which participants conceive of each other as 'real' people who have lives outside of the computer screen. I believe that this recognition marks an interesting difference between discussion on these groups and the 'hi, what are you wearing?' conversations held on many other newsgroups and in chatrooms. In these fat groups, the participants often choose to reveal to one another their real names and even where they work, while in other cases they prefer to communicate using a coded user name. In any case, what is most important is connection to the other group members.

In view of the unique temporal character of on-line conversations, little things like clashing schedules don't get in the way of fat people connecting to one another. In the case of both groups, participants can read other postings whenever they desire, and can post responses or start new threads that will either hang around for a few days on a public electronic bulletin board (in the case of FAS) or be delivered to the e-mail account of other list members (as in FD). My observations indicate that most participants, particularly those on FD, respond within hours (sometimes even minutes) to posts which interest them, thus preserving a sense of flow and continuity in the conversations. Postings to both sites happen at all times of day and on every day of the week.

Since these sites are not communities in the traditional sense, and because their primary purpose is the sharing of self-posted information, there is little need to divide 'labour' on the sites. On FD, the one person with a greater investment of time and labour than others is the list wrangler, who screens new subscribers for gender, and who occasionally reminds the members of the list's mission statement, should controversy arise. The FAS group is run by an automated server, ensuring that anything that is posted will be made available on the bulletin board.

Some of the continuing themes of discussion on either one or both sites include: the 'fit' of fat bodies within cyberspace vs. in real space; guarding borders (both of the group and of fat identity); and strategies for resignifying fat. The resulting interpretation of social rules and basic patterns of order on the sites should prove useful for understanding how communication at these sites both enables and constrains particular notions of fat identity. The word 'fit' here can be plumbed both for literal and metaphorical meaning: fat people are often criticized for their physical inability to fit within the 'proper' dimensions of a human body. Intolerance of this lack of fit creates stigma, thus making the fat person ill-fitted for social relationships as well. Appreciation of the existence of on-line fat communities runs deep among the users in both FD and FAS, who often claim that they (both in identity and in physicality) do not 'fit' in everyday encounters. One FD list member put it this way when confronted with some intra-list squabbling about the sexual orientation of its members: 'I have yet to find any community that I fit into one hundred percent perfectly, and so when I find a community that most of me fits into, like this list, I get really concerned that I continue to mostly fit in' (FD, 14 April 1997). Such a statement speaks not only to the vital social function of these communities but also to the way in which users perceive themselves as outsiders from their regularly inhabited communities. Other users concur: 'Thank goddess [*sic*] for this list; sometimes I feel like some kind of isolated freakozoid when I use how it feels to be out in the world as my only reality check' (FD, 20 April 1997), and 'I realized that I don't know any lesbians who identify as fat dykes outside of my cyber-acquaintances on this list!' (FD, 21 June 1996). One heated FD conflict about the male-oriented posts of heterosexual list members elicited this plea for continued discussion in a virtual realm where fat women could finally fit comfortably: 'I just really hate "being where I'm uncomfortable" (a familiar theme to many of us, I assume, fat being a common denominator) and don't like to step on toes! I feel really good here ...' (FD, 11 September 1995). The list is again praised as a comfort zone for women who don't seem to fit elsewhere.

Many posts outline important reasons for using the on-line space for communication: connection with other fat women, equalization of shyness, amount of control afforded by the lack of immediacy, and the 'global village' effect. However, another reason cited for the appeal of on-line fat community space is the discomfort fat people often feel when congregating with each other in real space. For many, apprehension about being perceived as some type of pitiful spectacle keeps them isolated. One woman gave an example of such an instance:

> My partner and I went on an all-gay cruise, and although 90 per cent of the passengers were gay men, there were a dozen or so lesbians on board. Only one other couple were fat and they couldn't deal even being SEEN with another fat couple, let alone striking up a conversation with 'them' (us).
>
> (FD, 19 June 1996)

For some subscribers, it is the anonymity of cyberspace that is most attractive: the fact that they exist on-line as only words detached from their bodies frees them for less self-conscious reflection about the nature of their embodied experiences:

> Although I'm new to this group, I'm sure it can go without saying that I've suffered abuse and humiliation as a lifelong large female. I've never had the anonymity to be able to just blurt that out and I'm stunned at how sad it is to take suffering for granted just because of a body feature.
>
> (FAS, 24 April 1997)

Other members point to the possibility that the on-line fat community space provides a space for the airing of contradictions that might be used against fat people by unsympathetic others. In one post, an FD member praises the list for the diversity of perspectives it presents regarding fat acceptance, specifically in response to another member who admitted that she wasn't as accepting of her own fat body as she would like to be:

> When people are just honest about where they are, while owning it as internalized oppression, what more can you ask? You won't make progress by pretending to be in some other place (not that I'm saying you are, but it seems that some folks want you to do that). And frankly that's what I think support groups (including this list) are *for*. You can't bring your fears and doubts and self-criticisms to the fat-phobes, they'd just say it proves their point. I think this is a great place for us to share

the process of learning to love ourselves ... It's unfortunate that some people have no tolerance for anything less than perfect self-love. Hell, if we all had that, why would we even need a movement?

(FD, 6 March 1997)

This post invokes issues of internal strife over who is allowed to speak on the list and what they're allowed to say. For now, my focus is on the author's recognition of the list as a safe space for exposing the contradictions that can be used against fat people by people who don't share their perspective of fat-acceptance.

Users on FD valorize the fat female form in cyberspace in other ways that mark them as outsiders from their communities. Frequently, their discussions of bodies and pleasures position fat women positively as active subjects of desire, encouraging them to take up much more space than they are usually considered entitled to:

I've rarely been in the presence of another woman who physically overwhelms me, and that is something I would dearly love to experience ... That is usually an experience that comes in the presence of men. It's not the 'maleness' of men that I fantasize about, but the physicality of them – height, breadth ... I do wish to have that feeling of being covered, surrounded, protected physically by another woman.

(FD, 15 April 1997)

Here, the on-line forum provides a place for the discursive affirmation of women whose bodies exert influence and take up space, an honour usually accorded to men.

Another reason why participants value the space of cyberspace, particularly in FD, is because it seems to provide a woman-only space so uncommon off-line. This gender parameter provokes significant discussion about the possibilities of organizing on-line from the borderlands of difference. One list member's anecdote about a 'real-world' experience of exclusion happened as the result of structural prohibitions against bisexuals and lesbians sharing the same floor at the annual Fat Women's Gathering on the West Coast. Her analysis of the event positions the FD list as an alternative space, large enough for everyone to participate in important conversations about fat:

I remember there was a lesbian caucus meeting ... and we had about forty women. Next door there was supposedly a bi women's meeting, but as I recall, only two or three women showed up so they cancelled it. That's *really* isolating, folks. I would not want to be a fat bi woman looking for my community, and find that the only meeting for me was cancelled and meanwhile, right next door, there's this huge meeting for fat women who love women, that I'm not allowed to go to. That sounds pretty damn depressing to me. Let's not let that happen again. I'd really like to see a more unified community. As fat women we don't have a lot of spaces in the world that are welcoming to us. Personally, I need all the allies I can get. And I sure don't want to make anyone feel isolated in the one place where they *should* feel they belong!

(FD, 19 July 1996)

Here, the freedom of electronic space is contrasted with the restrictions of the way social and political organizations are frequently organized off-line, by identity, which is presumed to be singular. This demonstrates the ways in which boundaries from different domains manage to inform and inflect one another.

If there is much at stake in deciding how identity is defined, there is also much at stake in choosing language to represent identities. Sometimes linguistic inventions can render identities intelligible even when their referents are ambiguous: take, for instance, the term 'queer', which FD members take to be a 'generic term ... which covers a multitude of sexualities' (FD, 16 April 1997). Depending on how you look at it, 'queer' may be a troubled term; some could argue that the term, and thus the identity, is colonized by people with very specific same-sex physical experiences, thus disallowing, say, a position of 'straight queerness'. This exclusivity arguably works to politically disadvantage groups who might otherwise benefit from such surprises of diffuseness. Others might argue that when such a term is bandied about and self-applied liberally by those who otherwise suffer none of the plights of gays, lesbians, bisexuals, and transgendered people, it loses all meaning or is incredibly patronizing. One FD member suggests that

the term queer did have a distasteful sound to it in the 1970s to 1980s ... [but] now that the younger 'Gender Fuck' gays and lesbians use it all the time, it has started to be more and more accepted. It still pisses me off when other people say it, though, but it's cool when we use the term. Reclaiming our Queerness!

(FD, 16 April 1997)

Using language to reclaim positive identity has been a project for fat communities, as well. Many have campaigned for public acceptance of the term 'fat' in place of euphemisms like 'big boned', 'overweight' and 'heavy set'. One list member claims that she is 'conscious of this list removing the badness from

the word fat. I use the word fatdyke from time to time and it shocks people and
I think "Yes! Go to work on your preconceived notions and biases!"' (FD, 10
February 1998). Still, nothing irks many fat people more than to hear a woman
five pounds over life insurance height-and-weight standards bemoan her
personally and culturally imagined status as a 'fat' person.[4] There is a sense on
the sites that the term 'fat' should be positively connoted, but not watered
down; again, not used to refer to bodies that really aren't fat. The question,
then, is what does pass muster as an authentically fat body? How is it
discursively constructed on-line, and need it strictly correlate with how the
same body is materially constructed in the 'real' world?

It is entirely possible that the fat bodies presented in these on-line sites
could be total inventions, but admitting that does not strip them of their
political volatility. In a language-only space where nobody can see your hips,
your belly, your legs, to say that you are fat is a strong, meaningful political
gesture that declares that fat will not be erased. Other than the narrative
assertion 'I am fat', accompanied by anecdotes about fat oppression suffered at
the hands of fat haters (an important part of fat 'credentialling' on these sites),
there is just no plain way to be sure. A preoccupation with attaining certainty
about real-world body types diminishes the meaning taken from on-line
performance. What *could be* becomes a much more interesting issue than what
is, especially when 'what *is*' is very much open to interpretation.

I am not trying to argue that these sites are purely creative zones where
everyone just happens to love fat and where participants float around in bodies
purchased with the currency of a few taps on the keyboard. Indeed, the space
of the on-line fat body is maintained through the quelling of dissent and
difference, mostly articulated by anti-fat flamers and spammers, but sometimes
voiced from within the groups.

In one instance, the occasion of internal dissent over appropriate minimum
weight requirements on FD compelled some list members to reflect on the
inherent relativity of *all* identities:

> on that 200 lb issue ... if someone weighs 200 lb, and is about ... 4' 10"
> or so ... she is probably as fat as I am and faces the same issues ... I still
> don't understand this arbitrary 200 lb thingy ... maybe we should have a
> height limit here ... (sorry, I couldn't resist).
>
> (FD, 2 April 1996)

This post gets at the difficulty of defining a real, essentially 'fat' identity; not
only is what is considered fat relative to a measure of height or other physical
descriptors, as this author points out, but it is also relative to cultural standards
and historical criteria.

One FD list member summed up her sense of the utility of the list by saying, 'You do what you can do and get by how you can. By creating supportive communities we work to accept ourselves, each other, and create change in the external world' (FD, 7 March 1997). At this point I hope that I have made a strong case that on-line communication about fat identity and politics has the power to resituate users within discourse. Some may ask for 'real' evidence, material indications that it's not all just 'talk', that these on-line conversations do contribute to a large-scale, external resignification of fatness. In response, I can cite a few examples of the small impacts that FD and FAS have had on the external world.

The first case deals with Fat Lip Readers Theater, a Bay Area theatre collective dedicated to the presentation of dramatic works which deal with issues of fat oppression. In April 1997, they posted a notice to the FD list which heralded a change in their organizational structure, perhaps modelled after the organizational structure of FD itself:

> Fat Lip has thus far been a closed group ... This will be changing. Instead we will have a central group of women ... which will guide the activities of the group, but the general membership of the group will be fluid, allowing interested women to participate on a project-to-project basis ... Fat Lip will continue to be for fat women only, but we'll continue to work with other size-acceptance groups to strengthen our community. [The central group, known as 'the Hub'] has come up with a mission statement: 'The Hub is a coalition dedicated to increasing the visibility and availability of size-positive activities, resources, and organizations in the greater San Francisco Bay Area.'
>
> (FD, 18 April 1997)

What I find most compelling about this is the move away from an organization based on shared essential traits, towards affinities of action. While there is still some identity-based core, the new emphasis is on working with others to achieve similar goals.

Other fat groups around the country borrow the cultural agitation tactics of the Lesbian Avengers (see Schulman, 1994), preferring spectacularly staged events to boring political rallies as a means of exhibiting their subjectivity. Frequently, users post notices about events, such as a group scale-smashing under Seattle's Space Needle, a collective scale-toss from the Golden Gate Bridge, a 'No Diet Day' bookmarking in a large New York City bookstore's Self-Help section, and even an ice-cream eat-in on the front lawn of a busy Boston Jenny Craig diet centre. Another fun form of direct action, possible from the comfort of one's own living room, involves applying 'Feed This

Woman' stickers to ads featuring anorexic models and sending the ads back to the companies.[5] Judging from the on-line discussion of these types of events both before and after, the fat site users aren't just a damp bunch of pasty-skinned computer geeks whose only light is the flicker of their monitors; they're as physically active and bold (and of course, sometimes as couch-potatoey and mild) as they are on-line. Their subversion of mainstream standards of acceptable physicality is small, dispersed and local, but it is exactly this kind of subversion that provides the best (because most radically democratic) opportunities for re-imagining what counts as healthy and beautiful.

To sum up, fatness can be reconfigured from a spoiled identity to a proudly inhabited one by using any number of strategies aimed at entering fat bodies into discourse proudly and publicly. This task, though, is never easy, and is very risky. One FD list member who has been working at the task for years says, 'It takes all of my strength every damn day to get out there and be myself, stay centred in my being, come across as the woman I truly feel myself to be and not think about or take in people's negative response to my physical being' (FD, 6 March 1997). Still, the sense I get from the two groups is that the possibility of resignifying fat – of finally (though partially) inhabiting the position of 'subject' rather than constantly 'subjugated' – is well worth the effort and the risk.

Throughout this attempt to enter fat bodies into academic discourse, I have tried to pay particular attention to the contradictions inherent in the conversations on-line. Mara Math, an FD list member, talked about the will to innocence that one encounters in most groups which are striving to invigorate their individual subject positions:

> My experience has been that every movement has its excesses around the cusp of first gaining power. Remember the days when the line was that all lesbian sex was perfect? As were all lesbian relationships? (And there are often far crueller excesses as well.) I suspect that this rush-of-power/reverse of the pendulum re. Fat Lib takes the same route: fat is unequivocally good, and absolutely the only thing wrong is social oppression. I think paying attention to these contradictions (without yielding to oppressive bullshit) would serve us well.
>
> (FD, 8 February 1998)

This chapter, then, is intended to place those contradictions under a magnifying glass in an effort to debunk the strategic efficacy of innocence, in favour of a more complex scheme for recognizing the contested character of fat identity. Elizabeth Grosz recognizes that the realization that 'one's struggles are inherently *impure*, bound up with what one struggles against' (Grosz, 1995: 62) is troubling, in that it 'refuses the idea of a space beyond or outside, the fantasy of a position insulated from what it criticizes and disdains' (*ibid.*). We see complicity happening in cyberspace: those seeking to reconfigure the fat body *must*, to some degree, work in tandem with the kinds of ideas and ideal bodies they are trying to destroy.

Patricia Mann writes that 'those of us who are not physically assimilable stand upon previously unremarked boundaries of liberal universalism, representing its de facto exclusionary capacities for all to see', but also assures us that 'it is [our] ... visible physical markings ... that allow us to represent our political agency most vividly' (Mann, 1994: 158). Though the spaces I have examined are text-based, they work to represent a politicized surface for the fat body. It is remarkably apparent from posts like the last one that the on-line groups can provide a steady anchoring point, as well as a point of departure, for fat subjectivity.

In *Gender Trouble*, Judith Butler argues that the body's surface is politically constructed (Butler, 1990: x). While her focus is on issues of sex/gender construction, my efforts are directed at denaturalizing and resignifying categories of body size and shape. Butler accomplishes her task by highlighting the subversive potential of parodic practices, which certainly find their parallels in fat politics in the guise of events like fat lingerie shows and fat *Star Trek* conventions, campier even than the draggiest drag. Though in these on-line sites there is not such a strong visual sense of parody, users have indeed appropriated and reworked vocabularies and symbols from the dominant mainstream to their own advantage; the prevalence of the word 'fat' in the movement, instead of euphemisms like 'heavy-set', is a case in point. Butler points to other areas where 'discourse reiterate[s] injury such that the various efforts to recontextualize and resignify a given term meet their limit in this other, more brutal, and relentless form of repetition' (*ibid.*: 223), citing the success of reworking the word 'queer' and the failure of reappropriating 'nigger'. I believe that a resignification of 'fat' is poised somewhere in between these two; in some kind of aural slide, being called 'phat' is the freshest form of flattery,[6] but it's still disconcerting to be told you're looking chunky. The comfort with which on-line participants freely use 'fat' to describe themselves positively is still challenged by the brutally negative cultural repetitions of the adjective as a put-down.

It appears that the strategies mobilized on-line in the instances I have examined allow fat people to claim their subjectivity, while they slowly and unevenly rework the rules of what counts as healthy and beautiful. The participants assume the position of the speaking subject within their on-line language communities, providing a frame of reference for their citation as healthy and beautiful within the larger language communities in which they operate. The strengths of the groups are their flexibility and continuing dedication to discussing the difficulties of pragmatic struggle over the resignification of fat.

These conversations are effective forms of political action. Butler claims that power relations both constrain and constitute the very possibilities of volition: one cannot withdraw or refuse power, only redeploy it (*ibid.*: 124). While I don't imagine that a bunch of fat people sitting in front of their computers typing away is likely to be read as an attempted coup or transcendence of oppressive relations around body size and shape towards limitless pleasure in the fat body, I would argue that the conversations they engage in do subversively redeploy a sense of entitlement about the possibilities of taking pleasure in and by fat bodies. They are not taking over the universe, and have no plans for some kind of fat separatist utopia; instead, their power is more of what Butler describes as

> a kind of diffuse corporeal agency generated from a number of different centers of power. Indeed, the source of personal and political agency comes not from within the individual, but in and through the complex cultural exchanges among bodies in which identity itself is ever-shifting, indeed where identity itself is constructed, disintegrated, and recirculated only within the context of a dynamic field of cultural relations.
>
> (*ibid.*: 127)

She argues for 'the production of new subject-positions, new political signifiers, and new linkages to become the rallying points for politicization' (Butler, 1993: 193), and while fat site users rarely explicitly indicate their intentions, the project of their discussions is to revamp their subjectivities, accord new usefulness to the signifier of fat, and to explore new linkages of affinity and action. As I have shown, they squabble all the way through these processes, but their factionalization does not produce political paralysis. Instead, I want to plumb their sense of *dis*-identification with each other for its political merits, as Butler claims that 'the affirmation of that slippage, that failure of identification is itself the point of departure for a more democratizing affirmation of internal difference' (*ibid.*: 219).

What is vital is that users do not let their squabbling get in the way of their continued self-signification, so essential to future possibilities for citing fat as healthy and beautiful and powerful. Curiously, though, members keep talking to each other, in a move reminiscent of Butler's 'double movement'; they 'invoke the category [of fatness] and, hence, provisionally ... institute an identity and at the same time ... open the category as a site of permanent political contest' (*ibid.*: 221–2). Though users utilize identity terms with almost every utterance, they also constantly question them.

Notes

1. According to Butler, 'the abject designates those "unlivable" and "uninhabitable" zones of social life which are nevertheless densely populated by those who do not enjoy the status of the subject, but whose living under the sign of the "unlivable" is required to circumscribe the domain of the subject' (Butler, 1993: 3).
2. I use the abbreviations FAS and FD to stand in for the full names of the newsgroup and the listserver. While privacy was not mentioned as a huge concern for those on the public FAS bulletin board, many members of FD expressed concern about the maintenance of their privacy on what was considered by some to be their 'private' electronic mailing list. Thus, I agreed to conceal the name of the group.
3. One FAS subscriber portrays the list as composed of classic overachievers: 'I've heard of an inordinate number of graduate degrees on this board (I'm working on my third right now). I also posted a few weeks ago that I had noticed that whenever I come into work on a holiday or weekend, or early or late, it is the larger people who are here, never the thin ones ... And it isn't because we don't have lives outside of work ... It seems that the only thing we forego is sleep' (FAS, 26 June 1996). One might also make an educated guess that the participants benefit from some degree of social class advantage, given their knowledge of computer use and their relative ease of access to computer equipment.
4. One FD member says that 'when average-sized women say they are fat, it makes above average-sized women mad. There is no universally agreed-on weight that divides the average-sized from the fat, and fat includes a very wide range of sizes. The same average-sized women who calls herself too fat will rush to tell you you are not fat if you make a good appearance and she likes you' (FD, 5 February 1998).
5. One FAS post recommended Kaz Cooke's book *Real Gorgeous*, which prescribes sending the following type of letter to fashion magazine editors: 'Dear Editor, the model on page 72 of your latest issue looks like a sick whippet. I want to know what the clothes look like on a size 14. And PS, please give that model some lunch before she faints. Signed, Reasonably Outraged, Come to Think About It' (FAS, 8 March 1997).
6. William Safire explains the origins of 'phat': 'Though some have postulated the origin of *phat* as an acronym for "pretty hips and thighs" or even more lascivious constructions, the word is more likely a deliberate misspelling of *fat*, which has for centuries had a slang meaning of "rich", as in "fat and happy"' (Safire, 1998: 12).

Bibliography

Butler, J. (1990) *Gender Trouble: Feminism and the Subversion of Identity* (New York: Routledge).

Butler, J. (1993) *Bodies That Matter: On the Discursive Limits of 'Sex'* (New York: Routledge).

Fraser, N. (1992) 'Rethinking the public sphere: a contribution to the critique of actually existing democracy', in C. Calhoun (ed.), *Habermas and the Public Sphere* (Cambridge, MA: MIT Press), pp. 109–42.

Grosz, E. (1995) *Space, Time, and Perversion: Essays on the Politics of Bodies* (New York: Routledge).

Mann, P. S. (1994) *Micropolitics: Agency in a Postfeminist Era* (Minneapolis: University of Minnesota Press).

National Institutes of Health (NIH) Technology Assessment Conference Panel (1993) 'Methods for voluntary weight loss and control', *Annals of Internal Medicine*, 119(7) Part 2 (1 October): 764–70.

Safire, W. (1998) 'All phat! and a bag of chips', *New York Times Magazine*, 17 May, p. 30.

Schulman, S. (1994) *My American History: Lesbian and Gay Life During the Reagan/Bush Years* (New York: Routledge).

12

The projection of geographical communities into cyberspace[1]

DUNCAN SANDERSON AND ANDRÉE FORTIN

Municipal community networks, projects for digital cities, and a host of bulletin boards and web sites for place-based organizations large and small all attest to processes of 'urban development' in cyberspace. To use an analogy, it is as though geographical communities are being projected into cyberspace. In this chapter we want to highlight the strong links that exist between traditional place-based communities and particular uses of the Web. Certainly, there are also electronically mediated communities of interest which transcend place (other chapters in this book provide examples), but here we want to emphasize the 'localization' of existing social groups in cyberspace (Guédon, 1996), and explore the difficulties and contradictions which this practice also brings with it. In particular, one can interpret much of the emerging activity in virtual space as an affirmation of local social identities, as a manifestation of local social networks of community organizations, and as visible signs of both local and global orientations (Fortin, 1995; Lefebvre and Tremblay, 1998).

We outline a typology (or a map) of place-based web pages. The presentation and discussion of this typology will help the reader to spot certain key features of cyberspace as it is currently taking shape (Guédon, 1996), as well as the relationships between this space and socio-geographic space, as manifested in local organizations, villages, and cities. Examples of each are drawn from current web sites in Quebec, Canada, although we are confident that similar examples could be found in several countries.[2] We will explore the electronic and social web which underpins place-oriented cyberspace. Key phenomena defined and described include the density and scope of links, the degree of local or outward orientation, social and institutional action to occupy cyberspace, the liveliness and visibility of a site, the promotion of local actions in cyberspace (meetings, club activities, celebrations), and ways in which local identities may influence and be observed through a web site.

We also explore possible tensions and distortions between local electronic and geographical space: for example, a municipality may have more than one web site. A municipality can have only one geographical site, but it may exhibit multiple 'personalities' when it enters into cyberspace. Some localities may become relatively dominant in cyberspace when compared to their stature in geographic space — signs of hidden social ambitions perhaps? Finally, we discuss the dynamics of information produced by people in socio-geographic communities, and the production of information within local or global orientations. We also return to the concepts and analogies which we have proposed for the analysis of the intersections between cyber and geographic space, and highlight various issues which we see emerging as geographic communities occupy cyberspace.

The social and communication context framing the projection of local communities into cyberspace

The reflections and observations presented here can be situated within a broad set of questions about the nature of public space, collective identities, and the role of communication. A public communication space in which a society debates its orientations and concerns has always existed. With the Internet, a new form of public space has appeared, one which is at the same time interpersonal (for example, e-mail) and mediated (web pages). It is a communication space which allows new relationships between self, physical space, and others.

One of the conditions for these relationships is a common culture, and a 'common geographical space', which depends on the reciprocity of communication as discussed by Habermas (1979). In this respect, we can observe two contradictory tendencies. On the one hand, sociability seems to be reduced to the metaphorical, in the sense that people have no shared relationship to actual geographical place. Thus some identities are not based on place, but rather on personal and cultural characteristics, such as sex, age, tastes and lifestyles. Such forms of identity give rise to social networks, the collective form of the pure relationship discussed by Giddens (1991). This is the tendency which most analyses of the Internet tend to focus on, namely the virtual community and forms of sociability which are displayed there (Fernback, 1999). On the other hand, this medium can also be used to reinforce identities based on geographical space, and then it becomes a medium in which local identities can be projected and expressed, heard and recognized (much as Taylor, 1992, discusses the politics of recognition). It is a medium in which the colours of a region, association or organization can be seen and observed. The 'reading' of these identities on the Web is especially interesting, in that collective identities emerge which are being projected and constructed at the same time as the media space itself is being built. Our long-term objective is to identify and describe this dynamic.

There is currently both an interest in international developments and problems, as well as a desire to 'act locally' and to improve local networks (Rheingold, 1995). The twin analogies of 'orienting to the world' and 'focusing in on one's own place', help to illuminate contemporary social relations. These are also analogies which can be used to understand the uses which are being made of the Internet. On the one hand, academics and entrepreneurs alike represent the Internet as a 'universal technology', one that cuts across cultures and countries. In theory, we can engage in conversations with numerous others in diverse cultures across the world. On the other hand, the narrowing of focus can be observed in electronic communities of interest founded on particular facets of our identity, or certain interests: for example, in distribution lists for gays, or home gardening web sites.

As a global phenomenon, the Internet initially appears to have few local geographical roots. The metaphor of 'the Web' emphasizes the connections, rather than the myriad individuals and organizations which nourish it. Rather, it is useful to consider that part of the process of producing the Web is analogous to back-yard and roof-top gardening – it is produced by local people in specific but sometimes out-of-the-way places. In essence, we argue that the Web is not free of spatial anchoring. The Internet is not only used to 'visit' or connect with people and cultures in far-away places but also to find out about one's neighbour and events in one's own municipality. Indeed, what interests us here are the social uses of the Internet, and particularly those found in somewhat isolated areas or relatively small communities. We believe that the practices in these places will help us to perceive not only a general orientation to the world but also a simultaneous interest in one's local community.

A typology of web pages

Aside from research and scientific sites, and virtual communities,[3] we have identified four types of web site which have a direct connection with place and local social organizations. These are: a) industrial, tourism and municipal showcases; b) institutional sites; c) social and community organizations; and d) community networks. This typology and the short descriptions which follow are based on an examination of about a hundred municipal and organizational sites in Quebec. These are ideal types, since in practice a given web site may be an example of two or more of these types.

Industrial, tourism and municipal showcases

These are sites which are primarily oriented towards people from outside of the municipality or region. These sites provide local information such as tourist attractions and facilities, or attempt to sell local products. An example of this type of site is http://saglac.qc.ca, which includes links to pages which describe small municipalities. Links may be provided to pages which describe local businesses and manufacturing companies, and invariably include details about their business objectives and how to contact them.

Institutional sites

These sites are oriented towards the activities and resources of local or regional institutions. They may be health or education oriented: for example, a college or university web site. The sites may also provide information on economic and political networks which promote regional development. These sites can be distinguished from showcase sites in two respects: first, they generally provide more detailed information than is the case with a showcase site, in terms of tools, texts, or contacts; and second, they specifically target information to local users. A good example of an institutional site in Quebec is an organization for local development, SADC (Sociétés d'aide au développement des collectivités: http://www.reseau-sadc.qc.ca). This site provides pointers to other organizations which are oriented towards employment creation or regional development.

Social and community organizations

Social and community organizations may also have a 'presence' on the Web. This type of page represents the community equivalent of the business or municipal page. The pages present the organization and usually its objectives and main activities, and sometimes a contact person is identified. As with the other types of web site, the pages at these sites may be relatively independent of each other, or there may be a central 'portal' site which provides a restricted view onto a set of community organizations. An example of a portal community organizations site is the Community Development Corporation in Victoriaville,

Quebec (http://www.cdcbf.qc.ca/cdcbf/). The organizations represented by this type of page may or may not be part of a community network.

Community networks

Community networks are oriented towards a specific geographic space and to
the people who inhabit it. The organizers of community networks generally
adhere to certain objectives: wide access to the Internet or other electronic
network by the general population within a given locality (and this may include
public access points), some form of co-ordination among those who promote the
use of the Internet within the community, an attempt to include a variety of
institutions, and a desire to use the Internet as a medium for local organizing
initiatives and information distribution.[4] There may also be an objective of
making local government more responsive and democratic (Tsagarousianou, *et
al.*, 1998). There is usually a central web site, which acts as a portal to pages
provided by diverse organizations, such as community organizations,
municipal government, or leisure and cultural groups. An example in Quebec
is http://www.icrdl.net/basques/org-comm.htm, and in Brighton
in the UK, http://community.pavilion.net/ (Fig. 12.1). This
illustration presents an overview of the different kinds of local information
available at the site (as of May 1999).

The important point here is that the form of community network which we
are describing is composed of people in a specific geographical location with a
diversity of interests. The topics that are presented and the organizations that
are represented are relevant to people in that locality, but not necessarily to
those from elsewhere. Often, it becomes apparent that there are real people
behind the page, who want to tell the surfer about their part of the world. Yet
the surfer only sees what people from that part of the world want him or her to
see. This form of network is a product of, and attests to, a regional dynamic
which is oriented towards local needs. The place-based web sites identified by
this typology can be analysed from two perspectives. First, with respect to
their 'material' nature, and second, in terms of their connections with local
social groups and structures.

A site's place and character in cyberspace

Just as humans are situated within a dense network of relationships, so too are
web sites. The notion of integration within cyberspace refers to a page or site's
connections and 'sociality'. Part of this notion could be measured empirically,

Figure 12.1 Brighton `http://community.pavilion.net`

by establishing the number of links to a given site. For example, if a site is registered with several search engines, or if a site is referred to by several other page creators, then it would have relatively high integration. The number of references to a site is an indicator of the integration of a site within the virtual world.

A site may have a number of other characteristics with spatial or social dimensions. For example, certain connotations may be created through links to particular sites. A site is also likely to have a local or external orientation – a surfer could be led by links to consult or discover organizations within the same locality, or if there is an external orientation, he or she could be referred to sites elsewhere in the country or world. Visitors may come who live nearby or far away. Sites may also have a degree of attractiveness which could be assessed by the number of voluntary repeat visitors. Some sites may also exhibit signs of being more or less provincial or cosmopolitan, as indicated by the variety of languages available, possible signs of the nationality of visitors, and the local or universal nature of the content of the site.

A site as a signpost to a social and geographical community

Web links on specific sites are indicators of the status or role of an organization within its locality. For example, the community development organization noted earlier (http://www.cdcbf.qc.ca/cdcbf/) is clearly the lead one within the site, and it acts on behalf of other organizations. If an organization provides contact information about other organizations, or links to their pages, there is a strong chance that they have a co-ordinating role within the actual locality and that the organization's leaders have social contacts with other organizations. Conversely, if sites, particularly portal sites, do not provide such information, this may suggest conflict, lack of contact, or some other social breakdown. If many links exist, this suggests that the organization occupies a pivotal role within the community. Similarly, it would be interesting to explore absence and presence in cyberspace communities, specifically with respect to powerful and marginalized social groups in geographic communities.

Municipal sites also vary with respect to their coverage of local organizations and activities, with a wide or narrow listing of attractions, industry, community events, work or industrial opportunities, culture, sport, leisure, health and educational institutions. It appears that the large urban centres are more likely to have complete lists of community organizations and their contact information (for example, in Montreal there is http://netpop.cam.org/). Sites may also offer information which can only be of interest to local people: for example, who else but the local population would be interested in the name and phone number of the scout master or items in the classified ads? Some sites may also offer visitors 'perks' which, in at least one case, we have observed to be of value only to local people. For example, a local Internet service provider offers coupons for purchase rebates (http://www.ivic.qc.ca).

We have also noticed that some site designers attempt to communicate the 'realness' and sociability of the people represented by the web site. This may be achieved by including photographs of places or groups or events, or by providing web space in which individuals can identify and describe themselves and their interests, and leave their telephone number. To us, it seems that the name of the site host or sponsors, organizational documents, as well as announcements for local events and attractions, have the effect of reinstating the realness and concreteness of the place and people which are presented by a web page.

Relationships between geographic, social, and cyberspace

Certain aspects of our geography are being translated into or imprinted on cyberspace. This gives rise to a more general question: what is the relationship between a municipality, as it may be represented in web sites, and the community which directly or indirectly (through organizational leaders) creates the web sites? An example from Quebec illustrates these relationships. Figure 12.2 reveals what we would see if we were to access the web page for the Basques region (in Quebec). Although this page provides an entry into a region, with links to municipalities, companies, and organizations, the browser is not obliged to pass through this page in order to obtain local information, and could also go directly to a municipal page. For example, one could go directly to the web page for Trois-Pistoles (Figure 12.3). Or one could go to the page for

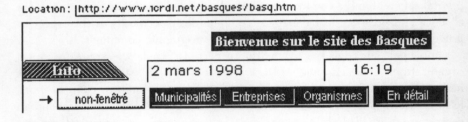

Figure 12.2 Basques.

Figure 12.3 Trois-Pistoles.

Location: http://www.icrdl.net/basques/clor_aci.htm

Figure 12.4 Saint-Clément.

Saint-Clément (Figure 12.4). These different entry points suggest an ambiguous relationship between the regional entity which put the web site together and the municipalities in the region. On the one hand, the user or browser can access the regional pages and obtain information about organizations in the region. On the other, it is apparent that a city (Trois-Pistoles) and a village (Saint-Clément) are associated with this region, and that it is also possible to obtain more information about this city and village. Also, the regional Basques site is accessed by an address which is the same length (at the same level) as the local addresses for Saint-Clément or Trois-Pistoles. A zoom onto the Basques region is not necessarily followed by a further zoom down to the municipalities. The architecture of the web site does not indicate to the person from out of town that Trois-Pistoles or Saint-Clément are subelements within the Basques region.

It is also possible that the surfer forms false impressions in relation to these municipalities. Based on their apparently equal importance (given an equal number of web pages), it might appear that Trois-Pistoles (population 3,890) and Saint-Clément (population 600) have equal importance in regional affairs. Nor is it obvious, at first glance, that there are two other municipalities within the region, without web sites, which have a larger population than Saint-Clément. A presence in cyberspace is not necessarily an indicator of geographical size or political importance.

Is there some special reason that helps to explain why Saint-Clément has a web site? Possible clues can be found in the political history of the village. For example, a post office which had been scheduled for closure by Canada Post was occupied by the local population (Beaudry and Dionne, 1996). This suggests a well-organized population, with strong local identity. In this case, the appropriation of cyberspace by the local population, in the creation of a web site for Saint-Clément, appears to be closely linked to social and community dynamics. In this example, a symbolic information space has been constructed which is potentially different from actual geographic space and administrative structures. With the apparent importance of Saint-Clément and the lack of information about other larger municipalities, a distortion has been created between the image communicated by the web sites and the socio-economic reality. A desire to communicate a distinctive social identity is operating: Saint-Clément was apparently anxious to 'put itself on the electronic map'.

Moreover, the administrative configuration of villages, cities, and regional government is relatively fixed. A village cannot easily leave regional government, and usually a person can only live in *one* municipality. However, these relationships are not so fixed in the electronic world. If the citizens of Saint-Clément feel at some point that their village is not well served by the Basques' web site, they could easily create their own site which could be hosted by a server in some other city.[5] It would also be possible to have a municipal site located in more than one region, or to be grouped with other similar cities (e.g. culturally or politically) rather than by region. In sum, a given relationship between geographical identities, territorial administrations and cyberspace is not necessarily fixed for ever. We can foresee (and see already) changing alliances and electronic identities and associations which are different from territorial identities.

The negotiation of relationships between organizations in cyberspace and the ambiguities that are part of this were highlighted in an interview in the spring of 1999 with a local development organization in the city of Victoriaville, Quebec. The organization first of all wanted to be associated with other organizations which had similar mandates. Thus, because of a youth job-placement service, the organization was keen to be associated 'horizontally' with youth agencies and services, or with employment services. However, the organization had a mandate for regional development, and also wanted people to be able to 'zoom' vertically down to its level in a classic progression of general to specific, Canada to Quebec to regional development organization. Thus a vertical spatial metaphor of national down to local (one of the desired web page structures) reflected this organization's understanding of its place within an organizational environment. A conceptual clash appeared though, as it also wanted to accommodate other affinity relationships with youth and employment services.

A case study of the production of information by local people and organizations

One of the fundamental characteristics of the Web as a communication medium is that sites and pages can be produced by people with relatively modest means. It is useful to study the social dynamics which underlie the creation of web sites, and to consider the social and communication objectives of the people who are behind the page. We can illustrate some of these dynamics through the example of a medium-sized city, Victoriaville, Quebec (population 40,000). Web sites were produced by the local ISP (the Internet service provider: http://www.ivic.qc.ca/), the Community Development Corporation (http://www.cdcbf.qc.ca/cdcbf/), the City of Victoriaville (http://www.ivic.qc.ca/ville/), and the Economic Development Corporation (www.cdebf.qc.ca/home3.html). The observations reported here are based on our inspection of these web sites and on interviews with a representative from each organization.

In Victoriaville, aside from the Internet service provider, the process of creating the web pages required that people in these organizations transmit information that they had acquired to specialized web page designers. The organizations had to use internal budgets in order to pay for the web page design. The four organizations indicated that they were satisfied with what they had done, and three out of four had specific plans for further expansion or embellishments. In spite of the effort and expense required to produce the web sites, the organizations had a strong desire to provide information about themselves and the place where they lived. In a very real sense, they wanted their organization to become visible in cyberspace.

We also observed a relatively decentralized development dynamic, at least for Victoriaville: each of the four organizations was aware of the others, although there was little overt co-ordination between them. For instance, there was no common web page for organizations in the city, and there were few or no links to help navigate from one organization to another. Thus, just as there are very real proximities and barriers between buildings in a city or town, in the electronic world there are also proximities (through links) or barriers (a lack of links). However, we are not able at this time to indicate whether or not there is a relationship between the density of web links between organizations in a locality and the social network for that locality. Logically, the more that local organizations are aware of the electronic activities of others, and the more that actual social contacts are established between them, the more likely it would be that web links would be added to take the surfer to neighbour organizations in his or her locality. Still, this did not seem to hold true in Victoriaville: in spite of a strong history of community organizations (Ninacs, 1993), there were very few links between the four organizations which we identified.

This can be contrasted with another development trajectory, in which there is a strong effort to co-ordinate information about local organizations and events. In the UK, for example, there is a community networking initiative in Brighton which is reflected in a relatively inclusive web site

(http://www.brighton.co.uk/welcome.htm). This central site provides links to business, community, government, education and tourist
organizations. In spite of the large number of organizations in this city which
had developed their own web sites, the participants were able to co-ordinate
themselves and invest the time necessary to create a focal information centre
for the area.

Local, linguistic and global orientations

From our initial overview of web sites in Quebec, it became apparent that web
page producers anticipated either a local, provincial, or global audience. The
local orientation was found for example in classified ads, local community
events, the identification of local chapters of organizations (Scouts, Lions
Club), and even sales coupons for local stores. In particular, the development
plans for the City of Victoriaville included providing more information about
the city administration and services to local citizens. The ISP was also
committed to providing local information (it designed and hosted many free
web pages about local organizations and activities). This orientation was seen
as providing value to its clientele and helping to distinguish itself from other
national ISPs. In one sense, the potential access to the local information from
anywhere in the world was superfluous, as the authors clearly did not envisage
that its primary users would live far away.

Occasionally, though, the information was oriented towards a more distant
audience, as suggested by information concerning local sites of interest, tourist
attractions, or industrial opportunities. Still, almost all of the sites in
Victoriaville were in French only, and this was generally true for other sites
we visited in French majority municipalities across the province. For this
reason, we would qualify the intended audience of some pages as primarily
'linguistic' in scope, specifically serving French-speaking populations. One
interesting exception was the 'Festival international de musique actuelle de
Victoriaville', which attracts many out-of-town and international visitors, and
for this reason provided translations in English. This site clearly had a national
and global orientation.

Conclusion

Many geographically located organizations and communities are projecting
themselves into cyberspace through web pages and sites. Virtual communities
do form on the Internet, but one must also be aware of the ways in which our

socio-geographical localities influence the creation and use of information which is found there. We have suggested that geographical communities do not die in cyberspace, but in fact help to shape it.

Further, geographical communities also appear to use the Internet to reassert their social and political identities. Most municipalities have at least one web page, usually sponsored by the municipal administration, and often local organizations and institutions also provide pages which describe themselves and their activities. These create a sort of social and cultural geography in cyberspace: central sites (for example, a welcome page for a community network) become a landmark or signpost which connects otherwise isolated outposts. We consider initiatives which tie together otherwise isolated sites to be of particular significance. This effort suggests a desire to colonize cyberspace on behalf of place-based social and geographical identities.

We have suggested a number of conceptual hooks into this phenomenon. Sites are more or less integrated into a virtual world, and indicate with more or less fidelity the integration and social networking of their creators within their geographical communities. The sites have varying topographies, with some giving more emphasis than others to tourism, local services, culture, local events and so on. The web sites of a given locality may be tightly linked between themselves, or there may be barriers, and these too may or may not reflect the ties and barriers in the geographical communities. Also, the authors of these web sites may try ardently to communicate the realness and actual location of the people and organizations that create these sites, through various visual and symbolic devices.

In Quebec, and we believe the same holds true elsewhere, three sorts of orientation or space were discernible: the local (information about local events); a linguistic space (information of general interest to a given linguistic group); and the cosmopolitan or global (information destined for people from anywhere or diverse linguistic groups). This suggests an area for further reflection: historically, geographic space has been a natural protector of languages and cultures. The Web, on the other hand, potentially opens up communities, when there is a common language, to people from elsewhere. Yet this remains theoretical if the information on a web site is indecipherable to them, and the site remains similarly distant as when people had to travel to another continent. The Web closely juxtaposes linguistic spaces and communities which until now have usually been geographically separate, while simultaneously allowing these spaces to remain distinct. Thus, while the Web is a globalizing force, allowing forms of access to distant communities, it also allows local communities to display and maintain some individuality, through parochial information and local languages.

We also noted the likelihood that new social and administrative ambiguities emerge because of the ways in which geographical place is present or represented on the Web. Web sites may combine resources and references from more than one municipality, and it may not be clear where these are physically located, or how one is to find them in real space. Organizations may become members of more than one geographic community, through multiple references or links. Organizations may decide to move their home location from municipality to municipality, from ISP to ISP, or even from country to country.

Place and geographic community will continue to be one of the defining elements of identity, and the absence of this information will introduce social and communication ambiguities. If one receives an e-mail from Jean_Thibeault@mail.com, the question will naturally surface: but where is Jean? The Jean of Victoriaville is not the same person in our imagination as the Jean from Paris. In this respect, it will be interesting to see if e-mail addresses evolve to allow place markers, and whether these place markers will be local or national or some combination (for example, Jean_Thibeault@Victoriaville.Quebec.Ca). The inclusion of photographs of groups of people and of buildings and natural landmarks in web sites can be interpreted in much the same way, as information that is there to remind us that real people in real places created this site. People and places are being represented in cyberspace in ways which attempt to render this space human, located and tangible.

Finally, although our analysis has centred on the organizations and communities which we have seen on the Internet, it will also be instructive to examine which organizations and localities are not present on the Web, or represented only to a minor degree. Some organizations and places may not want to be seen: for example, one can easily imagine that some traditional communities may not agree with the very notion of the Internet, and would certainly not want their communities to be represented on it. In an interview with a member of a community organization, the person indicated that since the core values of the organization were human contact and face-to-face communication, they were hesitant about using the Internet because of a concern that these values and practices could be undermined. It could be instructive to seek out organizations and communities which resist naming or describing themselves on the Web, and to seek to identify any reasons for this.

Indeed, such issues point to an uneasy relationship that we see developing between geographical communities and the Internet. Centuries of practice and legislation have codified the relationship between place, citizens, local organizations, and local government. Geographic identity will surely continue to be a strong orientating force. However, the Web introduces a new freedom of association between communities, and encourages new actors (not just elected officials) to create and project unofficial representations of those communities. The governing bodies that exist for physical communities do not control this new information space. Small community groups can claim a different visual and symbolic space on the Web than that which may be occupied by local government. Groups and institutions could band together and claim that they provide the most legitimate and accurate information about their community. The example that we gave of the Basques region indicates that some communities may symbolically expand and augment their importance in cyberspace. In other cases, organizations may individually stake out a claim in cyberspace, and exercise their independence, as we observed in Victoriaville, Quebec. Still others will co-ordinate their actions through community or civic networks. We will surely witness new structures appearing on the Web which are at the intersection of the persistence of place-based social structures and identities, and the desire to create new relationships and identities.

Notes

1. The authors are grateful for research project funding by the Social Sciences and Humanities Research Council of Canada (410–99–1102). This is a rewritten version of two articles which first appeared in French: Andrée Fortin and Duncan Sanderson (1999), 'Espace social, communautaire et virtuel: continuités et discontinuités', *Le Géographe canadien*, 43(2): 184–90; and Andrée Fortin and Duncan Sanderson (2000), 'Les dynamiques communautaires et territoriales derrière la page', in D. Lafontaine and N. Thivièrge (eds), *Le Développement et l'aménagement des régions fragiles à l'ère des mutations globales: nouveaux modèles, nouvelles cultures de coopération* (Rimonski, Quebec: GRIDEQ/GRIR), pp. 135–49. The authors would like to thank Sally Munt for her helpful editorial comments.
2. In a research project sponsored by British Telecommunications, Duncan Sanderson (1997) examined a number of community networks in the UK and several UK municipal web sites.
3. An example of a virtual community can be found at
   http://community.s-one.net.sg/
   All web addresses given were active as of May 1999.
4. For more information on community networks, one could consult
   http://www.communities.org.uk/
   or Schuler (1996), or Casapulla *et al.* (1998).
5. This is not just hypothetical. The city of Lachute had its site hosted by an organization in another city:
   http://www.mtl.net/solidarite/lachute/lachute2.htm

Bibliography

Beaudry, Raymond and Dionne, Hugues (1996) 'Vivre quelque part comme agir subversif: les solidarités territoriales', *Recherches sociographiques*, 37(3): 537–57.

Casapulla, G., De Cindio, Fiorella, Gentile, Oliverio and Sonnante, Leonardo (1998) 'A citizen-driven civic network as stimulating context for designing on-line public services', in R. Chatfield, S. Kuhn, M. Muller (eds), *PDC '98 Proceedings of the Participatory Design Conference*, Seattle, November, pp. 65–74.

Fernback, J. (1999) 'There is a there there: notes toward a definition of cybercommunity', in S. Jones (ed.), *Doing Internet Research. Critical Issues and Methods for Examining the Net* (Thousand Oaks, CA: Sage), pp. 203–20.

Fortin, A. (1995) 'L'ancrage improbable de l'international dans le régional: la "musique actuelle" à Victoriaville', in F. Harvey and A. Fortin (eds), *La Nouvelle Culture régionale* (Quebec: Institut Québécois de Recherche sur la Culture), pp. 155–96.

Giddens, A. (1991) *Modernity and Self-Identity. Self and Society in the Late Modern Age* (Stanford: Stanford University Press).

Guédon, J.-C. (1996) *La Planète cyber. Internet et cyberespace* (Paris: Gallimard).

Habermas, J. (1979) *Communication and the Evolution of Society* (Boston: Beacon Press).

Lefebvre, A. and Tremblay, G. (eds) 1998 *Autoroutes de l'information et dynamiques territoriales* (Sainte-Foy and Toulouse: Presses de l'Université du Québec and Presses Universitaires du Mirail).

Ninacs, W. (1993) 'The Bois-Francs experience: reflections on two decades of community development', in E. Shragge (ed.), *Community Economic Development: In Search of Empowerment* (Montreal: Black Rose Books), pp. 93–114.

Rheingold, H. (1995) *The Virtual Community: Finding Connections in a Computerised World* (London: Minerva).

Sanderson, D. (1997) *Assumptions and Potential Issues Related to Community Networks and Current and Near-Term Internet Technologies* (Ipswich: Report to British Telecommunications, November).

Schuler, D. (1996) *New Community Networks: Wired for Change* (Reading, MA: Addison-Wesley).

Taylor, C. (1992) *Multiculturalism and 'The politics of recognition'* (Princeton: Princeton University Press).

Tsagarousianou, R., Tambini, D., and Bryan, C. (eds) (1998) *Cyberdemocracy: Technology, Cities, and Civic Networks* (London: Routledge).

13

In the company of strangers

Mobile phones and the conception of space

SUSSEX TECHNOLOGY GROUP

We are in the presence of something like a mutation in built space itself ... We ourselves, the human subjects who happen to inhabit this new space, have not kept pace with that evolution ... We do not yet possess the perceptual equipment to match this new hyperspace ...

(Jameson, 1984: 81)

Introduction

Mobile phones link us together while we are apart. They join, in virtual communion, workers with workplaces, children with parents, lovers with lovers, friends with friends and families with each other. The mobile phone is a significant object; it is a guarantee of connection in (and to) the dislocated social world of modernity; a world in which, as Anthony Giddens points out, we increasingly 'make ourselves available' to others at a distance (Giddens, 1993: 184). But how do we use mobiles? Are they perceived as machines for public use, or as devices for private talk in the company of strangers?

Pilot research concerning users' perceptions of the mobile phone was undertaken in Brighton, UK, at various times of the day and at different public locations in the summer of 1996. The aim of the research was to identify social and cultural issues emerging around the use and ownership of mobile phones at a transitional period in the technology's uptake. The research was conducted by the Sussex Technology Group[1] based at the University of Sussex, via a series of forty recorded interviews with locals and visitors to the town, all of whom were using or visibly displaying a mobile phone. Interview questions were intended to allow phone users to define the significance of this particular

technology within their everyday lives. Although the interview questions
reflected the research group's tentative foci, two things became apparent: first,
that a diversity of competing claims and discourses was in circulation around
the object of the mobile phone, and, second, that these multiple discourses
reflected a preoccupation among users with the tactics and practice of space.

In the period during which the research was completed approximately 12.5
per cent of the UK population had mobile phones. Even at that time
penetration was rising rapidly and growth was expected to continue.[2] By
winter 2000, the expected growth rate had been exceeded and four in ten
people in the UK owned a mobile phone.[3] Mobile telephony has become an
established feature of everyday life. Our sense, however, looking back on this
research, is that many of the questions and concerns raised in the original study
in the transitional period of adoption remain relevant — and largely
unanswered — today. We hope therefore that this picture of the practices of
early users might contribute to a developing body of research work focusing
on the cultural context of mobile communications.

Our intention was to define emerging issues around practices of use and
their possible implications, rather than offering quantitative assessments of
mobile phone use. Mobile phone use adds up to more than caller, telephone,
receiver, physical environment. It includes the cultural space in which use is
embedded. Communicating in the company of strangers can, after all, be a
symbol of status, an annoyance, or an anxiety; it can be something to be
carelessly indulged in, or something to be carefully managed.

Mapping spatial practices

Distinct zones of technological action and appropriation, each reflecting
different spatial awarenesses on the part of users, emerged in the interviews.
We characterized these zones as:

- performative space
- public/private space
- physical space
- psychological space

This paper treats each of these divisions in turn. It should, however, be noted
that these spaces cannot be entirely separated out from one another; the
existence of each is dependent on its interrelationship with the others. Moving
from the performative space to the psychological, we are zooming in on
different aspects of the practice of use, moving from the most external to the

most internal of socio-cultural processes. While recognizing the interconnection of these processes at all levels, we have also found it useful to define each modality of use as follows:

Performative space

Performative space, the space in which one displays oneself as 'a user', is theorized as a way of presenting a 'just-in-time lifestyle' which might also be understood to create a mechanism of inclusion/exclusion (a division between high-technology 'haves' and 'have-nots'). Here we were influenced by Erving Goffman's (1990) theories of the presentation of self. Performative space also acts as a limit point in the study. A problem, given that our research considered public use and was conducted around streets, beaches, promenades, cafés and railway stations, was that invisible users choosing not to display their mobile phones were difficult to spot and are not well represented in our survey. This could account for a bias in favour of male interviewees in the study – one conclusion we reached very early on was that women do not (currently at least) display phones in the same way that men do. Not only use, but use practices (i.e. the hip-holster versus the handbag) are gendered.

Public/private space

The space mapped out here relates to the blurring of what has been addressed traditionally as public/private space. It is suggested that Hannah Arendt's conception of private *intimacy* as an essential counterpart to public visibility might usefully interrogate tactics of use and help explore the manner in which – and the degree to which – the mobile phone can allow the intimate to recolonize arenas of publicity in new ways. Arendt's necessary 'reliable hiding place from the public world' (Arendt, 1989: 71) becomes peculiarly virtual.

Physical space

Physical space plays a particularly interesting role in the study given the specificities of Brighton itself as a location. This modality of mobile phone use is related to the spaces of Brighton beach and the meanings which have accrued around Brighton as a seaside holiday resort and liminal space (Shields, 1991). Mobility is self-evidently part of the technology under consideration, but it does not follow that the technology is therefore dislocated from its embedded use, which must be conditioned, to some extent, by the physical location which acts as a 'back-drop'.

Psychological space

The psychological space is perhaps the most jealously guarded by users: questions regarding the psychological impacts of the technology provoked a defensive set of responses. 'Dependency' upon the mobile phone was something users in our study strenuously denied. This defensiveness – or even hostility – could be contextualized via an examination of the 'masculine' cultural ideals of self-sufficiency. Briefly considering Baudrillard's (1993) theory of the 'revenge of the object', we suggest that, paradoxically, the physical portability of the mobile phone may result in a lessening of internal or psychological mobility; as one interviewee, nervously joking that his head is 'glued to the phone',[4] suggests.

The performative space

A: 'I'm not just a man with a mobile phone.'[5]

Do mobile phones – the visible possession of a phone, the using of a phone, the wearing of a phone – say something about the people using them? Our research suggests that mobile phones are implicated in the presentation of a self. First, interviewees were aware of their own performance as mobile users. They were aware that to use the phone to communicate with people at a distance is also to communicate something to the people in the immediate physical locale. There are those who bask in the visual and aural ambience of phone use.

The display of self

Most of those we talked to explicitly denied that the phone was a part of their image. This denial was also articulated less directly through declared strategies of technological indifference; users often claimed they did not 'choose' their phones, they simply 'bought' the most sensible one. As they said: 'It's just a phone'.[6] One interviewee claimed he was 'forced' to buy his phone. Some stressed that their technology choices are not about enthusiasm, but practicality. Others declared that the phone is about work (where again the stress is on the functional) and was not bought for the pleasure of ownership itself.

In practice, we observed something slightly different. Many of our male interviewees wore their phones visibly. They carried them either in their hands or on their belts, or left them lying on café tables, often prominently. These were all public announcements of ownership. This kind of visible display appeared to be gendered. We had problems finding women phone-owners, when they were not visibly using their phones.

Talk itself also matters in the display of self in the local setting (the setting of the taking and making of calls from the mobile, as opposed to the direct communication between caller and receiver), even if it is ostensibly not 'directed' there, but is rather ambient. Many of those interviewed thought that other people listened in when they made calls — some admitting they did this themselves. What is said then, as well as what is done, is regarded as part of 'being on display' when the mobile is used publicly.

Talk might be regarded as less important in terms of self-presentation *in situ*, hence a number of interviewees claimed indifference — saying they did not care who listened in. On the other hand, a significant chunk of interviewees apparently self-censor their own calls, explaining that they only leave 'messages', talk about 'business', make particular kinds of calls which are in general unrevealing. They also suggest that calling at all in some places, such as restaurants, will expose them as acting inappropriately.

Other people

The ways in which interviewees understood display to function appeared to come less from a consideration of their own experiences as users — although this was largely what they were asked to reflect on — and more in response to their experience of 'other' users, real and imagined. In particular, everyone we interviewed, in different ways, presented their own use and ownership of a mobile as standing in contrast to the spectre of a less well-adjusted user — what we could call Mobile Man.

The composite picture of Mobile Man which emerges from these interviews looks something like this: Mobile Man is a man displaying his masculinity. Mobile Man does not use his phone appropriately — he uses it in restaurants, for instance. Nor does he invest in his phone appropriately — he cares about it in the 'wrong' way, for instance as a technological gizmo; it is not 'just a phone'. Mobile Man is an 'old wave user' rather than a modern pragmatic user with the 'correct' investment. And Mobile Man does not display his phone modestly — he might be said to inappropriately over-display it.

In various ways the majority of those interviewed were at pains to ensure that they distance themselves from this stereotype, which they often invoked explicitly. On the other hand, they often also displayed some of the characteristics they repudiated: they displayed their phones on the streets, and they displayed to us their considerable technological competence. How can this conflict be understood? We should like to suggest, first, that the spectre of Mobile Man rules out for many of our interviewees the notion that mobile phone technology itself could enhance their prestige. They reject suggestions that the mobile could be adopted as a part of their image. This would be to come too close to Mobile Man, whom they renounce.

Second, most of those we interviewed suggested they believed that mobile phone ownership reflects upon them very differently 'these days'. Mobile Man is a figure from 'the past'. As a user said: 'Two years ago people used to look at me really funny.'[7] Mobile Man certainly exists as a mythical construct for these users; they defined their use in contrast to him. It used to be peculiar and possibly 'nerdy' to own and use a phone; now it is to be regarded as 'normal'.

This transition – and some of its implications – is clear when responses to a different set of questions are considered. The implications of mobile ownership were seen in a different light when the direction switched from questions about how/whether the technology might be displayed, to questions about its use. Here responses were far more expansive, and less defensive. For our interviewees, it is not style *per se* but lifestyle which is displayed (and displayed positively) by carrying/using a mobile. In our interviews they presented themselves to us as people who need to juggle busy, full lives: their lives, they imply, *warrant* phones. Their phones and their phone calls are statements that they are people-in-demand, that they live their lives at a certain speed. Technology returns here, not as object – the phone itself – but as speed. What is being valorized, displayed, using the mobile phone, is a just-in-time lifestyle.

Finally, we should like to suggest that the mobile – which might once have been about a display of technological edgemanship – is beginning to be socially inclusive. We were told by our respondents that phone ownership is now normal, acceptable, just fine:

A: 'It's not a novelty any more. Everybody's got them.'
Q: 'What reaction do you get when you use the mobile phone?'
A: 'To be honest, all my friends have got mobiles now. It's not a novelty.'[8]

Within this discourse 'everybody' is an apparent term of inclusion which nevertheless operates against an excluded other. Many of our interviewees recognize that mobile use is still relative. As a woman user who is also a care worker pointed out, what seems normal – no longer about display to 'haves' on the inside – may be precisely about display to 'have-nots' on the outside. Her comment is about her own office:

Q: 'And do you think it's part of your image?'
A: 'Yeah, I mean in the office I'm sort of, you know, everybody's got them anyway. But maybe outside ... I work as a youth worker, the kids probably think "Whoa, look – she's got her mobile phone, she's got her switch card". Ehm, yes, so maybe it is a part of my image.'[9]

Perhaps being seen with a mobile, therefore, might be said to be partly about displaying membership of a network of inclusion, and partly also about displaying a technologically enhanced quality of life, rather than about showing off a technological competence. Post-Mobile Man has gone beyond a simple display of ownership; although he still needs the phone as a symbol of that going-beyond – hence the interviewee, encountered on Brighton beach, who explained to us that he 'was not just a man with a mobile phone'[10] – even as he fiddled with the one he held in his hand.

Private/public space

Why do so many people choose to speak loudly in public by means of a telecommunications device? And why do some people claim they use their mobile for that most private of talk – sex-talk? The mobile phone places actions conventionally banished into the sphere of the intimate and private realm back into the realm of the public. Mobile phone users therefore have to – or choose to – negotiate speech acts in a sphere which is not clearly 'private' but which might not be 'public' either. In addition, in our research mobile phone users often blurred another related distinction, drawing no clear line between private and business calls. The mobile phone has implications for theories of the public and private sphere and for our understanding of how the shift between public and private is negotiated.

Appropriation – or the individual's effort of self-creation

Many of our interviewees reacted defensively regarding the purpose of their phone purchase – underlining its business use and character, when it soon became clear as the interview progressed that the main use could be characterized as private:

Q: 'So, why did you buy your phone in the first place?'
A: 'For business, I need to call people ...'
Q: 'And ... who do you call most often?'
A: 'Oahh ... probably my girlfriend to be honest.'[11]

Given the history of the mobile phone and its original promotion as a business tool – used overwhelmingly by business men in public arenas – it does not come as a big surprise that this discourse still throws shadows on how people think about the proper or prescribed use of mobiles. However, private usage is increasingly important and what is considered 'proper' might be changing. The question is how the mobile is making this transition into the everyday. How is it being appropriated as an object of consumption? Roger Silverstone and Eric Hirsch suggest that appropriation can be central to an individual's or a household's effort at self-creation: defining and distinguishing the individual or the household from what is outside, and allying those within a household to each other:

> An object – a technology, a message – is appropriated at the point at which it is sold, at the point at which it leaves the world of the commodity and the generalised system of equivalence and exchange, and it is taken possession of by an individual or households and owned. It is through their appropriation that artefacts become authentic (commodities become objects) and achieve significance.
>
> (Silverstone and Hirsch, 1992: 21)

As the phone becomes appropriated, as people make the mobile their own in efforts of self-creation, the two categories of use – private and public – are becoming indistinguishable for mobile phone users. The following response is representative:

Q: 'Who do you call most frequently?'
A: 'Ahh, it's probably, (pause) pfff, probably, (pause) work and friends. I couldn't distinguish between the two, so it's both ...'[12]

By virtue of the mobile phone, the public sphere is infiltrated by private talk. In this case, though, the public sphere cannot be understood in the sense of a Classical Greek understanding of speaking out and to another, or even in a Habermasian sense of the public sphere. Rather, mobile phone talk infiltrates a sphere thought of as public with matters of the private. We suggest the increasing appropriation of the mobile for private purposes blows private talk-bubbles into a public world.

Sex-talk and other 'deviations'

Some of our respondents stressed that they use their mobile not only for business or for private conversation but also for phone-sex:

Q: 'Who do you call most frequently?'
A: 'Him!' (Gestures at boyfriend at the table)
Q: 'And where do you use it …'
A: 'Ahmmh … in the car.'
Q: 'Do you think people listen to you when you're making your calls?'
A: 'Ahhmmhh … it would be interesting if, if they did, so – yeah, possibly' (laughs).
Q: 'And what kind of calls do you get mostly —'
A: (interrupts question) 'Phone-sex!'[13]

There are a number of issues raised by this interview sample, which we would like to consider in the light of Hannah Arendt's *The Public and the Private Realm* (first published 1958). Here, Arendt discusses the home as an essential 'hiding place':

> The four walls of one's private property offer the only reliable hiding place from the common public world, not only from the common public world, not only from everything that goes on in it but also from its very publicity, from being seen and being heard. A life spent entirely in public, in the presence of others, becomes, as we should say, shallow.
>
> (Arendt, 1989: 71)

However, Arendt also discusses the role of the presence of others, 'the formality of the public constituted by one's peers', in the production of what she calls 'excellence' (*ibid.*: 49). This paradox – between the necessity of the public, and the need for the private or intimate sphere – seems very relevant in thinking through the dynamic involved in mobile phones and intimate talk of all kinds.

When using a mobile phone outside the home, we definitely – and consciously – leave the only reliable hiding place from the common public world behind. We're left with the mobile phone as a less reliable hiding place – in which we retain a certain sense of the possibility of intimate contact, but in which we also have to assume the possibility of being overheard by strangers. When performing in public spaces we are individuals who are private (in our conversation), and public (due to our physical presence) at the same time. We are, in other words, bringing private issues under public scrutiny. Here then is the possibility of 'excellence', but also threat of the loss of that intimacy which deepens our lives, which ensures that they are not, as Arendt puts it, 'shallow'.

The notion that people get pleasure out of intimate talk (and deeds) in public and semi-public places is not new, but the mobile phone can bring in a new dimension. Sex-talk on a mobile is a slightly more unusual form of this kind of exhibitionism. An activity which, in Arendt's words, might attain, through the combination of the feelings of anxiety and pleasure it triggers, an 'excellence' never matched in privacy. Depending on the extent to which we are used to the mobile situation, pleasure may override anxiety and vice versa.

Private and other kinds of business

Q: 'First of all, why did you buy your phone?'
A: 'Ahm, because, ahm, I, because of the job I do. [I travel] around the country and I need to keep in touch with my friends.'
Q: '... and who do you use it [for], what do you use it for most often?'
A: 'Ahhm (laughing), I use it most of the time to call my friends ... my parents ...'[14]

As this research project suggests, the distinction between business and private talk is not only blurred in the ways people subscribe to these categories. We need to distinguish those users who explained that they bought a mobile phone not *for* the job they are doing (that is, for dealing with business matters) but *because* of the job they are involved in (that is, they are often in transit and need to be able to manage domestic tasks from a distance). Although many interviewees classify this kind of use as 'business', we appear to be looking, in fact, at private business:

Q: 'And what kinds of calls do you get mostly?'
A: 'Ahh, just calls of friends saying how you're doing. But it's then sometimes business, you know ... [sorting out] my direct debit and things in Ireland.'[15]

In many of the interviews where our respondents insisted that they use their mobile strictly for business (work) purposes another interesting pattern emerged:

Q: 'Who do you call most frequently?'
A: '... work, work, work ... and work' (laughs).
Q: 'What kinds of call do you mostly receive?'

A: '... business, friends and family, right.'[16]
Q: 'And who do you most frequently call?'
A: 'The office.'
Q: 'And what kind of calls do you mostly receive?'
A: 'Errr, personal calls.'[17]

The importance of private and personal communication surfaces even in those cases where a strong or predominant business use is established. Then, the outgoing calls are business related, but the incoming calls are private. Once again, the private bubble slips across into the public realm.

Finally, the group of people where the distinction between business and private talk seemed most clearly defined was the one which had been given a mobile phone by their employers. Within this group there was a strong sense of surveillance – in that they either received calls from the office or had to report to the office during certain periods of the day:

Q: 'And who do you call most frequently?'
A: 'The office.'
Q: 'And when do you use it?'
A: '(pause, nervous laughter) Usually to tell people where I am. ... When I leave the office I usually call people every second hour just to confirm my whereabouts, yeah.'[18]

Q: 'So why did you buy a mobile phone?'
A: 'It was given to me ... . It was a surplus requirement for the guy I work with ...'
Q: 'Who do you call most frequently on your phone?'
A: 'I have an agent in London ... It's like an office, really.'
Q: 'When is it switched on?'
A: 'So, really, when I'm ... it's like on [during my] free time, but when I'm working I don't want it switched on, because I don't like to be interrupted.'[19]

Private use in these cases was hesitant and sporadic. It appears that being monitored – or perhaps being available for interruption – makes users more conscious of the inscribed business purpose. As a consequence they are more keen to switch the mobile off whenever they can (e.g. after a day's work) rather than using it for private talk. Switching the phone off is one of many tactics employed to avoid business interfering with private matters – the bubble may float both ways.

Just how potentially dominant private tactics really are is demonstrated when the need for business calls declines (change of occupation, or, more dramatically, job loss) but the mobile is still kept on, and is redefined as a tool for private networking:

Q: 'Why did you buy your mobile phone?'
A: 'Ahem, well, I bought one at the time it was ... it was going to be useful for my work. I was selling advertising at the time for a Brighton magazine; so I was moving up to London, but I was gonna carry on and sell it ...'
Q: '[The mobile phone] helped in what way? In your business? ...'
A: 'Not in a business sense, 'cause I'm not doing, I'm not doing that business any more, but in a social, for my social life. It sort of helped from that point of view, because I'm always around, out and about.'[20]

In conclusion, mobile telephony appears to alter perceptions of private and public spheres, of where private talk and business-related talk properly takes place, and how it is validated. To what extent this could contribute to a wider technologically mediated collapse of the private/public dichotomy remains to be seen.

Physical space

Place can be about the public/private divide, it may mean a place inside or outside, a real place or an imagined place, a geographical space or a communication zone, or it may refer to mechanisms of creating space around oneself which criss-cross these divides. We have already suggested that for our interviewees the mobile might work to create a permeable sense of place – a place at once public and private, opaque and transparent, a 'here' and 'there' which also *oscillates* between these states. This sense of place – one which is technologically mediated – is of course to be understood also within the context of a particular location. Brighton itself, the 'real' place where our interviews took place, is also a place on the margin. It is on the periphery as a physical location (a coastal town) as well as on the margin of the 'mainstream' agenda (it is the place of amusement, the 'dirty weekend' town, the gay capital of the UK). Part of this is image rather than reality – but the distinction between the two seems fluid.

To conduct research concerning place of use of a particular technology brings certain questions with it. How far does 'where people are' influence what they say? In the case of Brighton, can the mobile be part of an expression of marginality, as well as one of inclusion? Certainly in the interviews which took place on the beach our interviewees adopted a more relaxed attitude to our research — and in fact more people agreed to be interviewed there than anywhere else. This was in marked contrast to railway station interviews, which were rushed and sometimes terse, despite the fact that at the station people were *waiting*, while on the beach they were *doing* leisure.

Our interviewees certainly perceived phone use — including their own — as located. A number suggested that attitudes towards the mobile were different depending on whether it was being used in a big city or a smaller town. In London, they claimed, mobile phones are hardly noticed 'these days':

Q: 'And what reaction do you get when you use the mobile phone? ... People are just sort of taking it really?'
A: 'I suspect 'cause of the kind of places that I go to, people are used to seeing mobile phones, ... I mean, in the centre of London ...'[21]

Another 'place' people claimed mobiles went unnoticed was the big event. Two specific ones mentioned in the interviews were the Edinburgh Festival[22] and Lesbian and Gay Pride.[23] At these events 'everyone has one' and therefore the mobile becomes invisible by virtue of its own mass. Interviewees, however, felt that in smaller places, and locations with fewer 'cultural activities', mobile phone use was still remarked upon. To some extent carrying a mobile — at least in a place like Brighton — is understood to be read by others as a symbol of 'cosmopolitan' or 'hip' behaviour — even though the interviewees themselves were at pains to suggest that their use is normal to them.

Visual place and aural space

Users were noticeably vague when asked to explain exactly where they used their own phones, although they could offer many accounts of other people's use. Only one person responded with a specific place — the toilet. Others mentioned cars, while the majority simply stated 'Anywhere ... everywhere'.[24] Many stressed that they used the phone while 'on the move'. This indifference about place could be compared with the far more extensive accounts interviewees gave of how they organize an intimate aural space around themselves when using the phone. In the organization of this space the issue of hearing and overhearing emerges as key. We have said that some interviewees do not use the mobile in public at all, generally because they could be overheard. They know, from their own experience of overhearing other people, that calls are in some sense public:

Q: 'Do you think people actually listen to your calls?'
A: 'Yes. ... Because I listen to other people's calls ...'
Q: 'So you're assuming that everyone else does the same?'
A: 'Yeah.'[25]

Some mobile phone users said they tried to control where they make or take calls:

Q: '... and what reactions do you get when you use the phone in public?'
A: '... I try not to be "Loud Person on Mobile Phone" ... if it's on the bus or train I would say I phone them back, or something ... very annoying.'[26]

Another interviewee told us about running out of the supermarket when receiving a call to avoid being seen using the phone and/or being heard talking in public.[27] Users also take control of where and how they receive calls by turning their machines off. Several others discussed mechanisms like the vibrating phone as a means of avoiding calling attention to themselves while remaining connected:

Q: 'What are your reactions to other people's use of the phone? ...'
A: '... the vibrating phone ... which you can put on to switch off and it ... just vibrates in your pocket ... You can take the call or leave it.'[28]

Finally, a different group of users said that the fact they might be overheard did not affect their phone practice. Rather, they use their own understanding of a public/private divide to produce a private space around themselves; for these users their mobile calls are private *despite* being carried out 'in public' because they are simply not addressed to those in the immediate physical location. The company of strangers is in this sense both 'there' and 'not there'; they choose to understand the 'hearing space' the phone creates as private – even though they 'know' it is permeable.

Psychological space

Does the mobile phone control its user, or does the user control it? In considering the psychological space we ask how the mobile phone figures within users' most intensely personal concerns: those of the subjective freedom to act, and the creation of symbolic potency. Our research suggests that users negotiate a trade-off: in purchasing security they are also buying into a minimization of control.

Control or be controlled? This was the final question we asked our respondents. In only one interview was the binary itself directly rejected. In an interview conducted with a German couple, the male partner was the one who responded:

Q: 'Do you control the phone or does the phone control you?'
A: 'Really, both.'[29]

The woman added to this response by stating that her male partner was 'crazy for his handy' (this is German slang for the mobile phone), claiming 'he couldn't live without it'. Her partner was led to interject 'all right, all *right*', as if to terminate these accusations of an 'un-masculine' dependency on an object. This – potentially gendered – use of the mobile phone is also clearly illustrated in the responses of one male interviewee:

A: 'It's my girlfriend's, but I did buy it for her ...'
Q: 'And when you bought it for her why did you choose it?'
A: 'Because she is bloody hard to find (laughs) ... So I can always get hold of her.'[30]

In this case, the mobile had self-consciously been purchased, by the male partner, with the aim of increasing the accountability and control of his female partner. However – although the mobile was 'the girlfriend's' it was (at least temporarily) in 'the boyfriend's' possession.

In general, answers to the direct question on control were among the most curt of all responses garnered. They produced anxiety and defensiveness in a number of cases, as respondents either rejected the slant of the question, or clearly struggled (certainly in relation to earlier more articulate comments) to provide an 'acceptable' response:

Q: 'Does it control you or do you control it?'
A: '... errrmmm, I errr control it, because I've got an answer machine on it ... so that ... – it helps.'[31]

Interviewees were noticeably hesitant:

A: 'Itssss ... I got rid of it and found that I needed it, so, ah, possibly a bit, a bit of both really ... just ... I *do* need it from time to time.'[32]

The first example illustrates the pattern of assertion followed by backtracking: I control my mobile – why? – because I've got an answering machine. And what does that do? – it helps. The implication is not that the user controls his mobile, but rather that he is 'helped' by the addition of an answerphone in his ongoing struggle to manage the demands made via the mobile phone. But 'help' is not always enough. In answer to the question, 'Do you sometimes feel dependent on your phone?', this interviewee responded by showing an unusual acceptance of dependency – 'Yes, sometimes'.

In some cases, the issue of control was perceived as a financial issue:

> A: 'I am in control of the phone ... I have the lowest, lowest bills ever ...
> of anyone in the world ... the worst customer that Vodaphone has.
> One of my bills for a month, on my outgoing calls, is £2.50.'[33]

This user evidently equates 'control' with imposing strict limits on his outgoing calls. He is also careful to switch off the phone when he is working, 'because I don't like being interrupted'.

These brief examples imply that the mobile works ambivalently, rendering the subject available within networks of emotional support and contact, but also opening up the continued possibility of critical scrutiny and surveillance:

> Q: 'Has the mobile phone had unexpected drawbacks or benefits for you?'
> A: 'It makes me feel secure.'[34]

The 'object weight of communication' implied by the mobile has to be read through the individual's psychological projections of its significance. The mobile can play the part of a technological *injunction* ('you will never ignore my demands upon you, you will never be free of my intrusion') as much as a technological *conjunction* ('you will never be outside the network of always-immediately-available presence, you will always be able to reach me').

The ambivalence of the mobile phone could be read as an example of Baudrillard's (1993) 'revenge of the object', in which the object confronts the subject as something always enigmatic and indeterminate, something which the subject attempts to know/seduce/use. The revenge of the mobile phone consists of the ruses of mobility, users can be pinned down and made immobile. The 'lightness' of the mobile, which sells itself as a practical and portable tool, is always emphasized. But this masks both the object weight of communication and the weight of self-responsibility and moral obligation which the phone can offer to its users.

What we have is a discursively framed zone in which the subject will pursue feelings of security and in which the issue of a controlling or controlled technology is likely to threaten this desired (or partially achieved) security.

Again the play between security and control has a bearing on negotiating subjectivity:

Q: 'How often do you use it [your mobile phone]?'
A: '... Well, Janie's suggested that I could have it [the mobile] surgically removed from the side of my head.'[35]

In a scenario where self-sufficiency is the ideal, and where the self is supposed to act as a source of its own ground, value and destination, the trope of dependency or addiction becomes the fault-line which reveals the impossibility of achieving any kind of pristine subjectivity.

Conclusion

In this study we have aimed to locate negotiations which appear in users' perceptions of the mobile phone: for example, negotiations over 'old yuppie' versus 'new normal' usage, or 'public' versus 'private' call-types. We conclude that the central metaphor which emerged from users' comments was that of space. The preoccupation with space and its metaphors (reflected in the manner in which we have structured the paper) certainly occurs at almost every level of mobile use and perception, from public performativity through to intensely private practices in space.

The contradictory dimensions of the mobile – the manner in which it brings previously 'hidden' aspects of private communication into the visible and public spaces of the street – appeared to produce anxiety in a number of respondents. One interviewee recalled the first time that his mobile went off:

A: 'I was in the middle of the supermarket when it started ringing and I just sort of went into a panic and I dropped my purse, just ran out and I was really flushing, really embarrassed and I was really conscious of being in public and using this ...'[36]

Embarrassment, inhibition, ostentation and enjoyment are 'structures of feeling'[37] which often accompany mobile phone use. These are all emotional states which might be said to correlate with the individual's perception that s/he is breaking a social rule. Display, and feelings of inhibition or self-censorship, therefore, can be regarded as two sides of the same coin.

The focus on space and spatial metaphors, through which many of these issues are articulated, is to be expected, given that the mobile disrupts established socially defined boundaries and regulations concerning the use of space. Talking to a lover or even a work colleague while in the company of strangers can be disconcerting. New forms of social conduct and regulatory mechanisms (initially at the level of individual conduct, and then also through increasing social sanctions) can be expected to evolve in order to 'contain' the technological challenges to public/private divisions presented by mobile telephony.

Notes

1. Caroline Bassett, Liz Cameron, Maren Hartmann, Matthew Hills, Irmi Karl, Ben Morgan and Bridgette Wessels.
2. Figures from the 1996 Mobile Phone Report, quoted in the *Financial Times*, 15 October 1996.
3. *The Guardian*, 6 January 2000.
4. Interview 8, Friday, 12 July 1996. All subsequent dates are also in 1996.
5. Interview 5, Friday, 12 July.
6. Interview 3, Saturday, 13 July.
7. Interview 7, Saturday, 13 July.
8. *Ibid*.
9. *Ibid*.
10. Interview 5, Friday, 12 July.
11. Interview 4, Friday, 12 July.
12. Interview 5, Saturday, 13 July.
13. Interview 2, Friday, 12 July.
14. Interview 3, Friday, 12 July.
15. *Ibid*.
16. Interview 6, Saturday, 13 July (our translation).
17. Interview 1, Friday, 12 July.
18. *Ibid*.
19. Interview 7, Friday, 12 July.
20. Interview 8, Friday, 12 July.
21. Interview 7, Friday, 12 July.
22. *Ibid*.
23. Interview 8, Friday, 12 July.
24. Interview 1, Friday, 12 July.
25. Interview 8, Friday, 12 July.
26. Interview 5, Friday, 12 July.
27. Interview 8, Friday, 12 July.
28. Interview 3, Saturday, 13 July.
29. Interview 2, Saturday, 13 July (our translation).
30. Interview 6, Friday, 12 July.
31. Interview 1, Friday, 12 July.

32. Interview 2, Friday, 12 July.
33. Interview 7, Friday, 12 July.
34. Interview 1, Saturday, 13 July.
35. Interview 8, Friday, 12 July.
36. *Ibid.*
37. To appropriate Williams (1961), p. 64.

Bibliography

Arendt, H. (1989) *The Public and the Private Realm* (1958), reprinted in *The Human Condition* (Chicago and London: University of Chicago Press).

Baudrillard, J. (1993) *The Transparency of Evil: Essays on Extreme Phenomena* (London: Verso).

Giddens, A. (1993), in P. Cassell (ed.), *The Giddens Reader* (Basingstoke: Macmillan).

Goffman, E. (1990) *The Presentation of Self in Everyday Life* (London: Penguin) (first published 1959).

Jameson, F. (1984) 'Postmodernism, or the cultural logic of late capitalism', *New Left Review*, 146: 81–4.

Shields, R. (1991) *Places on the Margin – Alternative Geographies of Modernity* (London and New York: Routledge).

Silverstone, R. and Hirsch, E. (eds) (1992) *Consuming Technologies – Media and Information in Domestic Spaces* (London and New York: Routledge).

Williams, R. (1961) *The Long Revolution* (London: Pelican).

14

Playing with Lara in virtual space

KATE O'RIORDAN

Introduction

Computer games have become part of the cultural practice of a wide range of social groups and although the many environments in which they are played remain socially stratified, this chapter relates specifically to their use in domestic space. I will discuss the traditional evaluation of computer game space as a male-dominated realm, and suggest that this assumption requires some revision. I intend to explore how computer game playing is a transformative process which offers identifications for a plurality of subject positions, sometimes beyond gender binaries. The main aim of the chapter, then, is to articulate the relationship between the player and the game, concentrating on the categories of subjectivity and identity. The technologies of gaming are significant sites of socialization which offer material interpellation to the subject. I will use two metaphorical constructs to articulate the relationship between the player and the game: symbiosis and the cyborg, demonstrated through a case study of specific game material, Lara Croft©.

I deal specifically in this discussion with console games, played in a domestic environment and represented on a television screen, for example, PlayStation® and Nintendo 64®. Although these game consoles are often referred to as media for video games, this is a misleading association. The games consoles are computers and the appearance of graphics on the television screen does not relate game material significantly to video (although I will mention some of the formal connections below). These types of game remain in the realm of computing and to refer to them as video games decontextualizes them. In this construction, the element which differentiates them from other media is the physical involvement demanded by the game. This involvement is unlike either television viewing or the consumption of other traditional off-line media, which demand a psychic and discursive involvement with the content, but limit physical involvement to the form of the media. For example, when I view television I can physically change channels but I cannot change the production of an image within the channel. Through the methods outlined, I will offer an interpretation of game space which reflects upon the ontology of playing.

Games: historical and cultural contexts

Spacewar was the first computer game, and was developed at the Massachusetts Institute of Technology in 1962. This program required the use of large and expensive hardware and was never developed for popular use. The first games to enter into the public domain were *Pong* (1973) and *Space Invaders* (1976), which really mark the emergence of computer games as a form of popular culture. As well as these arcade games, in 1975 the Atari Corporation (USA) developed a games console for the home. Home *Pong* sold very successfully but it is *Pac Man* (1982) which has become an enduring cultural icon.

Although the 1960s and 1970s had seen developments in the games industry, particularly in the public realm of arcade games, domestic computer games did not begin to enter the mainstream until the 1980s when the industry developed and diversified. This coincided with such factors as acclimatization to computer use, an increase in economic viability, decreasing hardware size and an increasing leisure market. Games consoles which could be used to play many different games at home were developed; hand-held games like the *Game Boy* and the *Game and Watch* became relatively cheap and accessible to consumers all over the world. The 1980s and 1990s have seen the emergence of a global market in console games, which are played by a wide variety of social groups on an everyday basis.

The computer game in the late 1990s offers a filmic, photo-realistic world which presents the opportunity for the player to take on the character of choice and make identifications in the negotiation of imaginary worlds. These opportunities are constrained, however, by the limitations of the cultural values they reflect. Computer games, like many other media texts, reproduce cultural narratives about colonialization, exploration, domination and aggression. Computer game playing and production are historically gendered: the public nature of the video/leisure arcade, the cinema lobby, pubs, bars and clubs has encouraged a male domination of this activity. As in other public leisure spaces, a male presence has predominated. The inception period of the 1960s and 1970s is traditionally viewed as having been dominated by masculine user-based practices, although in the 1980s and 1990s the gender imbalance of use has become somewhat less polarized. The creation of computer games is also seen as male dominated. The traditional educational segregation in the West of 'feminized' arts and humanities and 'masculinized' sciences has created, through the conflation of sex and gender, a working public that predominantly employs men in the engineering and programming sectors which produce ICTs (information and communication technologies).

However, cultural values do change; public space is not as male dominated as has been traditionally assumed and with the miniaturization of technologies, gaming has become a predominantly domestic occupation which is conversely, historically and discursively assumed to be the location of the feminine. This relocation of games to the domestic sphere destabilizes any assumptions drawn from studies of public/private, masculine/feminine space. Programming departments now employ women, and academic and industrial segregation has seen organizational shifts. High levels of photo-realism have introduced artistic and design-based elements into game production. It is still true of computer games that they largely reproduce the cultural context of male, white and heterosexual ideologies, which remain entrenched in narratives of violence, domination, quest and colonialism. The feminine is largely represented as an object of reward or rescue, or as a titillating vehicle employed as a hook for the plot of the game. However, these generalizations must be further qualified by both the shift in location from public to domestic and a consideration of the different games markets. Games aimed specifically at young children, for example, deploy colour and music as major features, although games directed at young men still feature heavy armoury, darkness and gore.

However, design companies like Purple Moon, founded by Brenda Laurel (1991), have researched extensively into the ways that girls play.[1] After two and a half years of research Purple Moon started developing games that would appeal to girl gamers and have so far enjoyed commercial success. Their web page provides a 'safe space' for girls (although anyone can access the pages), in marked contrast to the male-dominated web pages of Games Quest and Gamespot, which promised: 'Kick Some Bot Butt with Epic MegaGames' Latest 3D Killer' in its July 1999 headline.[2] The Purple Moon site and the products associated with it tend, though, to be based on a philosophy that not only defines play as gender differentiated but conflates sex with gender. It is not clear that game *playing*, as opposed to design, is dominated by any gender and I will suggest that games, like other media, offer a multiplicity of identities despite the fact that the culture around them remains relatively masculine.

The shared spaces of television and computer games

The realization of computer games on the television screen is indicative of media convergence. The imaginary space of the screen had been utilized by computer games well before the emergence of digital television, in the literal sense of the technological convergence of traditional programming. The cultural practices of television viewing are also of significance now when we talk about computer games: who watches and when and where are all factors to be considered. Of further significance is the assimilation of computer games into the narrative and images of television, and vice versa. Who uses the television, when and in what modes of viewing are issues of ethnography which are well covered in separate work.[3] In this section I discuss specifically the assimilation of computer games into television narrative and of television narrative into computer games.

The visual space of off-line computer games on the television screen has a close operating relationship to the traditional reception of audio-visual media. The television is an imaginative space, pre-populated with narrative and images. Computer games allow active intervention into this space. I am not reasserting the following binary: television = passive/new media = active; television viewing is both active and interactive in a number of senses. However, computer games operate at different levels of participation, particularly at the physical and material one. This assertion must be qualified by both cultural considerations and the fact that computer games offer a very limited interactivity, in the sense that they are pre-programmed, providing a restricted paradigm of both imagery and narrative.

I wish to emphasize some qualifications before continuing this discussion, because it is important not to accept uncritically a utopian vision of the freedom of computer interactivity. Computer games are partially interactive at present, they can only offer certain freedoms and a qualified experience of entertainment. They are primarily, however, spaces of constraint with clearly defined parameters. Generic market leaders are quest, popular sport and combat scenarios with simplistic plots and linear narratives. The whole games market is too prolific to analyse in depth here, but the following contemporary sample gives an indicator of what leads it. *PlayStation Magazine* (1999) provides reviews, game information and a demonstration disk of forthcoming games among its services. The demonstration disk features *Soul Reaver*, *Rollcage*, *Viva Football*, *Warzone 2100*, *A Bug's Life*, and *All Star Tennis* as its playable games. The names are self-descriptive, apart from *Soul Reaver*, which stars a male-configured ghoul, and *Rollcage*, which is a racing game. Of these, only *All Star Tennis* features any female avatars. The cultural context from which the market emerges is largely being reproduced: popular sport simulations, the theme of war and film merchandising all contribute to traditional, conformist scenarios. Product synthesis comes into play with *A Bug's Life*, aimed at children and rendered from the graphics of a computer-animated film of the same name. This kind of merger has led to the vernacular 'Silliwood' to indicate the convergence between products associated with Silicon Valley and that of Hollywood.

Television is a medium in which games are both closely related and significantly different, in both material and psychological ways. One factor which they both share is the screen, but the spatial barrier between screen and viewer is transformed through game technologies. The screen of the television film or programme is a flat surface which bars the viewer from material interpellation; it only offers a psychic location. The television screen provides a material barrier of glass that informs the discursive symbolism of our notions of viewing: off screen and on screen are seen as entirely distinct. The material barrier of the screen seems proof of the division, and even technologies like the remote control and 3-D glasses have not challenged the distinction between on screen and off screen. Technologies of computer games, however, challenge the material and discursive barrier of the screen because although the material barrier is still there, its meaning is changed through locating the viewer, with a strong identificatory presence, *on* the screen.

In several significant ways, the viewer/participant temporarily inhabits game space. Although there is no 'real' space, there is an imaginative sense of space 'behind' the screen. The significant difference between watching a programme and playing a game is that the viewer of the game interacts with the material on the screen by exerting some control over it. There is a direct effect caused on the screen by the participant. Games are therefore partially interactive spaces and developments in authoring skills have led to some of them being labelled 'interactive cinema' (Friedman, 1995: 77). Through a joystick and control panel, the player controls the actions of the avatar, thus the traditional unfolding of the programme narrative is transformed into a manipulation of the action on screen. The actions of the player determine the actions on screen via a direct physical motor link.

The participant, then, 'inhabits' the screen space in terms of sight, sound, spatial organization and control. The spatial organization of the participant is transferred to that of the game space. The mental process of motion is applied to the game space so that the participants experience moving through a physical space as they are enacting the temporal narrative. The sensory perceptions and physical motion of the body become both divided and extended. The neural sensorium extends to the screen, visualizing an interiority; interaction is not only on the screen, it is visibly below or behind the screen. Screen space has an interiority developed by the use of graphical perspective, and it is this interiority that the player is activating and exploring through a kinaesthetic relationship.

By representing computer games on the television screen through consoles like the PlayStation® by Sony, game space is inserted into the architecture of television. The images are imposed on an imaginary space in which we are culturally acclimatized to viewing images that reflect certain aspects of reality. Spatial arrangement is one of these aspects: it is a feature of screens that a flat surface can reflect the Cartesian perspective of points about a three-dimensional axis, which is the phenomenological experience of real space. We are acclimatized to viewing a representation of space on the television that visually reflects our material belief in three-dimensional space. In computer games a slightly less realistic representation is often presented which occasionally deploys a two-dimensional representation; however, game space offers a reflection of the *experience* of actual space through the ability offered to the player to intervene in this representation. This contrast between the television's reflection of an understanding of space, and the game's reflection of an experience of space, is one of the most significant differences between these media.

The gap between the convincing images of television and the less highly resolved ones of games is one which technological advances are rapidly closing: the instances of two-dimensionality which used to be prolific are deployed less and less as game producers compete with each other to simulate increasingly virtual representations.[4] Despite the diversity of materials available on television, it is a technological space which is widely accepted as reproducing reality: documentary, news, camcorder footage and CCTV images prevail. Computer games join the assembly of television material but they are selected at the point of consumption (like videos, which also share the same commercial outlets), and are widely accepted as fictitious, imaginary play spaces. These texts, whether fictions or simulations of the actual, share the same credible spatial paradigm that is presented by the television screen.

In the same way that the television screen approximates a representation of reality, computer games offer a representation of virtual reality. They are not 'true' virtual reality, which would be totally immersive, but neither are televisual images true off-line reality. Computer games are only partially immersive because of this feature of the screen, which although offering representations of three-dimensionality, is flat. Another significant difference between the experience of television programme images and the images of computer games as they stand is that the player has a physical as well as a psychical relationship to the narrative space. In the mode of television viewing there is no *direct* physical connection between the representations on screen and the viewer.

In the mode of game playing, the player is connected to the narrative space through a handset. This can be a multi-game application with buttons, or can be a dedicated aspect of a particular game. The game *Die Hard Trilogy*, for example, supplies a gun-shaped handset which projects a light and appears to 'kill' figures on the screen. This brings the game experience closer to that of virtual reality, but there still remains the barrier of the screen to the full immersion promised by virtual reality. When viewing television the screen is the material, impermeable barrier which renders the images 'unreal'. When playing, the screen has a psychological semi-permeability which occurs because the player appears to affect the screen space, penetrating the boundaries of the technology with human input.

This psychological and physical intervention into game space connects off-line game playing to other interactive media such as virtual reality, the Internet and on-line games. If television represents the simulacra argued by the post-modern paradigm (Baudrillard, 1981), computer game playing inserts the human agent into the circuit of simulation. The physical continuum between the player and the space of the game reinforces the psychical one to the extent that the experiences represented on the screen are not the same as the vicarious ones of television. The poles of active and passive, represented and received, player and viewer are collapsed into a new paradigm of experience and subjectivity: 'Everywhere ... in which the distinction between these two poles can no longer be maintained, one enters into simulation' (Baudrillard, 1981: 31). Baudrillard's assertion that this collapse in polarity means that everything in the experience of the postmodern is shifted into the realm of representation is destabilized if we consider the relationship between the avatar and player. As I will elaborate through an evaluation of Lara Croft©, the symbolic realm of representation has a material relationship with the consumer through computer games because the identity of the player is required to activate the meaning of the game.

Avatars and symbiosis

The avatar is the player's point of intersection with the narrative of the game and his/her virtual presence in that space as a cyberbody or virtual self. The avatar is the point of entry into the simulation. Avatars, also known as game sprites or iconic representations, come in a variety of forms, with a subsequent variation in behavioural paradigms, perspectives and appearances. The element which is common to most off-line avatars at the time of writing is that they are pre-designed. The player has a choice of different avatars in some games, but is seldom active in the design process. This means that the avatar adds to the constraining factors of game play as well as providing a point of insertion.

This point of insertion can be articulated through the metaphors of symbiosis and the cyborg. Symbiosis infers an organic-to-organic relationship which grants too much agency to the computer. However, it is a useful model which has helped to describe the relationship between player and game:

> It is very hard to describe what it feels like when one is 'lost' inside a computer game precisely because at that moment one's sense of self has been fundamentally transformed. Flowing through a continuous series of decisions made almost automatically, hardly aware of the passage of time, the player forms a symbiotic circuit with the computer, a version of the cyborgian consciousness described by Donna Haraway (1985) in her influential 'Manifesto for Cyborgs'. The computer comes to feel like an organic extension of one's consciousness, and the player may feel like an extension of the computer itself.
>
> (Friedman, 1995: 83)

This material and psychological symbiosis is composed of the continuum between the player holding the controls and the actions of the avatar on screen. It is also created by the immersion experienced by the player while his/her identification is transferred to the game space. Processes of communication with the immediate and actual environment are transferred to the simulated environment.

This relationship has been understood in different ways, as liberatory — 'Today at the end of the twentieth century, many of our children have access to the one to five rooms inside their apartments. Video game technologies expand the space of their imagination' (Cassell and Jenkins, 1999: 265–6) – and as destructive – 'Video games can thus be understood as a paranoiac environment that induces a sense of paranoia by dissolving any distinction between the doer and the viewer' (Robins and Levidow, 1995: 109). These responses point both to the social significance of this site and to its difference from other media. The assertion that these spaces can expand the imagination is an optimistic reaction, which we must qualify by reminding ourselves of the limitations of game space. The judgement of this relationship as 'paranoiac' suggests that this psychological continuum is understood as a disturbing infliction, a notion which I would dispute as simplistically deterministic and technophobic. This assertion is informed by social debates[5] which range over two main areas: content and form. Content involves the already familiar debate about violence in the media, its effects, and censorship. Form refers to whether or not technologies have a propensity for damage in themselves, in fears ranging from eye strain to disorientation or neural damage, epilepsy and strokes. These are fears which are regardless of actual game content but arise from the physical processes of repetitive playing. These latter debates unfortunately arise from a deterministic view which ignores the social relations which structure technological development.

However, Robins and Levidow's definition of games as paranoiac environments emphasizes the significance, impact and proliferation of the relationships between avatar and player in contemporary postmodern experience. The negation of this experience, through the connotations of the term 'paranoiac', denies the imaginative dimension of the subject positions offered to the player. The experience that the consumer has of most media texts is one of material interjection into the form only (turning the pages of books, choosing the video, using fast forward, rewind or changing channels); interjection into the material content of games is a different experience which offers an expansion of space, not a retraction. This symbiotic model ignores the social relations which structure this relationship, and for this reason I will employ a further model which provides us with a way of realigning this paradigm.

The cyborg is a useful model to articulate the relationship between player and avatar: 'A cyborg is a cybernetic organism, a hybrid of machine and organism, a creature of social reality as well as science fiction' (Haraway, 1991: 149). The cyborg has the advantage of implying a relationship between an organism and technology which is much closer to the actual relationship between player and game. It recognizes the game as a static artefact which is only activated by organic agency, highlighting the power that the player has in this relationship, usefully bringing us away from dystopian visions of psychic damage and technological determinism. Although new technologies can provide new sources of agency, they are still structured through human relations. We should embrace this model cautiously in view of the more sinister implications of the word 'cyborg', whilst also seeing how it positively opens up a space to explore the potential freedoms involved in our increasingly enmeshed relationship with developing technologies.

A case study: Lara Croft©

Paradoxically, the most famous current avatar of these game spaces is represented as female: this is Lara Croft©, the avatar of the games *Tomb Raider* (1997), *Tomb Raider II* (1998), *Tomb Raider III* (1999) and *Tomb Raider: The Final Revelation* (forthcoming). Fanzines receive letters which are purportedly written to Lara by gamers. Lara Croft© shares some representational similarities with James Bond and has also been proposed by British government ministers to serve as an iconic 'ambassador' for scientific excellence.[6] Douglas Coupland, a popular writer, claims to be in love with her (Coupland and Ward, 1998), and in a recent survey (Shurville, 1998), 70 per cent of male respondents claimed to be sexually attracted to Lara. Although female contributions to the same survey were few, both heterosexual and lesbian female respondents claimed to identify with Lara. As well as in the mainstream, Lara also appears as a popular figure in the lesbian press.[7] A whole market of commodities has emerged around 'her', including a promised film and an appearance in a high-energy soft drinks advert for Lucozade.

Lara's cultural popularity is an indicator of how far computer games and their imagery have interjected into non-computer-mediated communication, appearing as significant sites of commodification within the symbolic and material processes of representation in the circuit of culture (Hall, 1997). Games and their avatars provide a new point of identification in culture for the consumer. Potentially, different subjective positions can be developed and arguably new kinds of subjectivity may arise through this relationship between player and avatar, within larger domains of representation.

Lara is a group of pixels arranged in a shape which indicates a young woman of twentysomething. The player does not see much of her face and although the angle of view can be changed, it defaults to a point slightly to the rear of Lara (Fig. 14.1). This means that it is her profile from behind that is most

Figure 14.1 Lara Croft[©]. Image supplied courtesy of Core Design Limited. Lara Croft[©] and TM Core Design Limited. All rights reserved.

234   *Kate O'Riordan*

Figure 14.2 Lara Croft©. Image supplied courtesy of Core Design Limited. Lara Croft© and TM Core Design Limited. All rights reserved.

reinforced to the player as a position of identification. During some action in the game a more extended profile is displayed when she goes into a pre-programmed sequence, such as swimming or shooting (Fig. 14.2). The external profile of her entire body is viewed by the player eventually, through the completion of the game narrative. In the advancement through the narrative, the player is rewarded by a developed disclosure of the entire external appearance of Lara.

Lara is represented as wearing minimal clothing: for most of *Tomb Raider III* she wears shorts and a vest, a gun belt and boots, her brown hair usually in a practical long plait. There is a degree of appropriateness and functionality in some scenes: she wears a coat, gloves and trousers in Antarctica, for example. The clothes are always figure-hugging and thus retain the shape of her body image. She is a classic phallic fantasy figure: long legs, large breasts and a small waist. Her physiology is improbable, representing a Barbified caricature, suggesting the possibility of ironic play to enter into any identification with Lara. At the point of reception there is ample opportunity to enjoy Lara as a representation of hegemonic desirability which can be identified either with or against. There is evidence to suggest that heterosexual men and women and lesbians can all read her as desirable.[8] It is not problematic to imagine that any subject position could find her desirable, as she is represented symbolically as the desirable phallic woman: 'the Uzi-toting cyberbabe'.[9] As with any successful mainstream figure, then, Lara provides a wide range of subject identifications which can interpellate the game player.

The features of Lara's visible appearance conform to certain stereotypes: the pin-up figure and the clothing are informed by existing images of intensely heteronormative femininity. Some of her preconfigured movements also strongly connote sexuality, such as the crawl — for this move Lara gets down on her hands and knees and crawls away from the player who is positioned to view her from behind. What makes Lara so resonant of sexuality is that the plot of the game focuses on the player's manipulation of her virtual body. The aim of *Tomb Raider* is to learn how to 'propel' Lara as proficiently as possible.

However, this is not the model of control it might first appear, because the player is also 'Lara' during game play. The rhetoric of gamers indicates the extent to which a partial identification occurs: 'Having fought your way past the thrills of speeding tube trains that bowl you along the track and the pneumatic drill that will certainly have killed you a few times' (*PlayStation Magazine*, 1999: 127). The writer of this review is addressing a *you* who is both Lara and the player. When playing *Tomb Raider*, players often refer to Lara as 'I'. These rhetorical references indicate the partial transfer of subjectivity which can occur. Although the player is positioned as a voyeur by the default perspective which always returns to a point behind Lara, the active relationship between the Lara icon and the player repositions the voyeur as the voyeur/actor. This incorporation of self into avatar while playing renders debates about objectification and stereotyping rather less tenable, because Lara is not entirely an object of control, but rather a process of interaction within the paradigms of the game.

The subjectivity of the player experienced in *Tomb Raider* is surprisingly complex. Several positions are held in tension at once in the process of playing: that of the player, that of Lara and that of the 'player in action'. The 'player in action' is simultaneously Lara Croft in the game world, the self in the game world and the self external to the game world. The self external to the game world cannot be analysed here, because this 'self' is the individual player as well as a conceptual realm. Such analysis would require a more detailed interviewing of players. What we can analyse is the textual representation of Lara in which the player's self is imaginatively inserted, partially transferring self to avatar. Through the partial transference of subjectivity which occurs, neither the player nor Lara's paradigm of behaviour is completely determined. The active role of the player in the *Tomb Raider* games provides a forum for a range of subject positions to be experienced through playing with Lara. One could spend the whole time in the game space headbutting a wall if one so desired (but not much narrative would develop). Lara does not have a discrete identity but neither does the player-as-Lara, and this confusion of the paradigms of identity and narrative allows for some freedom of identification. The continuity between the subject position of the player and the iconic representation of Lara allows for a cyborgian model to be employed in analysing this relationship, as the pixels on the screen have a continuous relationship with the effects of the self of the player. While playing, the body is directly connected to the action on the screen, entering into an affective physical relationship with the programming code. Through the physical and psychological continuum with Lara, the player enters into a symbiotic hybridity which negotiates game space so that the self becomes the self-and-avatar, in a diffuse but distinct relationship between person and machine.

Computer games – a different social space

The model of the cyborg abounds in computer literature, popular culture, science fiction and critical theory. Along with symbiosis, it provides a useful metaphor to articulate the blurring of the boundaries of human identity and technology. As I have explored in the case study above, even in one of the least immersive and paradigmatically constrained models of computer games, the off-line, television console game, the self is projected into the circuit of simulation. Even through the medium of television, game technologies draw upon a more involved relationship with the player, eroding the complete distinction between the medium and the self.

The possibilities for constructing a partial, and always contingent, sense of self in the realms of virtual reality, cyberspace and computer-mediated communication are extensive. By exploring the real-world model of the games console, which has already found its way largely unnoticed into the living room of domestic space, I hope to have illustrated aspects of the complex relationship between the players and images that appear on our screens. The screen-as-mirror can now be physically related to, and a new reflection of self can be played with. The image in the mirror has still been put there by professional designers, but the viewer can enter in a projected guise and temporarily embody it with his/her own self, however gendered. Through these means the closed circuit of simulacra comes to refer to the real – the player. Computer games are significantly different from either imagined narratives, television, or narratives of fiction, because the computer game has physical presence: it provides a prosthesis for embodying the imagination and is an extension of the body, offering a consolidation of embodiment, putting 'you' or 'I' into the game.

The game technologies discussed here are already being superseded (for example, digital video disk, DVD). Interactivity is becoming more entrenched in popular culture, cyborgian practices are being increasingly explored. What this reveals is that between the medium and the consumer is a dynamic which prohibits the analysis of either the medium, the material or the consumer in isolation. The complexity of the relationship between the player and the game destabilizes any easy object/subject formation and questions the polarity between the consumer and the media. Cyberspace is with us in many forms, and game space is the most enduringly popular. Although it is clear that the architecture of such space is not new, the relationship that the consumer has with the material and medium is increasingly different, changing the ways we conceptualize separate domains of self and other. It is clear, then, that different theoretical constructions are required to analyse, rather than observe, the collapses which are occurring.

Acknowledgements

Acknowledgements and thanks are due to Irmi Karl, Dr Sally Munt and Dr Simon Shurville for their generous advice and contributions.

Images supplied courtesy of Core Design Limited. Lara Croft© and TM Core Design Limited. All rights reserved.

Notes

1. Laurel is a researcher, author and software designer of long standing in the industry. Her company web site is www.purple_moon.com (accessed May 1999).
2. www.bigbig.com/gq and www.gamespot.com (accessed May 1999).
3. See, for example, Gauntlett and Hill (1999), Silverstone (1992) and Ang (1991).
4. Exceptions are the popular *Abe* games: *Oddysee* and *Exoddus*.
5. These debates are ongoing but have been returned to specifically in the wake of several news events, most recently the Littleton shootings in Colorado in April 1999. See, for example, 'In the line of fire' by Paul Keegan (1999), pp. 2–3.
6. On the BBC web site, and reported in the mainstream press.
7. She was the 'cover girl' in the June 1999 issue of the magazine *Lesbians on the Loose* (Australia), for example.
8. These groups were the only ones who identified themselves by their sexuality in Simon Shurville's survey, and I don't wish to imply that people who identify with other sexualities are excluded from this.
9. http://news2.thls.bbc.co.uk/hi/english/sci/tech/ newsid%5F225000/225615.stm (accessed July 1999).

Bibliography

Ang, Ien (1991) *Desperately Seeking an Audience* (London: Routledge).

Baudrillard, Jean (1981) *Simulacra and Simulation*, trans. S. F. Glaser, 1994 (Michigan: University of Michigan Press).

Cassell, Justine and Jenkins, Henry (1999) *From Barbie to Mortal Combat: Gender and Computer Games* (Cambridge, MA: MIT Press).

Coupland, Douglas and Ward, K. (1998) *Lara's Book: Lara Croft and the Tomb Raider Phenomenon* (Rocklin, CA: Prima Publishing).

Friedman, Ted (1995) 'Making sense of software: computer games and interactive textuality', in Steven G. Jones (ed.), *Cybersociety: Computer-Mediated Communication and Society* (Thousand Oaks, CA: Sage).

Gauntlett, David and Hill, Annette (1999) *TV Living – Television, Culture and Everyday Life* (London: Routledge).

Hall, S. (1997) *Representation: Cultural Representations and Signifying Practices* (London: Sage/OUP).

Haraway, Donna J. (1985) 'Manifesto for cyborgs: science, technology and socialist feminism in the 1980s', *Socialist Review*, 80: 65–108.

Haraway, Donna J. (1991) *Simians, Cyborgs and Women: The Reinvention of Nature* (London: Free Association Books).

Keegan, Paul (1999) 'In the line of fire', *Guardian*, Tuesday 1 June (UK), pp. 2–3.

Laurel, Brenda (1991) *Computers as Theatre* (Reading, MA: Addison-Wesley).

Lesbians on the Loose (1999), June (Australia), cover page.

PlayStation Magazine (1999), 'Top Secret', 43, March 1999 (UK), p. 127.

Robins, Kevin and Levidow, Les (1995) 'Soldier, cyborg, citizen', in James Brook and Iain Boal (eds), *Resisting the Virtual Life: The Culture and Politics of Information* (San Francisco: City Lights Books).

Shurville, Simon (1998) *Lara Survey* June http://www.gamespot.co.uk.

Silverstone, Roger (ed.) (1992) *Consuming Technologies: Media and Information in Domestic Spaces* (London: Routledge).

15

Personal stereos and the aural reconfiguration of representational space

MICHAEL BULL

Inhabited space transcends geometrical space.

(G. Bachelard, *The Poetics of Space*)

For twenty-five centuries Western knowledge has tried to look upon the world. It has failed to understand that the world is not for beholding. It is for hearing ... Now we must learn to judge a society by its noise.

(J. Attali, *Noise: The Political Economy of Music*)

What? What are you talking about? The Sony Walkman has done more to change human perception than any virtual reality gadget. I can't remember any technological experience since that was quite so wonderful as being able to take music and move it through landscapes and architecture.

(William Gibson, *Time Out*)

This chapter investigates the manner in which personal-stereo users lay claim to the urban spaces that they transitorily inhabit. Since 1979 when personal stereos were introduced to the commercial market by the Sony Corporation, they have become firmly embedded in the social world and are increasingly inscribed in the daily rituals and journeys of millions of people. Personal stereos are distinctive, as they are built and designed to be used on the move. Mobility is inscribed in the personal stereo and thus any analysis should not restrict itself to fixed locations such as the office or the home as other forms of research into the use of communication technologies have often done (Lull, 1990). Indeed the personal stereo, following Baudrillard,[1] might be conceptualized as a form of 'mobile home' in which, for example, the street itself becomes a 'mobile' site of consumption. In effect, personal-stereo use disrupts conventional notions of private and public behaviour and space, thereby raising questions concerning the adequacy of such dichotomous notions. The reordering of the meaning and significance of these concepts is rendered understandable through an analysis of personal-stereo users' capacity to inscribe 'public' space with 'private' meaning. The use of personal stereos thus sheds light upon the meanings that users attach to public and private spaces through the disclosing of an underlying set of assumptions attached to users' sense of their own constitution, volition and social horizon. This, in turn, directs the investigation into the complex nature of the relationship between forms of communication technologies, the constitution of subjective behaviour and the cultural and historical nature of urban culture experienced by personal-stereo users.

The personal stereo is a very direct and powerful form of technological artefact, which re-prioritizes the auditory nature of experience with an unusual immediacy. In the following pages I analyse the nature and meaning of this prioritization of aural experience constituted through the technological artefact of both the personal stereo and recorded 'sound'. In doing so I argue that personal-stereo use changes the nature of the user's cognition, thereby enabling the effective subjective management of a wide range of everyday behaviour. Personal-stereo users manage and organize the flow of experience through the use of their personal stereo and in doing so, their experience of space and place is brought under their control. Personal-stereo users habitually operationalize a variety of behavioural strategies that enable them to successfully prioritize their own experience, personally, inter-personally and geographically through the mediated use of the personal stereo. Personal-stereo users not only manage their flow of thoughts and emotions but also engage in interpersonal strategies in which they control the nature and duration of interaction. For example, personal-stereo use enables the construction of forms of auditized 'looking', whereby users either escape the 'look' of others or engage in strategies of 'looking' without being 'seen'. Personal-stereo use plays an active role in making the urban environment 'what it is' for users. Users can aestheticize urban space, others or their own personal experience at will. The urban spaces of daily habitation thereby become subjectively managed and controlled in a variety of ways through use, thus giving users a sense of empowerment. Importantly, the contingent nature of the everyday and the attendant awareness of risk become mediated and reduced through the structural possibilities of personal-stereo use. In this sense urban experience becomes, in a significant manner, technological experience.

Critical theory and the relational nature of auditory experience

If personal-stereo use aurally reorganizes the experience of space and place of users, then we need to formulate an epistemologically appropriate framework to explain such use. If the world is for hearing, as Attali suggests, then there exists an unexplored gulf between the world according to sound and the world according to sight. Going down the auditory path requires taking a fresh look at what has been written of the senses, technology and everyday experience. Sound has its own distinctive relational qualities: as Berkeley observed, 'sounds are as near to us as our thoughts' (quoted in Rée, 1999: 36). Sound is essentially non-spatial in character, or rather sound engulfs the spatial, thus making the relation between subject and object problematic. Sound inhabits the subject just as the subject might be said to inhabit sound, whereas vision, in contrast to sound, represents distance, the singular, the objectifying (Jay, 1993). Personal-stereo use therefore needs to be situated and articulated through the specific relational qualities attached to sound in space. Critical theorists were aware of the way in which mechanically reproduced sound transforms urban spaces of habitation: 'Loudspeakers installed in the smallest night clubs to amplify the sound until it becomes literally unbearable: everything is to sound like the radio' (Adorno, 1991: 58). Adorno's explanation of the relational qualities of the auditory is useful to our understanding of personal-stereo use, which takes place within a reconstituted and 'privatized' representational space that has even greater immediacy for users than described by Adorno in the 1930s. Adorno makes the point that the club and the radio appear similar, with the club becoming 'like' the radio. Spatial specificity is overlain by an alternative presence, an identity in which the present becomes consumed by the 'far away'. Likewise, in the following account the isolated space inhabited by the individual disappears:

> Even in the cafe, where one wants to roll up into a ball like a porcupine and become aware of one's insignificance, an imposing loudspeaker effaces every trace of private existence. The announcements it blares forth dominate the space of the concert intermissions.
>
> (Kracauer, 1995: 333)

Adorno (1976), Benjamin (1973) and Kracauer (1995) in particular investigated the ambiguous and dialectical nature of cognition in relation to transformed and technologized urban spaces. A close reading of their work demonstrates a nuanced approach to the relationship between experience, technology and culture which has been largely ignored in urban and cultural theory. Adorno questions the relationship of the experiencing subject to representational space through a precise understanding of the role of the auditory. This transformed relational experience is described as 'we-ness'. 'We-ness' describes the ambivalent relationship of subjective experience to representational space and is constituted through forms of communication technologies. As such, Adorno's concept of 'we-ness' can be appropriated in order to adequately understand the experience of personal-stereo users.

States of 'we-ness' can be understood as being built into our reception of polyphonic music, together with other forms of representation and reception from opera, soaps, radio chat shows to news programmes. Everyday life thus undergoes a process of 'de-privatization' which is dialectically related to the notion of 'we-ness'. De-privatization signifies the industrially produced construction of an illusory private realm which confounds traditional notions of private and public. It is in reference to the contradictory nature of the creation of a perfectly private personal sphere by personal-stereo users to which Adorno's following observation appears most relevant:

By circling them, by enveloping them as inherent in the musical phenomenon – and turning them as listeners into participants, it contributes ideologically to the integration which modern society never tires of achieving in reality. It leaves no room for conceptual reflection between itself and the subject, and so it creates an illusion of immediacy in a totally mediated world, of proximity between strangers, the warmth of those who come to feel a chill of unmitigated struggle of all against all.
(Horkheimer and Adorno, 1973: 46)

Adorno and Horkheimer point to the powerful aural quality of music and the social construction of states of 'we-ness' within it. The site of experience in Adorno's work collapses within the historical transformation of the subject's 'interiority', which becomes increasingly mediated by and constituted through the use of everyday products of the 'culture industry'. The drift towards conceiving experience as colonized is, however, also present within Lefebvre's understanding of representational space. He sometimes appears to claim that lived space is passively experienced as a 'given' with the imaginary or symbolic activity of the individual appearing to be fully colonized by saturated forms of representational space:

Living bodies – the bodies of 'users' – are caught up not only in the toils of parcelised space, but also in the web of what philosophers call 'analgons'; images, signs, symbols. These bodies are transported out of themselves and emptied out, as it were, via the eyes; every kind of appeal, incitement and seduction is mobilised to tempt them with doubles of themselves in prettified, smiling and happy poses; this campaign to void them succeeds exactly to the degree that the images proposed correspond to the 'needs' that those same images have helped fashion. So it is that a massive influx of information, of messages, runs head into an inverse flow constituted by the evacuation from the innermost body of all life and desire. Even cars may fulfil the function of analgons, for they are at once extensions of the body and mobile homes, so to speak, fully equipped to receive these wandering bodies.

(Lefebvre, 1991: 99)

Representational space becomes saturated as the subject's eyes consume the 'analgons' which 'void' the subject of the occupancy of their own experience. For Lefebvre, even the 'overlaying' of physical space by the imagination merely constitutes an additional form of superimposed or structurally determined meaning. Adorno's analysis of auditory experience, in which structural imperatives take precedent in the constitution of an 'imaginary', appears, at times, to be similar to Lefebvre's. This potential weakness in their work needs to be addressed in order to gain a more dynamic understanding of personal-stereo use. I argue, somewhat generously perhaps, that their understanding of the colonization of experience that manifests itself in aspects of their work goes against the grain of their own theoretical frameworks, in which there can be no mimetic, one-to-one relationship between subject and object, as this would reflect a collapse of the dialectical nature of experience, where a tension exists between technology as invasion and technology as resistance. This drift into determinism I see as a consequence of insufficient attention to empirical study in both of their works.

Kracauer, however, brings out the ambiguous nature of a technologically mediated aural transformation of urban experience in the following description of radio listeners in the early 1930s:

Who could resist the invitation of those dainty headphones? They gleam in living rooms and entwine themselves around heads all by themselves; and instead of fostering cultivated conversation (which certainly can be a bore), one becomes a playground for Eiffel noises that, regardless of their potentially active boredom, do not even grant one's modest right to personal boredom. Silent and lifeless, people sit side by side as if their souls were wandering about far away. But these souls are not wandering according to their own preferences; they are badgered by the news hounds, and soon no one can tell who is the hunter and who is the hunted.

(Kracauer, 1995: 333)

The transformation of experience through the privatized act of listening places personal stereos within a historical trajectory of technologized experience that incorporates the daily use of other communication technologies such as radio, television and film. Kracauer points to the ambiguous and seductive nature of these new domestic communication technologies: 'Who could resist the invitation of those dainty headphones?' But what is it about those headphones that is so attractive? Is it that they wrap themselves snugly around the head of the user, hinting at some kind of an auditory intimacy? Yet Kracauer is equally concerned with what the technology appears to achieve. His radio users transcend geographical space, listening takes them away from the mundanity of their domestic space. They no longer commune with those in physical proximity, but with the voices transmitted through the ether, which is seen as preferable to any discussion with the person next to them. The technology of the radio and the headphones enables users to prioritize their experience socially. Kracauer in this description addresses the nature of cognitive, aesthetic and moral spatial practices of urban life, but he does so through the technologization of these realms. Kracauer's subjects appear to be retreating into mediated forms of public inwardness which transform both the 'site' and 'horizon' of their experience. With this framework in mind I now move on to consider the transformation of representational space and the 'site' of experience as described by personal-stereo users in their accounts of everyday use. The ethnographic material drawn upon in the following pages derives from a study carried out primarily in London over a two-year period, from 1994 to 1996, and consisting of in-depth qualitative interviews with over sixty personal-stereo users. Interviews were conducted both with individual users and in groups. Supplementary material was also gained through the use of user diaries. The subjects represented a cross-section of users in terms of age, gender, ethnicity and occupation.

Reconfiguring the site and horizon of urban experience: an ethnography of personal-stereo use

Personal-stereo use reorientates and re-spatializes the user's experience, with users often describing it in solipsistic and aesthetic terms. Personal stereos appear to provide an invisible shell for the user within which the boundaries of both cognitive and physical space become reformulated. Take this comment from one user:

> I don't necessarily feel that I'm there. Especially if I'm listening to the radio. I feel I'm there, where the radio is, because of the way, that is, he's talking to me and only me and no one else around me is listening to that.

So I feel like, I know I'm really on the train, but I'm not really . . . I like the fact that there's someone still there.

(Mandy)

Personal-stereo users often describe habitation in terms of an imaginary communion with the source of communication. Mandy is twenty-one. She spends four hours each day travelling across London and uses her personal stereo throughout this time. She likes to listen to both the radio and to taped music on her machine. She listens to music habitually, waking up to it and going to sleep with it. Her description of listening sheds some light upon the connections between technology, experience and place. Using a personal stereo appears to constitute a form of company for her when she is alone, through its creation of a zone of intimacy and immediacy. This sensibility, following Adorno, appears to be built into the very structure of the auditory medium itself. The headphones of her machine fit snugly into the ears to provide sound which fills the space of cognition. The 'space' in which reception occurs is decisive, for just as the situation of the television in the home changes the structuring of experience there, so the use of a personal stereo changes the structuring of experience wherever it is used. Mandy describes herself as being where the 'music' or the 'DJ' is. She constructs an imaginary journey within a real journey each day. The space of reception becomes a form of 'mobile home' as she moves through the places of the city. The structuring of space through personal-stereo use is connected to other forms of communication strategies enacted via a range of communication technologies. Users live in a world of technologically mediated sounds and images. The imperative towards experiential states of 'we-ness' is usefully thought of as learned and embedded in the consumption of television, radio and music reception in the home and elsewhere. The desire for mediated forms of technologized experience becomes part of the sedimented meaning structure of users' everyday experience. This is demonstrated in the following remark by Mandy:

I can't go to sleep at night without my radio on. I'm one of those people. It's really strange. I find it very difficult. I don't like silence. I'm not that sort of person. I like hearing things around me. It's like hearing that there's a world going on, sort of thing. I'm not a very alone person. I will always have something on. I don't mind being by myself as long as I have something on.

(Mandy)

Mandy goes on to describe her feeling of centredness, of being secure with her personal stereo by excluding the extraneous noises of the city, or at least her ability to control this: 'Because I haven't got the external sort of noises around me I feel I'm in a bit of a world of my own because I can't really hear so much of what is going on around me' (Mandy). The use of a personal stereo either creates the experience of being 'cocooned' by separating the user from the outside world, or alternatively the user moves outwards into the public realm of communication 'culture' through a private act of reception. This demonstrates the dialectical nature of personal-stereo use: the user does not perceive herself as being 'alone' but understands that neither is she 'really there'. Using a personal stereo makes her feel more secure as it acts as a kind of 'boundary marker'. Boundary markers 'mark the line between two adjacent territories. Note when boundary markers are employed either on both sides of an individual or in front and back, they function as "spacers" ensuring the user personal space in a row or column' (Goffman, 1971: 66). Personal-stereo use thus provides an effective boundary surrounding the user with her 'own' aural bubble. Mandy's use of a personal stereo also transforms her experience of place and social distance. Through use, the nature and meaning of being 'connected' within a reconfiguration of subject and object itself becomes problematic. The very distinction between them appears to be blurred. The following description of situatedness is typical, in which the user describes use as filling 'The space while you're walking … also changes the atmosphere as well. If you listen to music, like, and you're feeling depressed it can change the atmosphere around you' (Sara). The site of experience is transformed from the inside out. Effectively it is colonized. Habitable space becomes both auratic and intimate:

> Because when you have the Walkman it's like having company. You don't feel lonely. It's your own environment. It's like you're doing something pleasurable you can do by yourself and enjoy it. I think it creates a sense of a kind of aura, sort of like. Even though it's directly in your ears you feel like it's all around your head. You're really aware it's just you, only you can hear it. It makes you feel individual … Listening also constitutes 'company': if there's the radio there's always somebody talking. There's always something happening.
>
> (Alice)

This is contrasted with the observation that nothing is happening if there is no musical accompaniment to experience. The auratic space of habitation collapses. The nature of a world of 'we-ness' is a world accompanied by mediated messages of culture and its social formation, in which patterns of habit exist along a gradient that moves in the direction of dependency. When the personal stereo is switched off the 'we-ness' falls away and the user is left in an experiential void often described with various degrees of apprehension or annoyance. Left to themselves with no distractions, users often experience feelings of anxiety. This is apparent in the many users who either put their personal stereos on to go to sleep or go to sleep with sound or music from their record/CD players or radios. The activity is of course pleasurable in its own right:

> I like something to sing me to sleep. Usually Bob Marley, because I don't like silence. It frightens me. If it's silent and it's dark as well. It helps me think. Because I have trouble sleeping, so if I have a song I like, it's sort of soothing. It's like your mum rocking you to sleep. I like someone to sing me to sleep.
>
> (Jana)

> I don't like silence. I hate it at night. I suppose it's at night and you're on your own. I just don't like being alone. I just have to have someone with me, or if not with me, some type of noise. That's why I have music on for. It kind of hides it. It just makes me feel comfortable.
>
> (Kim)

> Just having the noise. If it's not music I have the TV. If there's the radio there's always someone talking. There's something happening.
>
> (Sara)

These responses contextualize the role of personal stereos in relation to other forms of communication technology that also act as forms of 'we-ness'. Dorinda, a thirty-year-old mother, describes using her Walkman while cycling. For her the state of 'being with' is very specific. She plays one tape for months on end on her personal stereo. At present it is *Scott Walker Sings Jacques Brel*.[2] The tape has personal connotations for her and while listening she describes feeling confident, as if she's 'with' the singer. The sense of security she gains from this imagined familiarity is conveyed in the following remark: 'Yeh. It's me and Scott [Walker] on the bike' (Dorinda). Other users also describe this in terms of a feeling of being protected. Their own space becomes a protected zone where they are 'together' with the content of their personal stereo: 'If I'm in a difficult situation or in new surroundings, then I think nothing can affect you, you know. It's your space' (Paul).

Use appears to function as a substitute for company in these examples. Instead of company, sound installs itself, usually successfully. Jade, a habitual user, describes his relationship with his personal stereo in interpersonal terms, in which the machine becomes an extension of his body:

It's a little like another person. You can relate to it. You get something from it. They share the same things as you do. You relate to it as if it's another person. Though you can't speak to it. The silence is freaky for me. That is kind of scary. It's almost like a void, if you like.

(Jade)

The above extract is also indicative of the feeling of being 'deserted' when the music stops. This feeling might also be described in terms of communication technology enhancing the space and the time of the user. As such it becomes both taken for granted and 'everyday' in terms of the user's experience. Experience without it is seen as either void or at least inferior to experience through it. The spaces of experience can become transformed, as the following teenagers testify:

It fills the space while you're walking.

(Rebecca)

It also changes the atmosphere as well. If you listen to music you really like and you're feeling depressed, it can change the atmosphere around you. It livens everything up. Everything's on a higher level all the time. It makes you a bit busier. You get excited. Everything's happening.

(Sara)

The invigoration and heightening of the space of experience enacted through use collapses the distinction between private mood or orientation and the user's surroundings. The world becomes one with the experience of the user, as against the threatened disjunction between the two. Using a personal stereo colonizes space for these users, transforming their mood, orientation and the reach of their experience (Silverstone, 1994). The quality of these experiences is dependent upon the continued use of the personal stereo. This is graphically demonstrated by the following seventeen-year-old respondents who were asked in a group interview to describe how the atmosphere changes with the switching off of their personal stereos:

An empty feeling.

(Kayz)

Got nothing to do.

(Zoe)

Just sitting there and get bored.

(Donna)

It's like when you're in a pub and they stop the music. It's an anticlimax. Everyone just stops. You don't know what to say.

(Sara)

Switching off becomes tantamount to killing off their private world and returning them to the diminished space and duration of their disenchanted and perceived mundane outside world. The above comments appear to represent a world of use that is in itself technologized.

The heightening and colonizing nature of personal-stereo use is clearly brought out in the following examples of holiday use. Personal stereos are a popular holiday companion for users:

I use it lying on the beach. You need music when you're tanning yourself. There's the waves and everybody's around. You just need your music. On the plane we were listening to Enigma and things like that. It fitted in ... Not bored, it livens everything up. Everything's on a higher level all the time. It makes it seem a bit busier. You get excited. Everything's happening.

(Donna)

Donna isn't describing use as an antidote to boredom but as a form of harmonizing the environment to herself. Using a personal stereo 'enhances' her experience, helping her to create a 'perfect' environment. Use allows her to experience the environment through her mediated fantasies. The following user describes her holiday personal-stereo use thus:

I use it on the beach. I feel that I'd be listening to my music. I have the sea, I have the sand. I have the warmth but I don't have all the crap around me. I can eliminate that and I can get much more out of what the ocean has to offer me. I can enjoy. I feel that listening to my music, I can really pull those sun's rays. Not being disturbed by screaming kids and all that shouting, which is not why I went there. I went to have harmony with the sea and the sun. The plane journey, flying out and back and you listen to different music, but it just helps me to still my mind and to centre myself, and I feel that by taking this tape with me I'm carrying that all day and I feel that I'm able to take more from the day and give more to the day. Whether that's right or wrong I don't know, but that's how I feel.

(Jay)

The environment is reappropriated and experienced as part of the user's desire. Through her privatized auditory experience the listener gets 'more' out of the environment, not by interacting with it but precisely by not interacting. Jay focuses on herself as personally receiving the environment via her personal stereo. There is only the sun and the user's body and state of mind.

Actual environments, unadorned, are not normally sufficient for personal-stereo users. They are either populated with people (Jay) or merely mundane (Donna). Music listened to through the personal stereo makes them 'what they are' for the user and permits the re-creation of the desired space to accord with their wishes. This is achieved by the user repossessing space as part of, or constitutive of, their subjective desire. Personal-stereo users thus tend to colonize and appropriate the here-and-now by transforming it into a pleasurable habitable space precisely through the 'colonizing' of that space through an aural and privatized re-inscribing of it.

Personal-stereo use: home and auditory mnemonics

Personal-stereo use sheds light on the creation and meaning of forms of aural 'habitable' space. As personal-stereo users traverse the public spaces of the city, they often describe the experience in terms of never leaving 'home', understood either symbolically or sometimes literally. The aim here is not to reach outwards into a form of 'we-ness' but rather to negate distance, enabling the user to maintain a desired sense of security. Using a personal stereo is often described in womb-like terms of being surrounded or enveloped. This is what users frequently mean when they refer to feelings of being at 'home'. Only the auditory nature of experience appears to be so all encompassing and non-directional. The use of music that has personal associations or connotations heightens these feelings. Equally, personalized music enables the user to re-create a sense of narrative that overlays or re-inscribes journeying in public. This represents an alternative route 'home'. Jay typifies the first point:

I like to have a piece of my own world. Familiar and secure. It's a familiarity. Something you're taking with you from your home. You're not actually leaving home. You're taking it with you. You're in your own little bubble. You're in your own little world and you have a certain amount of control and you don't have so much interruption ... What it evokes for me is that I didn't really have to worry about it at all, because there's someone there who'll take care of me. In a sense like when you're little and you have your mum and dad. So that's what it would evoke for me, a feeling of security, that it will be all right ... I don't like it [the urban] to totally take over. I have to have a piece of my own world.

(Jay)

Jay listens to tapes that she associates with her own world and memories. She does not visualize this sense of home literally in terms of concrete memories but rather relates to it in terms of a sense of well-being and security. In this sense, she does not demonstrate an interest in an ongoing communicative process with a socially constructed public state of 'we-ness'. Rather, certain tunes or songs produce a heightened sense of well-being, reminding her of childhood and family.

Other users describe travelling back into their own narratives by visualizing situations or re-experiencing the sensation of pleasurable situations while listening to their personal stereos in discounted public spaces. Their imaginary journey takes precedence over their actual physical journey and their actual 'present' is overridden by their 'imaginary' present. While daydreaming is a common activity, users appear to have great difficulty conjuring up these feelings and images of home and narrative without using their personal stereos. As such, daydreaming becomes mediated, constructed and constituted through the technological medium of the personal stereo and music.

The control exerted over the external environment through use is also described in terms of clearing a 'space' for thoughts or the imagination. The random nature of the sounds of the street does not possess either an adequate configuration or force to successfully produce or create the focusing of thoughts in the desired direction. For users who are habitually accompanied by music, there arises a need for accompaniment as a constituent part of their experience. The world and their biography is recollected and accompanied by sound. This construction of a space or clearing for the imagination either to function in or be triggered by personal-stereo use appears to be connected to the habitualness of use rather than the type of environment within which the experience takes place. It often makes little difference to the user whether they are walking down a deserted street or travelling on a congested train, in terms of the production of the states of 'being' discussed here.

Home and narrative appear to be closely connected in the lifeworld of users. Personal stereos can be construed as functioning as a form of 'auditory mnemonic' in which users attempt to construct a sense of narrative within urban spaces that have relatively less narrative sense for them. The construction of a narrative becomes an attempt to maintain a sense of pleasurable coherence in those spaces that are perceived to be bereft of interest. Users describe a variety of situations relating to this point:

The music sparks off memories. Just like that. As soon as you hear the tunes.

(Kim)

I'll remember the place. I'll be there. I'll remember what I was doing when I was listening to that music.

(Jana)

If I'm listening to Ben E. King's 'Stand by Me', I can imagine myself walking down Leicester Square, because that's where I heard it with that guy.

(Mandy)

I'd visualize it. Like if I heard a certain song at a party or something and when I heard it again on my Walkman, I'd just be at that party again with my friends doing what I was doing.

(Zoe)

Sometimes it brings back memories. Like how you felt. Some types of music and songs like, you only listen to them at certain times with certain people, so you listen to them on your own and it brings back memories ... atmospheres.

(Sara)

Personal-stereo use therefore represents one form of biographical travelling. The narrative quality that users attach to music permits them to reconstruct these narrative memories at will in places where they would otherwise have difficulty in summoning them up. These memories provide the user with a feeling of being wrapped up in their own significance while existing in the perceived narrative anonymity or invisibility of their spatial present. Users' relations to representational space are transformed, enabling them to construct forms of 'habitable' space for themselves. In doing so, users can be described as creating a fragile and temporal world of certainty within a contingent world. Users tend not to like being left to their own thoughts: not for them the reveries of a Rousseau, who liked nothing more than walking in the solitude of the countryside in order to be alone with his own thoughts. Personal-stereo users prefer to be 'alone' with the mediated sounds of the culture industry. Users thus generate feelings of empowerment precisely by becoming dependent upon the habitual use of their personal stereos.

Concluding remarks

How should we understand the relationship between the site of reception and 'representational' space in this newly configured world of technologized experience? Critical theorists have argued that new forms of technologically orientated communications, such as the radio, prioritized the individual, thereby enhancing forms of existing individualism while simultaneously dispelling, substituting or transforming notions of community through the creation of alternative forms of interpersonal communication (Adorno, 1991; Horkheimer and Adorno, 1973). These values manifest themselves in the technological artefact and its production. This is what is meant by claiming that forms of mobility are inscribed into the meaning and design of the personal stereo. The social relations produced within culture via both technology and individualism act to enhance these selfsame processes. How should we understand the relationship between the site of reception and 'representational' space in this newly configured world of technologized experience? I have highlighted the ways in which users use the personal stereo both to construct a space of security and 'independence' while, at the same time, becoming dependent on the technology. In doing so I have highlighted the dialectical nature of a technologized aural experience within which the theoretical dichotomies of active and passive, public and private become problematized and questioned.

Notes

1. 'To each his own bubble, that is the law today' (Baudrillard, 1993: 39). While Baudrillard is describing car habitation, Walkman use provides an interesting reconfiguration of this formula.
2. Jacques Brel, most famous French singer of the 1960s, who died in 1978 of lung cancer. Scott Walker released an album of Brel songs in the early 1970s.

Bibliography

Adorno, T. (1976) *Introduction to the Sociology of Music* (New York: Continuum Press).
Adorno, T. (1991) *The Culture Industry: Selected Essays on Mass Culture* (London: Routledge).
Attali, J. (1985) *Noise: The Political Economy of Music* (Minneapolis: University of Minnesota Press).
Bachelard, G. (1994) *The Poetics of Space: The Classical Look at How We Experience Intimate Places* (Boston: Beacon Press).

Baudrillard, J. (1993) *Symbolic Exchange and Death* (London: Sage).

Benjamin, W. (1973) *Illuminations* (London: Penguin).

Du Gay, P. and Hall, S. (eds) (1997) *Doing Cultural Studies: The Story of the Sony Walkman* (London: Sage).

Gibson, W. (1993) *Time Out*, 6 October, p. 49.

Goffman, E. (1971) *Relations in Public: Microstudies of Public Order* (London: Penguin).

Horkheimer, M. and Adorno, T. (1973) *The Dialectic of Enlightenment* (London: Penguin).

Jay, M. (1993) *Downcast Eyes: The Denigration of Vision in Twentieth-Century French Thought* (Berkeley: University of California Press).

Kracauer, S. (1995) *The Mass Ornament: Weimar Essays* (Cambridge, MA: Harvard University Press).

Lefebvre, H. (1991) *The Production of Space* (Oxford: Blackwell).

Lull, J. (1990) *Inside Family Viewing* (London: Routledge).

Rée, J. (1999) *I See a Voice: Language, Deafness and the Senses, a Philosophical Enquiry* (London: HarperCollins).

Silverstone, R. (1994) *Television and Everyday Life* (London: Routledge).

Index